Friendgrief
An Absence Called Presence

by
Harold Ivan Smith, D.Min.

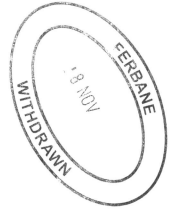

Death, Value and Meaning Series
Series Editor: John D. Morgan

CRC Press
Taylor & Francis Group
Boca Raton London New York

CRC Press is an imprint of the
Taylor & Francis Group, an **informa** business

CRC Press
Taylor & Francis Group
6000 Broken Sound Parkway NW, Suite 300
Boca Raton, FL 33487-2742

First issued in paperback 2018

© 2002 by Taylor and Francis Group, LLC
CRC Press is an imprint of Taylor & Francis Group, an Informa business

No claim to original U.S. Government works

ISBN-13: 978-0-89503-258-4 (hbk)
ISBN-13: 978-0-415-78470-2 (pbk)

Library of Congress Catalog Number: 2001025406

Library of Congress Cataloging-in-Publication Data

Smith, Harold Ivan, 1947-
    Friendgrief : an absence called presence / by Harold Ivan Smith.
        p. cm. - - (Death, value, and meaning series)
    Includes bibliographical references and index.
    ISBN 0-89503-258-9 (cloth)
    1. Grief. 2. Bereavement- -Psychological aspects. 3. Death- -Psychological aspects. 4.
Loss (Psychology) 5. Friendship- -Psychological aspects. I. Title. II. Series.

    BF575.G7 S585 2001
    155.9'37- -dc21   2001025406

Visit the Taylor & Francis Web site at
http://www.taylorandfrancis.com

and the CRC Press Web site at
http://www.crcpress.com

In Memoriam

No event has so corroborated my faith in the next world as Williams did simply by dying. When the idea of death and the idea of Williams thus met in my mind, it was the idea of death that was changed.

C. S. Lewis, 1946, p. xiv

They taught me a great deal about friendship. They taught me a great deal about dying. They are teaching me about remembering.

Twila Arbuckle
Denny Apple
Larry Baggett
Bob Benson
Hudson Butler
Alice Cobb
Tommy Cook
John Marquis Culver
Dorothy Culver
Harry Dickerson
Leon Doane
Billy "Rusty" Esposito
Anne Hargrove
Lois Hicks
Martin Alan King

M. E. Bud Lunn
Fred Marty
Elva McAllaster
Donnie Mesarosh
David Messenger
Milt Wieneche
John L. Moore
Pat O'Neil
Bunny & Chuck Oney
Cecil Paul
Gordon Phillips
Martha Shedd
Jean Stake
Billy Surratt
Mildred Bangs Wynkoop
R. T. Williams, Jr.

"Oh, but you have lots of friends . . ."
Left is the word they do not say.
That's what people told me when I mentioned
my friend's death.
Although I am blessed
with a rich bounty of friends
I am still diminished
by the loss of any one of them.
Because with each friend's passing
a chunk of my past and future ends.
Who will be there to ask,
"Do you remember the time?"

No one, these days,
has friends to spare.
It would be like saying
to the curator of an art museum
after a masterpiece had been stolen,
"Oh, but you still have lots of paintings . . ."
Perhaps.
"But I had only one that hung there."

Give your grief its voice.
Pay attention to your memories.
And count the ways you have been enriched
by having such a friend.

—*harold ivan smith*

Acknowledgments

Books do not just happen. Books begin with ideas, sometimes first heard out or received by friends. Sometimes one is lucky enough to hear a friend say, "Go for it" or "Write that book!"

Books go through drafts. My "cheerleader" friends have graciously read drafts and offered valuable suggestions. Several read with hearts well acquainted with friendgrief. I am grateful to Gregory DeBourgh, Susanne Fitzgerald, Emily Freeburg, Richard Gilbert, Ronald Attrell, Sandra Jacoby Klein, John Reid, and Paul Fitzgerald.

I am also grateful to Phyllis Silverman who helped me reconcile my verb tenses. Through her work on continuing bonds, I was able to eliminate *had* from a lot of sentences, especially "I *had* a friend." She helped me see that my friends who have waded the wide river are still part of my life. A rich part.

I am grateful to John Morgan for believing in my concept.

I am grateful to colleagues who write journal articles and books and for colleagues who do presentations and workshops at the Association for Death Education and Counseling. Through their ideas, my world is stretched.

Table of Contents

CHAPTER 1
An Introduction

In London attending a convention, I was stunned by two words in an obituary for a middle-aged adult who died suddenly: *"No mourning"* (Duncan, 1999, June 30, p. 24). When I called *The Times* seeking clarification, an editor assured me that I had read correctly, "No mourning. You know, no going on and on about it . . . crying and all that." After reflection, I realized that that published phrase captures the attitude of many individuals on this side of the Atlantic toward grief for a friend: no mourning.

I am a griever. I am a friendgriever. By grieving for friends, by crying and "all that" I am experiencing what Cable, Doka, Heflin-Wells, Martin, Nichols, Pine, Redmond, Sanders, and Schachter (2000) call "the hidden sorrow." At mid-life, I have lost more than my fair share of friends. Those losses have led to an appreciation for Lauren Bacall's assessment of losing friends, "As the number has shrunk, as the gaping holes multiply—as pieces of me go with those who leave this earth—I become more aware of my own mortality and the incredible sadness that endings bring" (1994, p. 152).

I am not alone. Between six and ten million Americans are annually impacted by the death of a friend, assuming three to five friends per death (Deck & Folta, 1989, p. 77). I have lost my grandparents and my parents, but the shaping losses of my life have been the deaths of my friends. My friendship network, in the words of the Timex commercial, "has taken a lickin' and kept on tickin'!"

I am grateful that these friends are part of my life—not were but *are*. My life, blessed by their presence, is now graced by their memory. If they had not been part of my life, if they had not demonstrated the meaning of friend and friendship, I would never have given my grieving for them a second thought and would have pursued some other stream of thanatological research.

Once I would have agreed with Pogrebin (1987): "Death is friendship's final closure" (p. 104) but the work of Klass, Silverman, and

Nickman (1996) has given me the courage to believe in "continuing bonds." Death is but a pause . . . between sentences. Someday my companions and I will resume our conversations, "Now where were we?" My understanding of life after death is influenced by my belief that somewhere "out yonder"—in the words of poet Doug Malloch (1915/1950)—Rusty and Elva and Martin and John and Twila and Bud and Pat and R. T. and Cecil and Bunny and all the others are enjoying the party and wondering when I will arrive. Gallup (1997) reports that most Americans believe in some form of existence after death. Lewis (1946) explains: "No event has so corroborated my faith in the next world as Williams did simply by dying. When the idea of death and the idea of Williams thus met in my mind, it was the idea of death that was changed" (p. xiv).

My friends, although dead, fill the bleachers of my memory. As I have sat at computers writing, in libraries reading, and listening—sometimes eavesdropping—to grief narratives of other friends, when I have wanted to abandon this project, they have protested. I learned so much from them in life; now, I am learning so much from them by paying attention to the accumulated grief. Friendgrief is like the task of Sisyphus in Greek mythology pushing the stone up the hill, only to have to do it again. And again. Smith (1996) wrote:

> I am again a traveler,
> wandering through a landscape for which Fodor
> has no guidebook—a land called Grief.
>   . . .
> Experiencing my friends' deaths has depleted my heart.
> My heart lies, collapsed, like a party balloon
> the morning after the celebration.
> No one understands my grief.
> I guess that's what I get for taking friendship so seriously (p. 9).

CONTEMPORARY FRIENDSHIP

I coined the term *friendgrief* based on the phrase "friend-griever" or one who grieves for a friend (Deck & Folta, 1989, p. 77). We friend—and why should *friend* not function as a verb rather than the more passive, befriend?—in a culture in which many are clueless as to how to establish and maintain a friendship. I agree with Ann Swindler's conclusion: "Modern friendship works in part because it isn't so demanding. It's turnonable, and turnoffable. Friends are like a line of credit at the bank, but you don't draw on them all the time" (as cited in Goodman &

O'Brien, 2000, p. 211). Friendship lite becomes a concession to busy schedules.

FRIENDSHIP VS. FRIENDLINESS

Many confuse friendship with friendliness. Individuals assume a person to be a friend because he is being friendly (Freeman, 1999). Women invest in friendships while men "act friendly." Women consider a friend to be a friend in all situations while men commonly preface requests of friends with the words, "If it's not asking too much." These days, too many consider any friendship to be disposable and replaceable. Jane Mansbridge finds contemporary friendships, "Fantastically voluntaristic" to the point, "I voluntarily enter; I voluntarily leave. You enter into friendships so long as they're good for you, and then you leave" (in Goodman & O'Brien, 2000, p. 212). Increasingly, friends interact when it is convenient. "So busy these days . . . would love to see you some time." But we never get around to scheduling some time. Because many friends are too hurried and too stressed to invest time in nurturing friendships (Putnam, 2000), friends drift in and out of our lives. "What ever happened to so-and-so? I never hear you talk about her anymore." In fact, some leave funeral or memorial services purposing to be a better friend only to be reminded of that failed promise at the next funeral of a friend.

THE ABSENCE OF A TIGHT DEFINITION

A definition is essential because defining friend or friendship in contemporary society is whatever I want friend to mean. It is not easy especially when a presidential candidate who has difficulty remembering names opens speeches, "My *friends*. . . ." Or when this sentence runs in a major metropolitan newspaper, "As 3,000 of his closest friends gathered at First Baptist Church on Friday . . . ." (Whitley, 1999, October 30, p. D-1). ("3,000 *closest* friends?" I want to ask how many *casual* friends did he have?) When former President George Bush writes in his memoirs: "One of my best friends died, C. Fred Chambers" (1999, p. 443) I stumble over *"one of my best friends."* What does Bush mean by *best* friend? Some would argue that one has *a* best friend rather than multiple best friends (Yager, 1999). Reading such statements, I concur with Nardi's assessment that "the word 'friend' is thrown around quite loosely and requires layers of explanation for coherent communication" (1999, p. 2) particularly in a clinical setting.

Goodman and O'Brien (2000) lament that Americans use friend to cover everyone from intimates to mere acquaintances. Steinsaltz (1999) charges that friend is "so vague in English" (p. 159) that the term, at times, covers relationships that may be anything but a friendship. "Some unfortunate people have no understanding of the word 'friend' beyond the dictionary definition. They have never experienced a deep friendship, so they do not even know that it exists, and are therefore missing something in their lives" (p. 161).

WHEN CLINICIANS DEFINE FRIENDSHIP

In a clinical setting, definition and clarification of operative terms are critical; definition frames the parameters in which research and practice are conducted. Nevertheless, clinicians tend to rely on their own experience to find the meanings of words like "friend." I opened a presentation on friendgrief at the Association for Death Education and Counseling (ADEC) with a definition of friend from *The New Shorter Oxford English Dictionary* (L. Brown, 1993), "A person joined by affection and intimacy to another, independent of sexual or family love" (p. 1028). Immediately, some participants challenged the definition. "I consider my spouse to be my best friend," and "All my research is in *groups* of widowed friends." I used the exercise to demonstrate the variety of definitions among clinicians attending the workshop.

Little has changed since Wright (1982) concluded that research on friendship is "rarely based on a clearly delineated conception of what friendship is." My experience at ADEC illustrates Wrights's conclusion that friendship has "broad and ambiguous boundaries, allowing for a great deal of variability in subjective definitions" (1982, p. 3). "I wouldn't call that a friend" has become a well-worn cliche. It is too easy for writers, researchers, clinicians, and friends to assume that others know or share a definition of "friend." These days, I have to say "No, I don't know. Tell me." Constructing an exact, universal definition for friendship may be as difficult as Justice Potter Stewart's experience on the Supreme Court with pornography: "I shall not attempt further to define . . . but I will know it when I see it" (Applewhite, Evans, & Frothingham, 1992, p. 449).

Gregory DeBourgh of the University of San Francisco, who critiqued an early draft of this manuscript, challenged me to define friend up-front. "If I were you, I would add an introduction and get the definition business done in the introduction. That way everyone would know what you mean by friend even if they do not happen to share that definition." So, for this book, I have constructed a definition of *friend* from two sources:

> A person joined by affection and intimacy to another, independent of sexual or family love (*The New Shorter Oxford English Dictionary*, 1993, p. 1028).

and

> A voluntary, personal relationship typically providing intimacy and assistance. . . . the two parties like each other and seek each other's company (Fehr, 1996, p. 20).

My working definition of friendship reads,

> Friendship is a voluntary, personal relationship providing intimacy and support. The participants, independently of sexual and family love, like each other and seek each other's company and comfort and highly value attributes such as trust, loyalty, and self-disclosure.

I concede that not everyone will concur with the exclusion of sexual or family relationships in this definition. Heterosexual and same-sex partners would challenge that exclusion (Clark, 1997; Nardi, 1999; Weinstock & Rothblum, 1996) insisting, "My spouse/partner *is* my best friend." Mitchell Wright, whose wife was killed in the schoolyard shooting in Jonesboro, Arkansas, confronted the convicted shooters in court before their sentencing: "I not only lost a wife, I lost my best friend, thanks to you" (Lieb, 1998, August 12, p. A38). Siblings such as Wiltshire (1994) would contend that brothers and sisters and other family members can be friends. Adult children may contend that some parents can be friends. Jarrett Payton (1999, November 21) writes, in reference to his father, Chicago Bears running back, Walter Payton, "He was my best friend and it's kind of hard when you lose your best friend and your father at the same time" (p. D8).

Certainly, some males identify wives as a best friend. For many males a wife is not only their best friend but possibly their *only* friend. For these men, a spouse/best friend's death is a duo grief. Rarely has a wife reported to me that her husband is her best friend. In some spousal and family relationships, boundaries blur and overlap but one relationship dominates (Weinstock & Rothblum, 1996). I conclude that an individual is either more spouse or more friend. So, in this study of friends-in-grief, I exclude spouses and family members.

WHAT ABOUT "MAN'S BEST FRIEND"?

I also exclude grief for a pet. Admittedly, some consider a pet a friend; a dog may well be a particular man's "best friend." Individuals may be reluctant to acknowledge their strong attachment to a pet "for fear of reprisal or being demeaned or ridiculed" (Jarolmen, 1998). One griever told me, "I am ashamed to admit this, but I wept more for my dog than I did for my mother." Without discounting the grief following the death of a pet, I leave this friendship to other researchers.

A WORKING DEFINITION OF GRIEF

Grief is also broadly defined. I chose the definition framed by Wolfelt (1988) "as the emotional suffering caused by death" or loss; a "constellation of thoughts, feelings and behaviors" (p. 1). Increasingly, in Western culture, grief is perceived to be a private matter, best experienced in the privacy of one's own residence, or better still, in the sanctuary of one's own mind and heart. For many, grief will have a short shelf life. I was amazed by a headline in *The Kansas City Star* on the fifth day after the death of twelve students in the bonfire collapse at Texas A & M, "Texas continues to mourn" (Texas continues to mourn, 1999, November 23, p. A2). *Continues?* How could anyone quickly get over the death of multiple friends?

The banishment of mourning from our vocabulary and our daily lives results in an epidemic of unresolved grief. For those who find public expression of grief for a family member discomforting, how much more so for someone who was "merely" a friend. In many respects, friends are not only disenfranchised but are "invisible grievers" (Silverman, 1999, p. 167) who mask their grief, sometimes through a flurry of activities of support for the friend's family. In a disposable society, you do not grieve—you replace.

Discounting grief for a friend's death is not new. Poet Alfred Lord Tennyson (1895) was chastised for exaggerating grief for his close friend, Arthur Hallam. Tennyson responds

One writes, that "Other friends remain,"
That "Loss is common to the race"—
And common is the commonplace,
And vacant chaff well meant for grain.
That loss is common would not make
My own less bitter, rather more (p. 18).

A WORKING DEFINITION OF FRIENDGRIEF

I define *friendgrief* as "the thoughts, feelings, or behaviors experienced when acknowledging and integrating a friend's death into our daily lives and into the narrative of our lives as well as into the narrative of the friendorbit in which we are participants." The friendorbit is a subset of persons in a social network who are available for socio-emotional aid or instrumental aid, or both (Thoits, 1982). Participants in a friendorbit provide emotional concern, instrumental aid (goods and services), information; and appraisal (House, 1981). In my friendorbit I have individuals to whom I look specifically for each of those gifts; a death will create an immediate void. The friendship network's boundaries must be renegotiated to accommodate losses. A particular death "can test the limits of friendship" (Barroso, 1997, p. 554) among those who compose the social support network. Some friends will rally together in the crisis, others will desert or drift away, especially when the deceased was the magnet that held friends together. How do I grieve when the friend who was always there for me is now *not* there?

SOCIAL NETWORK AS A CONVOY

Oltjenbruns (1995) introduced me to Kahn and Antonucci's (1980) paradigm for social support network: convoy. In World War I, as the German Navy disrupted British shipping lanes, war supplies were torpedoed to the bottom of the North Sea. Prime Minister Lloyd George ordered that cargo ships have escorts and travel in a protected group. The convoys reduced losses to just 1.1 percent of trade (Island, 1998, p. 19) and changed naval warfare.

Lofland (1982) argues that children need a "convoy of friends" to help them navigate childhood and Oltjenbruns (1995) insists that children require a convoy of support to survive the death of a childhood playmate-friend. I believe that adults and adolescents also need a convoy of "you-can-count-on-me" friends. Even when the network of friends is small or scattered geographically—a "I'll-be-there-for-you" friend comes through. The friendorbit assists an individual navigate through the minefield of life, especially bereavement.

According to Kahn and Antonucci (1980) in a convoy an individual moves "through the life cycle surrounded by a set of other people to whom he or she is related by the giving and receiving of social support." An individual's convoy "consists of the set of persons on whom he or she relies for support and those who rely on him or her for support" (p. 269). As an individual has a narrative, so does the convoy. When an individual dies, friends grieve individually but the friendorbit collectively grieves as well. Both the me and the we are "forever changed by the experience of grief" (Wolfelt, 1999) or by the avoidance of grief. Listen at a visitation or memorial service and you may hear, "Things will not be the same without Sallie!"

NEEDED: A CONTEMPORARY METAPHOR

However, working with younger adults—those for whom World War II is an experience perceived through movies and videos like *Saving Private Ryan* rather than memories—convinces me that *convoy* is dated. In an age of "Star Wars" something planetary seems appropriate for constructing a metaphor to facilitate the translation of the loss from the experience of the friend into the understanding of the clinician. Such a metaphor encourages the sharing and the hearing of the loss. Bolen reports, "One of the major functions of a friend or a therapist is being a witness to the life story of another person" (as cited in Ciardiello, 1993, November/December, p. 89).

The American myth of rugged individualism limits friendships and silences grievers throughout a support network. Confronted by the untimely or violent death of a friend, the surviving friend needs the aggressive support of others in the first moments of trying out the awareness of a friend's death, during initial rituals and gathering of friends, and long afterwards. Some co-friends may be unable or unwilling to provide support "over the long haul" a strategy that may force the friendgriever to attempt to go it alone which can be as dangerous to an individual as to a solo ship crossing the North Sea in 1917.

One day while enjoying fine Kansas City barbecue with a friend, Gregory DeBourgh, I attempted to explain my new analogy. Off the top of my head, I speculated that a friendship support system functions like the planetary system with orbiting friends. Soon we were sketching orbit configurations and variations. DeBourgh identifies this concept as a sociological paradigm which fosters understanding of the dynamics of friend networks impacted by death. The death of a friend—especially in the sparsely populated friend roster—results in significant changes and deprivation throughout the friendorbit.

THE ANALOGY IS NOT ORIGINAL

Attempts to conceptualize friend network are not new. Twenty-five hundred years ago, Aristotle (1987) talked about a "circle of friends" (p. 317). English cleric-poet, John Donne rejects isolation in the classic line, "No man is an island . . . ." Robert Louis Stevenson, eulogizing his childhood friend James Ferrier, commented, "There falls along with him a whole wing of the palace of our life" (Theroux, 1997, p. 279). Tennyson (1985) compared a friend's death to a "Slide from the bosom of the stars" (p. 31). In Theroux (1997), a passage leaped from the page:

> Every person is born into a particular quadrant of the heavens. Our friends hang like companion stars around us, giving us point and direction. We run to them when we have something to celebrate, fall back upon them when feeling ill-used or ill-defined (p. 279).

Working with individuals grieving for a friend, I have found friend-orbit an explainable metaphor that describes their social network.

THE FOUNDATION OF THIS BOOK

In *Friendgrief* I advance a set of core beliefs:

1. Friends have a right—as much a right as any griever—to mourn publicly and to be socially supported in their grief work before the death, during the dying, and after the death of a friend or friends.
2. Friendgrievers have a right to explore their own unique integration of the loss.
3. Friendgrievers have a right to maintain continuing bonds with that friend/friends.
4. Friendgrievers have a right to grieve regardless of the social status of the friend or the value assigned that individual by others.
5. Friendgrievers have a right to hear: "Your grief for a friend counts!"
6. Friendgrievers have to recruit support for the friendgrief.

"I MUST SEE YOU OFF ON THE ROAD"

Sometimes, theory is best supported by a story. Two men sat eating breakfast in 1871. For five years one had been lost in the jungles of Africa until the other, a reporter for *The New York Herald,* found him. The reporter's first words, "Doctor Livingstone, I presume" earned both men a niche in history and led to an intense friendship. Eventually, when Henry Morton Stanley had to return to New York, both realized that this would be their last meeting. Stanley, unable to eat, broke their shared silence, "And now we must part. There is no help for it. Good-bye" (Seaver, 1957, p. 595).

Livingstone interrupted: "Oh, I am coming with you a little way. I must see you off on the road" (Seaver, 1957, p. 595). As they walked, the friends talked about the future. Finally, Stanley stopped. "Now, my dear doctor, the best of friends must part. You have come far enough; let me beg you to turn back" (p. 596). Livingstone looked at his friend: "You have done what few men could do—far better than some great travellers I know. And I am grateful to you for what you have done for me" (p. 596).

According to Rosen (1996) "It is the task of therapy to assist clients in revising their old stories and in constructing new ones that have more relevance and meaning for their current and future lives" (p. 24). As clinicians listen, question, clarify, and "be with" the narratives of this particular friendgriever and this particular episode of friendgrief, we too "see them off" on the road to revision of their stories, reconciliation with the loss, and reorganization of their friendorbit.

CHAPTER 2

Losing a Friend

CHAPTER PREVIEW

Friends die. For many adults friendgrief is an occasional intrusion; for others a continual process: Who will be next? The death of a friend must be recognized so that the resulting grief can be enfranchised. Disenfranchisement in this culture—even by clinicians—is significant. Why should a clinician care about friendships or friendgrief? First, clinicians will have friends die. Secondly, clinicians will have clients devastated by the death of a friend. Although presenting other concerns, a client may also be impacted by unacknowledged grief for a friend. By understanding the dynamic nature of friendgrief, clinicians gain insight into friendships impacted and reshaped by death.

> The study of grief is more than the study of symptoms and possible pathology: it is the study of people and their most intimate relationships. Grief knows no bonds; it is undisciplined by marital law; uncontrolled by kinship boundaries; it floats free among those who love and were loved (Folta & Deck, 1976, p. 235).

Friendgrief is a significant reality for many individuals. Some senior adults' friendship networks shrink as friends die. Friendgrief is a daunting reality for participants in Schelps and Klein's (1998) study who have lost fifty or more friends and acquaintances due to AIDS (p. 57). Friendgrief is an inevitable consequence of natural disasters such as an earthquake in Turkey and by acts of violence such as the Columbine shootings. Friendgrief is a frightening reality in political hots spots like Sierra Leone, Rwanda, East Timmor, Kosovo, or ex-hot spots like Serbia and Cambodia where whole friendship networks dissolved in ethnic, religious, or political conflicts that result in genocide. How could friends allow distrust and hatred to escalate into wholesale ethnic cleansing? One survivor describes the chaos, "Looking at my neighbors, I thought they were my friends. I was very much surprised that they were among the people who came to try to kill us" (Berkeley, 1998, p. 25). Whole friendorbits vanished in a pipe line explosion in the small village of Jesse, Nigeria, in 1998. Friendorbits of members of the Mountoursville High School French Club had to be reconfigured after TWA Flight 800 crashed into the Atlantic in 1997. Widespread obliteration of friendships occurred on April 30, 1990 when 138,000 people drowned in a monsoon in Bangladesh (Dillard, 1999, p. 109). Throughout history friendship networks have been assaulted in plagues, wars, epidemics, natural disasters, and civil insurrections.

Friendship networks are snuffed-out for children in inner cities, grieving for friends killed in a culture of drugs, gang violence, drive by shootings, and domestic violence. How do school, neighborhood, and church friends—let alone clinicians who work with these friends—process the latest death, knowing other children and adolescents will die? Losses at such a vulnerable age will be a grief burden for a lifetime.

DEFINING A FRIENDSHIP

To any encounter with a client grieving for a friend clinicians bring their own understanding of friendship and grief. Take a moment to reflect on the following questions:

How old does an individual have to be to have a bonafide friendship and thus to grieve at a friend's death?

How long must an individual have known a friend to experience grief?

How does an individual respond when grief is discounted? "She was *only* a friend. . . ."

How does an individual grieve multiple deaths of friends in an accident or disaster?

How does an individual juggle the continual loss of friends?

How does an individual thoroughly grieve for a friend in a culture that aggressively discourages grief and encourages grievers, "Get over it!" or "Get on with life!"?

FRIENDGRIEF: A DISENFRANCHISED GRIEF

Doka (1989) recalls the experience of Arnold, the protagonist in *Torch Song Trilogy,* whose widowed mother's quells his grief for a "friend"—his lover—"How can you compare your loss to mine?" Doka contends that disenfranchisement occurs when an individual experiences "the loss of a meaningful and significant attachment" (p. xv) which "may not be recognized or validated by others" (p. xv) in the relational network. I have never forgotten the anger of a grieving parent upon learning of my research who demanded, "Surely you are not saying that the grief for some friend who has died is just as valid as my grief for my daughter!"

In this culture, friendgrievers are often overlooked. In the initial grieving period, accommodations may be made but friendgrievers are soon encouraged—and expected—to bounce back after this death with minimal inconvenience and disruption. Nevertheless, for some, a friend's death becomes the defining loss of an individual's life.

I am moved reading about the creation of the monument honoring the twenty-one young soldiers from Bedford, Virginia, who died in the landing at Omaha Beach on D-Day in 1944. Ray Nance recalls the lost comrades, "They were good friends, people I'd played cards with and joked with over the years." A reporter commented on the pain still in Nance's voice "56 years later." Another survivor in Bedford, summarizes friendgrief, "Life goes on, you never you quite get over the experience" (Murphy, 2000, June 6, p. A8). Nance captures the lingering disenfranchisement of friends in Bedford (pop. 3,200), by saying, "A lot of people don't talk about it still" (p. A-1).

FRIENDSHIP AND FRIEND LOSS

Friendship is a foundational reality and necessity for social and psychological survival in today's world (Ambrose, 1999), heightened by dysfunctional families and mobility, here today/elsewhere tomorrow. These days, we learn to hold friendships loosely. When individuals move into a neighborhood or community, few intend to be there in five years; increasingly, neighbor and friend are not synonyms. Upwardly mobile Americans easily trade "friends, familiarity and a larger yard for a bigger house, a better salary and the opportunities afforded by a larger city" (Walfoort, 1998, November 27, p. A5) for the next rung on the career ladder and a new batch of friends all the while promising to "keep in touch" with those left behind.

Too many settle for friendships maintained by a few scrawled lines of catching up across the bottom of a seasonal greeting card, family newsletter, or an occasional "How are you? I am fine!" E-mail or phone call. The lapses in communications lengthen until one day you realize you have not heard from this friend in a long time. It is no surprise that many adults settle for friendship "lite" or use the word "friend" generously. Losses of friendships are rehearsals for the deaths of friends.

A GRIEF DISENFRANCHISED IN THE LITERATURE

Browsing the book display at the annual meeting of the Association for Death Education and Counseling in 1998, I was reminded of the absence of acknowledgment and social validation of friendgrief. For me, a highlight of that annual conference is examining the books, some new, some classic, many written by presenters. Opening a book, I scan the table of contents and index looking for *friend*, a technique used by Deck and Folta (1989). I have learned to read between the lines in case *bereavement, friend* is included under a parallel or less-than-obvious heading such as *death, peer*.

Certainly, I found resources on the deterioration and death of a friend*ship,* such as Levinger's (1980) ABCDE theory (A is for attraction; B is for build-up; C is for continuation; D is for deterioration; and E is for ending). The progression of a friend*ship* can be explored, packaged in a theory emphasizing *formation, maintenance,* and *dissolution* (Zeggelink, 1993)—repackaged and expanded by other theorists in their books. If the ending of a friend*ship* can be the subject of scholarly research and publication, how can the death of friends be ignored in an American society with 2.3 million deaths each year (Neuharth, 1998, November 27, p. 11A) or a global society with 53.7 million deaths (Bureau of the Census, 1998, p. 470)? Increasingly, in a global culture, disasters such as the earthquake in Turkey which killed 25,000, impacts friends in this country as well. How can so common an experience be overlooked in the literature?

I skimmed books on the death of spouses, children, and pets; books on death from AIDS, cancer, and suicide. I skimmed books with theories for the post-Kübler-Ross era, books of poetry, and practical advice. I skimmed books for children, books for teens, and books for adults. I skimmed books on the deaths of gay uncles (or their roommates), grief in the inner city, and books on sudden infant death. Finally in Corr, Nabe, and Corr (1997) I found *friend* indexed between France and funeral director. Although not developed in the text, friendgrief is, at least, mentioned. Admittedly, had I read the books and resources line for line, I would have stumbled occasionally upon the word *friend* or brief anecdotes about friendships impacted by death. For example, while Wolfe (1993) comments on the deceased's friends in AIDS-related bereavement (Doka & Morgan, 1993), that discussion is not indexed.

From my perusal, I could make a case that one would never know that friends die and that friends grieve from the books on sale at this conference for grief professionals other than Smith (1996), *Grieving the Death of a Friend* (1996), and Gootman (1994), *When a Friend Dies: A Book for Teens about Grieving and Healing.* I find Deck and Folta's

(1989) assertion that the literature gives "no attention to friends as grievers" (p. 77) still valid. Only two empirical studies focus on the grief of friends (Roberto & Stanis, 1994; Sklar & Hartley, 1991-92). As a result of "theoretical silence" (Johnson, 1999, p. 11) or "conspicuous scarcity of research" (Roberto & Stanis, 1994, p. 19), many clinicians working with friendgrievers are hamstrung by the lack of sensitivity to and resources for this particular loss. Friendgrief although widely experienced, is rarely explicitly addressed in the literature. Austin and McClelland (1998) contend that many scholars publish: "to communicate our views and to address issues that have been left unexamined" (p. 641). *Unexamined* is an understatement when applied to the subject of the grief following the death of friends.

NEWSPAPER COVERAGE OF
GRIEVING FRIENDS

I make it a point to browse newspapers in cities where I lecture, work, or vacation. Even a quick perusal reminds me that friends die and that friends have roles in the grieving process and ritualizing. Some stories linger long after I discard the newspaper: "I saw my best friend, Natalie Brooks, get killed. She was shot in the head twice. I saw my friend laying down and in all this blood, and I just started running" words of Amber Vanoven, 11-year-old survivor of a school shooting ("Children lying everywhere," 1998, March 25, p. A-1).

Such accounts from Jonesboro, Arkansas, or the latest arena of violence, are hard to overlook. Schoolyard shootings, hyped by the media, the posturing of politicians, prompts widespread national public discussion and lamentation until the next shooting initiates a whole new cadre of friends into grief. Friends also die in hunting accidents, unsuccessful surgeries, commit suicide, die in homicides, or vehicular accidents.

> Dena McMillin never made it to her surprise 16th birthday party on Saturday. A two-hour drive with a friend was meant to divert her attention while her parents decorated. Minutes after the two left her father's house, they were in a car wreck that killed Dena (Hollingsworth, 1998, July 2, p. C-1).

WHEN A FRIEND OFFERS INSIGHT

Headlines catch my attention, particularly when friends clarify details or offer insights into a death. When actor Phil Hartman was shot and killed by his wife, one headline read: "The Hartmans—a Life of

Turmoil. Wife's temper led to fights, *friends* say" ("The Hartmans—a Life of Turmoil," 1998, p. A-2).

Friends supply missing details to help with meaning-making. Reporters seek out friends for comment and background, sometimes going through a string of friends before finding one willing to talk, on or off the record. Four years after the Oklahoma City bombing, when a survivor died in a single engine plane crash, reporters asked Arlene Blanchard, a friend, "How did he seem the last time you saw him?" Blanchard comments: "It seemed like he had a new lease on life. . . . That's what's so incredible, that he was able to survive [the bombing], and he dies like this" (Zizzo, 1998, October 13, p. 7).

But the media interest challenges friendorbits. Matthew Shepherd's death after a brutal gay-bashing attracted national coverage. People wanted to know what kind of guy—and secondarily, what kind of gay man—he was. Through Shepherd's friends, the public learned that Matthew was not an "in-your-face" gay activist. One friend comments, "Probably one of the most gentle people I've ever met in my life" (Kenworthy, 1998, October 10, p. A15). To keep the story alive, reporters explore new angles. When close friends will not talk, fringe friends are pursued. In Shepherd's case, some friends hopped "on the media bandwagon, and not to Matt's benefit" (Barrett, 1999, p. 28) angering Shepherd's family and other close friends who dismissed these "so-called" friends as opportunists. Some friends reluctantly break their silence to "set the record straight" or to correct misinformation from "so-called friends."

The deaths of the young, the rich, the famous, and celebrities are newsworthy. In the absence of strong friendships, the public creates pseudofriendships with the famous, the powerful, the wealthy, and the newsworthy (Pitts, 1998, November 27) and are impacted by their deaths, particularly violent or untimely deaths. "I feel like an old friend died" observations are common after celebrity deaths.

The celebrity friend's privacy and grief is invaded so that the curious public may have assistance in making sense—or attempting to make sense—of a celebrity death. "Inquiring minds want to know" captures the hunger. Rorem (1999) describes the press's relentless intrusion with what he considered irrelevant questions after his friend, Leonard Bernstein, died. "What was he really like? Did he smoke himself to death?" (p. 133). Perry Barlow, one of John Kennedy Jr.'s closest friends, contends that he "paid dearly for appearing on TV" to talk about their friendship. Barlow pointedly did not receive an invitation to the memorial service (Carlson, 1999, August 2, p. 31). Since Kennedy was a journalist, criticism erupted when fellow journalist-friends made themselves available for interviews during the rescue operation as well as during "wrap up" coverage of the story. Peter Jennings, a friend of Kennedy's and anchor for ABC News, declares: "I am offended that there are people on the air who identify themselves as his friend or claim to have a great intimate relationship with him. I think anybody who was a real friend of John Kennedy's would not say a word about him in public" (Roush, 1999, p. 43).

FRIENDGRIEF CAPTURED IN HEADLINES

Scanning newspaper headlines, I regularly find stories that link friendship, death, and friendgrief: "Woman tells of evening before *friend's* slaying" (Blakeman, 1998, April 22, p. B-2); "It's getting too hard to cope, *'friends* say after students' deaths" (Pardo, 1997, October 17, p. 1); "*Friends* remember slain man at vigil" (Crayton, 1998, May 12, p. B-5); and "Customers, *friends* mourn store owner" (Penn, 1998, May 8, p. C-1).

Some days, I become absorbed reading the grief dramas in which friends have major roles. In Seattle, I followed the story of the sentencing of Martin Pang, convicted of torching a family-owned warehouse—a blaze in which four firefighters died. One reporter captures the reaction of a colleague as a plea bargain was announced.

> At Fire Station 13 at Beacon Avenue and Spokane Street, where Brown, Shoemaker and Terlicker [three of the four deceased] served, the mood was quiet and somber yesterday. Firefighters described it as just another day, though they did gather around a television set to watch news of Pang's case.

> Dave Churchill, a firefighter who watched the floor collapse beneath his four friends, said he felt a sense of closure. "I think it's probably a good thing for the families and friends of the firefighters who died, rather than have it be a long, drawn-out trial and ordeal. But I still think he deserves a life sentence."

(Through a plea bargain the defendant avoided trial and a possible death sentence.) Churchill was only 15 feet away when the four firefighters fell through the floor ("Pang: Relatives look for more answers with lawsuits," 1998, p. A3). He saw his friends die.

Churchill's story haunted me during a long day of presentations. While I have lost friends, I have never had a quartet of friends die nor have I watched friends die in an inferno. How could Churchill continue working knowing that friends could die in the next fire? Suppose Churchill seeks out a clinician. Will the clinician fully appreciate the traumatic death of friends? What friend-friendly resources will the clinician recommend?

WHEN FRIENDS KILL

One headline and story still troubles me. "Doctor is convicted of killing friend in 1976." Surely, a friend killing a friend is more the stuff of a novel or a "made for TV" movie than real life. Friends do not kill friends. Or should I qualify that statement: *Real* friends do not kill friends. This particular murder periodically attracts widespread media attention.

> Montrose, PA—A doctor who for 21 years said his friend was killed in a trap-shooting accident was convicted Wednesday of murdering the man so he could marry his wife. Scher, an allergist, had said that his friend, lawyer Martin Dillion, tripped and shot himself on the 1976 outing while chasing a porcupine. The death initially was ruled an accident, but the case was reopened at the insistence of Dillion's father. ("Doctor is convicted of killing friend in 1976," 1997, October 23, p. A2).

How could a friend kill another friend? Maybe an *ex*-friend or a drug-deranged friend or drug-dealing friend. Increasingly, newspaper reports chronicle drug deals gone bad which involve a friend or friends killing a friend, "Ex-inmate convicted of murder. Man now faces life without parole in shooting of former friend at garage" (Lambe, 1998, October 22, p. C-1).

Sometimes tempers flair and a friend dies. Two friends, security guards in Springfield, Missouri, argued after one let a customer park in a particular space. As Friend A left the parking facility at the end of the shift, Friend B (still angry about the incident) shoved him in a stairway and he fell striking his head on a concrete sidewalk. When A died of a brain hemorrhage, the police charged the survivor-friend with involuntary manslaughter ("Stairwell death," 1998, October 7, p. C-3). Will the friend experience friendgrief in prison? If so, who will respond to his friendgrief? These stories prompt the question: Do I have any friend who might kill me? Certainly, I have friends who tease, "I could kill you for this" but I have never lost sleep over such comments.

WRONG OR "BAD" FRIENDS

A parent's nightmare is a son or daughter having "the wrong kind of friends." The phrase "Bad influence" carries a strong connotation. Many lives may be impacted when a friend is a negative influence. Two photos in *The Kansas City Star* illustrate this reality. The first is of a widow, sitting by the photo of her husband; the second is a senior yearbook picture of a smiling, clean-cut young male. The young man and a friend—the friend his mother had warned him to avoid—decided to rob a bulldozer operator working in an isolated area. However, as they approached him, for some reason, the young man in the picture opened fire. Then the boys fled. Eventually, a friend found the operator slouched over the controls, his wallet untouched. As a result, a young man, one year out of high school, who invested in a bad friendship, will spend the rest of his life in prison, without the possibility of parole; another man will have to long re-live the horror of finding a friend, bloodied and dead. The friendorbits of the operator and the killer, as well as readers of the paper, are left to wonder, "Why?" (Hoffman, 1998, September 25, pp. A-1, A-16).

FIFTEEN SECONDS OF FAME

The notion that everyone gets fifteen seconds of fame is attributed to Andy Warhol. Bebe Rebozo's death would have gone unnoticed in Miami, or been simply a local obituary rather than a story carried in newspapers across the nation, except for one detail. Rebozo had been Richard Nixon's faithful friend during Watergate. A brief news article summarizes the friendship: "Nixon found on Key Biscayne [Rebozo's home] the one thing his public life denied him: unconditional friendship, specifically that of Rebozo" ("Bebe Rebozo, Nixon friend, dies at age 85," 1998, May 9, p. A6). As I reread that sentence, I recalled that Henry Kissinger, Nixon's Secretary of State, once commented on Nixon's lack of friendships to Hugh Sidney, an aide, "Can you imagine what this man would have been had somebody loved him?" When Sidney sought clarification, Kissinger explained, "Had somebody in his life cared for him. I don't think anybody ever did, not his parents, not his peers. He would have been a great, great man had somebody loved him" (Ambrose, 1991, p. 588). So, Rebozo got fifteen seconds of fame for befriending a lonely, famous man. Nixon had long limited friendships: "I never wanted to be buddy-buddy even with close friends. . . . I believe you should keep your troubles to yourself" (Goodman & O'Brien, 2000, p. 55). Many follow that guidance and keep their grief to themselves.

WHEN AN EXPRESSION BECOMES A REALITY

Clinicians have heard and used the expression: "What happened to you? You look like you lost your best friend." For some that question is an agonizing reality. *The Louisville Courier-Journal* front-paged a photo of five hearses transporting family members killed in a car crash. In the accompanying story, a reporter notes that the high point of the joint funerals was a succession of friends sharing favorite stories about family members, particularly the mother, Robyn Jones. Jackie May, a close friend of Robyn, recalled the daily telephone chats that evoked teasing by Robyn's husband.

> With tears rolling down her face, May struggled to convey how much her friend's loss had hurt her. "Many times you have people say, 'You look like you lost your best friend.' Well, I have. My dear friend Robyn, so often I turn to you, to speak to you, only to realize that you aren't there. I miss you terribly" (Nord, 1998, June 13, p. A8).

But the missing is only beginning. *"You look like you lost your best friend"* will never sound the same to Jackie May or to those who acknowledge grief for a friend in a culture that discounts grief in general and friendgrief in particular. In time, some friends put on a happy face, if nothing else to avoid well-intentioned cliches such as, "She wouldn't want us to be sad." The intentional friendgriever will be challenged, "It was not like you lost a member of your family or something." Or *something*? For some co-friends and some clinicians, the goal is clear: reorganize the friendorbit and make new friends, or in other words, get over it. Klass, Silverman, and Nickman (1996) decry the demand that a griever "sever the bonds with the deceased in order to free the survivor to make new attachments" (p. 3) or friendships. Some individuals will, over time, experience the total depletion of their friendships. As Herman Hesse informs his friend, Thomas Mann, "As little by little they all vanish away, so that in the end we have more friends and intimates in the 'beyond' than here below" (as cited in Harris, 1999, p. 201).

RECOGNIZING MY GRIEF IN THE EXPERIENCED FRIENDGRIEF OF ANOTHER

Clinicians who have formed "friendly" relationships with clients will be touched by friendgrief. Also clinicians may be affected by psycho-dynamic links between a client's loss and the clinician's own life experience (Bennett & Kelaher, 1993). Some element in a client's friendgrief seems, sounds, feels, appears familiar or "reboots" the therapist's grief. In the Tate Museum in London, hangs the painting, *"Peace—Burial at Sea"* by British landscape artist J. M. W. Turner. The painting honors his friend, Sir David Wilkie, who died and was buried at sea. After critics fiercely attacked the painting as "too dark," Turner retorted,

"I only wish I had any colour to make them blacker" (Gaunt, 1971, p. 17). Viewing the painting and rereading the commentary in the guidebook, I mumbled, "I know what he means." I walked out of the Tate remembering friends who had died and feeling a new appreciation for Turner's art.

Friendgrief may be re-kindled by an experience as mundane as browsing new books in a bookstore when a stranger's string of written words stir the embers of grief for a friend. I found myself overwhelmed by a book about an individual driving a friend home from medical treatment in San Francisco—a cross-country trip. Admittedly, I wanted a "and they all lived happily ever after" ending. I wanted the author's friend to survive, even though my friends had not and my latest diagnosed friends, may not.

Although Connie died, the author writes, "But she does live in my memory, and I am reminded of her every time I look at her picture, which sits on my shelf" (Berry & Traeder, 1995, p. 198). The friendgrief is captured in elegant words:

> When we examine sunlight streaming through a window, we notice the dust motes sparkling, moving, dancing in the air. So it is with our memories of our friends and their memories of us. We may not even know they are there, unless the full light of our consciousness comes to rest on a memory. But they are always present, dancing, moving, swirling in our thoughts and around and through our souls (Berry & Traeder, 1995, p. 200).

FRIENDGRIEF IN THE OBITS

Broner (1994) writes about her father's habit, while reading the obituaries, of calling out, "Look, somebody wonderful lived" (p. 1). That observation captures the desire of many friendgrievers to acknowledge, "Look, somebody wonderful—*my friend*—lived." Faithful obituary readers are rewarded with unusual, extraordinary tidbits that lead to a voiced, "Imagine that!" or a confessed, "I wish I had a friend like that!" The individuals who make up today's obituaries probably leave friends, or at least a friend grieving, sometimes noted in the last line: "remembered by *a host of friends* or *numerous friends.*" Some samples from obituaries illustrate this.

> Everyone Craig met became his friend. He will be deeply missed by those he touched (Craig Anthony Huscher, 1998, p. B-3).

> Her many friends over the years will remember her for her sparkling wit (Lillian Elizabeth Freed, 1998, p. B-3).

Joan's life was a love song, a glorious duet with Lois; and a tender chorus with her dear friends and family. She is gone, but her music will live forever (M. Joan Driskill, 1998, November 9, p. B-2).

Notice that in the last obituary friends is intentionally mentioned first.

Friendgrief deserves not just the attention of other friends but of those who create and market sympathy cards, of clinicians—especially those who write books and articles and influence professional practice, of those who train and supervise clinicians, as well as of those who draft and interpret public and corporate policy on bereavement leave.

CONTROVERSY THINS FRIENDSHIP ROSTERS

Sometimes, a death stirs a hazy recollection, "Wasn't he the one who . . . ?" One's fifteen seconds of fame may be framed by notoriety or scandal. Thus, after the death, some friends grieve privately. Often when celebrities fall, many friends make themselves scarce. Al Campanis, for example, is not remembered for turning the Los Angeles Dodgers into baseball's world champions but for telling Ted Kopple on *Nightline* that blacks lacked "the necessities" to be managers of teams and baseball executives. A handful of words—by a tired man—provoked an uproar in organized baseball that banished Campanis from the game he loved. When Campanis died in 1998, headlines resurrected the controversy: "Ex-Dodger executive Campanis dies. 'Necessities' comment regarding black job candidate rocked sports 11 year ago" ("Ex-Dodger executive Campanis dies," 1998, June 22, p. C1).

No doubt, some readers concluded, after a quick glance at the story or headlines, "Oh that *bigot* died." However, buried in the story was an assessment by Tommy Lasorda, Campanis' longtime friend and former Dodgers manager: "He did more for black players, more for Latin players, than anybody. In all the years I've known him, I've never heard him say one racist thing" ("Ex-Dodger executive Campanis dies," 1998, p. C5). Only a devoted friend could offer such a gift. An incident, one poor choice of words must be placed in the context of a lifetime, and only a faithful friend like Lasorda can do that.

EVERYONE DESERVES A FRIEND

William Trollinger (1998), an opponent of capital punishment, befriended Samuel McDonald, a prisoner on Missouri's death row. Trollinger recalls, "[As] my friendship with Sam deepened, I tried not to think about the fact that the state of Missouri was determined to end his life" (p. 1059). When appeals were exhausted, McDonald asked Trollinger to be one of his "family and friend" witnesses at the execution. "I don't want to die alone, and I need to see you there" (p. 1059). Late one night, Trollinger found himself in a cramped observation booth,

> waiting and looking (initially through blinds) at a small fragment of my friend, I was overwhelmed by dread. As a middle-class, middle-aged white man who grew up in suburbia and has lived a secure and privileged life, I had never seen anyone die, much less be killed. Now I had a front-row seat.

> Just after midnight the guards raised the blinds. There, in a dazzling white room, lay Sam. He was on a gurney with a white sheet up to his neck. . . . He was speaking rapidly, but we could not hear anything. I repeatedly mouthed "I love you" to him (Trollinger, 1998, p. 1061).

After the injections terminated McDonald's life, Trollinger sat staring at his friend's body until a guard snapped the blinds shut and ushered out the witnesses. In another booth, sat friend witnesses of the off-duty policeman McDonald had shot to death. How was their friendgrief impacted by this execution?

Regardless of status or position in life, the death of a friend can have major impact. Stowe, Ross, Wodak, Thomas, and Larson (1993) report on the impact of grief on injecting drug users who have had a friend die. One wonders about gang members who have had numerous friends killed; a friend's death often prompts a retaliatory killing that results in fresh friendgrief in another gang. In every strata of society, individuals are touched by the death of a friend.

THE DEATH OF FIRST FRIEND

The friendship between Bill Clinton and Ron Brown began when a Southern governor, Clinton, decided to run for president and a political operative, Brown, decided to rejuvenate the Democratic Party after losses in 1980, 1984, and 1988. Slowly, through the primaries, the convention, and the presidential campaign in 1992, a friendship evolved and was deepened when Brown joined the Administration as Secretary of Commerce. The friendship was not always bound by protocol. Clinton (1998) explains, "As long as I live, I will remember the day Ron Brown forgot I was President and beat me at basketball"

(p. xiii) during a pick-up game between campaign stops in Los Angeles. "He took a few kids, and I took a few kids. All of a sudden he forgot who was President and how he got his day job" (Clinton, 1996, April 10, p. 2).

Living in the White House did not shield Bill Clinton from friendgrief. In 1996, the President called a friend (Alma, Brown's wife), "I wanted you to hear it from me first. Ron's plane is missing in Croatia" (Brown, 1998, p. 17). Clinton adds, "It was one of the saddest moments in her life" (p. xv). The next day, circumstances forced this friend to notify his, "Friend Alma, there are no survivors. They have identified Ron's body" (p. 25).

The rituals were exhausting for the President because his grief was both observed and scrutinized by the media as well as, given the times, political pundits. On Easter Eve, the President-friendgriever delivered remarks to about 1,000 people on the tarmac at Andrews Air Force Base and to more via cable (or who would see sound bytes on cable news broadcasts). The emotions of watching 33 flag-draped coffins unloaded, created, even for a veteran speaker, enormous pressure. In fact, President Clinton's words could have been spoken by friendgrievers in numerous settings. "Life is more than we can understand. Life is more, sometimes, than we can even bear" (Brown, 1998, p. 280). Days later, before 5,000 mourners at the National Cathedral funeral, eulogizing his friend, the President faced the Secretary's casket. "I want to say to my friend just one last time: Thank you. If it weren't for you, I wouldn't be here [as President]" (Clinton, 1996, April 10, p. 2).

Controversy erupted over video footage of the President laughing during the service. Critics immediately attacked Clinton's grief as "phoney" and a play for the public's sympathy. In the video clip, the President was filmed as he talked to a friend of mine, Tony Campolo. Tony had just whispered to the president a story about attending black funerals and the powerful impact of the singing of the hymn, "We Will Understand It Better." Clinton, having attended many funerals for African-American friends in Arkansas, knew the song well. Recalling it, he grinned, unaware that cameras were on him. Carlson (1996, April 22) defends the President, saying, "People laugh at funerals all the time. Only in the capital would someone stop doing so out of fear that it was used against him—as it was" (p. 24).

Bill Clinton surely felt the absence of his friend, especially during the Starr investigations and the impeachment trial. How might things have been different for the President had his close friend survived the crash? That same question will repeatedly come up in the minds of your clients: "What if my friend had lived . . . ?"

KEY CONCEPTS OF THIS CHAPTER

- Friendgrief must be openly acknowledged, socially validated, and publicly mourned in order to be thoroughly grieved.
- Friends have a right—as much a right as any griever—to give their grief its voice.
- Friendgrievers have a right to expect support in exploring their own unique journey path to reconciliation with the loss, whether their friend was Secretary of Commerce, an IV drug user, a disgraced baseball executive, a murderer, or the president of the local PTA.
- Because of the silence in the academic and professional literature, many clinicians are unaware of friendgrief and are insensitive to client friendgrievers.
- "You look like you've lost your best friend" is more than a cliche for some friends.
- Friendgrievers have a right to expect society, other friends, and clinicians to validate their grief.

.

CHAPTER 3

Defining a Friendship

CHAPTER PREVIEW

In this chapter, we will examine definitions of friendship to help clarify the scope of this study. Given the abundance of emotion-hued, feel-good definitions of friendship in this society, what does one mean by "friend?" In a clinical setting definition and clarification of operative terms are essential. A definition frames the parameters in which the friendship and the grief can be studied. Yager (1999) and Nardi and Sherrod (1994) identify three broad categories of friendship: "casual," "close," and "best" friend.

Friendgrief is shaped by the definition of the friendship at the time of death. An accurate assessment is critical for working with a grieving client. Definition becomes critical if a funeral ritual is designated private or if ritual space limits the number of participants.

> I think we're entirely too free in this country with the use of the word "friendship," when actually we're just favorably acquainted with someone, when we're their allies for the moment (Jim McDougal prepares for prison, 1997, May 20, p. A-5).

During the impeachment of President Clinton much was made of his friendship with James and Susan McDougal and the friendship of Monica Lewinsky and Linda Tripp. Some frustration revolved around the meaning of "friend." What does the word mean? A plaque on my office wall reminds me, "Words matter. Pay attention to them." As Humpty Dumpty informs Alice, "When I use a word, it means just what I choose it to mean—neither more or less." Alice protests, "The question is whether you can make words mean so many different things" (Carroll, 1960, p. 186). Alice's observation is appropriate for this study.

WHAT "FRIEND" MEANS

"Friend" can mean different things in an individual's vocabulary. The word is an umbrella covering a variety of relationships. One needs a qualifier to understand the statement, "My friend died last week." Because people use the term "friend" "loosely and often" (Fischer, 1982, p. 298), clinicians must be sensitive to the client's idiosyncracies and shadings in definitions. E. Klein (1998) examines the relationships of Jackie Kennedy Onassis, particularly her friendship with Maurice Templesman, whom *The New York Times* identifies as Mrs. Onassis' "longtime companion" (Kleinfield, 1999, p. A12) a phrase that implies, for some, a romantic connotation. One of Templesman's "oldest friends" (E. Klein, 1998, p. 330) contends that Onassis and Templesman were "very much in love" an assessment dismissed by "most of Jackie's friends" (p. 330). Which friends' evaluation is to be believed? Clinicians, family members, as well as friends in other orbits may be misled by a "friend" who exaggerates the relationship, especially after the death when the definition cannot be easily verified.

TIME VS. QUALITY MARKERS
OF FRIENDSHIPS

How long must you have known a friend to grieve? Do longtime or lifelong friends grieve significantly differently than new friends? In Vietnam, due to the constant rotation of personnel, friends knew each other briefly yet bonded instantly; survival depended on buddies looking out for each other. Robeson (1999) discloses his own ambush of friendgrief at the Vietnam Memorial while saying a delayed good-bye to "gallant and special friends" (p. 32). He recalls a teenage medic who, although wounded, nevertheless went to the aid of a new friend and was later found dead with his arm around him. The medic could have chosen safety but decided a new but "seriously injured friend facing a lonely and painful death need him" (p. 31).

Many Vietnam friendships evaporated upon return stateside. The promised letters were never written. Once home, many simply wanted to forget the experiences they had shared with "temporary" friends. Many found that stateside friends did not understand them or rejected them because the war was so unpopular (Howard, 1976; Shatan, 1973).

In contrast, soldiers in many Civil War units had grown up together, joined together, fought together, and died together; friends were often responsible for the initial battlefield burials or shipping bodies home (Dean, 1997). As lifelong friends, the grief resulting from a comrade's death was more disabling, especially when soldiers returned home.

Brevity also challenges the definition of friendship, such as between long or frequently hospitalized or institutionalized persons and health care providers. Close and continual contact creates something of a pragmatic friendship (Maxwell, 1996) or what Hoffman (1995) labels a "hospital friendship" (p. 33). Ethical issues arise when the patient becomes a friend (Carson, 1999) but nurses still "make friends" with patients; some write candidly about the friendship in the professional literature (Cochran, 1998; Hallock, 1994; Makrevis, 1994; Scott, 1994; Venturella, 1998). How much interaction does it take for a health care worker to create a relationship with a particular patient that would be considered a friendship by either party or by family members? In some instances—in many ways much as an interested party in legal proceedings may become a "friend of the court"—the nurse becomes a "friend of the patient," sometimes acting as a go-between, negotiator, or informal advisor in the medical maze (Cohen, 1995). Seefried (1999) describes friendship with "Jack": "The nature of our relationship allowed us several levels of intimacy that extended beyond the typical patient-nurse relationship" (p. 156). Still, grief for a patient-now-friend is disenfranchised (Murphy, 1999).

FRIEND REQUIRES QUALIFICATION

A friendship is created and maintained by participants, "without the benefits of any formalized guidelines" (Nardi, 1999, p. 128) or legal structures or definition. Friendship may be the only affectional relationship that operates voluntarily, without societal or contractual regulation (Wiseman, 1986). The absence of legal or societal regulation encourages freedom to define the word without challenge or clarification. Many friends make up expectations as they go (Goodman & O'Brien, 2000). Who is defining *friend:* a social scientist, a clinician, a participant in a graduate student's research, a child, a resident in a retirement facility, a closeted gay, a person "who never meets a stranger?"

- Definition becomes critical if a friend dies in a scandal or is discovered to be a serial murderer. Those identified as friends quickly distance themselves and redefine the friendship, "Oh, I hardly knew him" or "We *used* to be friends . . . but certainly not any more." Some abandon others in the friendorbit to avoid stigma contamination.
- Definition becomes critical if a funeral ritual is designated private. Which friends are close enough to be included? Which will protest the exclusion, "I sure thought we were friends." The designated

funeral space may require—sometimes conveniently—restrictions so that attendance must be limited to close friends. Who defines "close?" Edward Kennedy wanted John Kennedy Jr.'s memorial service to be held in "a cavernous cathedral" but Caroline, the chief mourner—instead chose a small Manhattan church. Her decision meant many self-defined, as contrasted with family-recognized, friends could not attend (Carlson, 1999, August 2).

- Definitions become important when corporate bereavement management policies—or a supervisor who interprets the policies—do not appreciate a definition of friend. When one employee asked off to attend a friend's funeral, the supervisor replied, "You know, I had a friend die one time and I only went to the visitation." One friend had to plead, "He was a really *good* friend. We've been friends since high school" to gain the supervisor's authorization.

- Definitions come into play in hospital settings when a friend is dying. What can a friend do when a nurse devalues closeness and insists, "*Family only!*" One by-product of the AIDS epidemic, is that increasingly nurses bend the rules to accommodate close friends (Gordon, 1997). Health care professionals are discovering that friends comprise a critical element in caregiving, particularly for the unmarried and unfamilied.

- Definitions come into play in expectation of social support, both short-term and long-term. Some families expect more support from best or close friends than from casual friends.

- Definitions come into play in the selection of individuals for direct participation in the rituals like a eulogist, pallbearer, etc.

- Definitions come into play in evaluating advice and soliciting support. Advice from a "close" friend might be valued more than advice from a "casual" friend. Friend support is a valued resource for individuals coping with loss (Gamino, Sewell, & Easterling, 1998).

- Definitions come into play in evaluating narratives of friendgrief. Friends construct personal definitions, expectations, and fine nuances based on their own experiences of (and need for) being friended and being a friend. Thus listeners filter the narratives of others through what Taylor (1998) calls "a listener's own history with the word" (p. 7). Over the past generation the definition of friendship has so changed that the word is impaired. Individuals are significantly impacted by their encounters with friendship, especially the inevitable blacks and blues of rejection and betrayal. The phrase "fair weather friend" is well-known shorthand for an unpredictable friend. Most adults have been disillusioned by a friendship and lament, "Some friend she turned out to be!"

THE TROUBLESOME ABSENCE OF A
CLEAR DEFINITION

Because "works for me" definitions are common, the contemporary meaning of friendship is ambiguous (Zeggelink, 1993). Cheney (as cited in Yager, 1999) illustrates this reality in a cartoon of two individuals looking at sympathy cards. "Well, she's not my best best friend, or a really close friend, but she is a good friend, if not a great friend" (p. 154). In practice or research, however, definition and clarification of operative terms are essential to delimit the boundaries. Willmott (1987) voices regrets that dictionaries are not more definitive. *The Oxford English Dictionary* (1978) devotes three pages to friend and chronicles how impoverished our vocabulary has become with the loss of once-useful words such as *friended, friendstrong, backfriend, friendable, friendess, friendstead,* and *friendful* (pp. 545-547). The words may be changing, as Putnam (2000) documents, because the friendships are changing as people spend less time with friends.

Friend resists airtight defining even among friends and undergoes continual evaluation. Ask me about those close friends who did not respond following my mother's death. Do I still consider them close friends or "just" friends?

Fluid definitions for "close" friend, for example, confuse dialogue. What one client considers a close friend, might be a casual friend to another client. By comparison, "spouse" has a common as well as legal definition; when someone uses spouse there is a clear legal definition: wife or husband (gays and lesbians who have had holy unions may also use spouse). In few friendships are expectations rarely stated explicitly, a factor that leads to disappointments and strained friendships (Vanzant, 1998). Friendships are hampered by contradictory and unstated expectations. In seeking and nurturing friendships, adults often formulate particular expectations for friends (Rawlins, 1992) particularly in times of crisis.

Yager (1999) and Nardi and Sherrod (1994) identify three broad categories: "casual," "close," and "best" friend after a review of the literature demonstrates "that people typically employ such categories when describing their friends" (p. 191). These categories work as something of a relational shorthand.

Casual friend   "Someone who is more than an acquaintance, but not a close friend, your commitment would probably not extend beyond the circumstances that bring you together; for example, a work friend or neighbor" (p. 191).

Close friend   "Someone to whom you feel a sense of mutual commitment and continuing closeness; a person with whom you talk fairly openly and feel comfortable spending time" (p. 191).

Best friend   "The friend to whom you feel the greatest commitment and closeness; the one who accepts you 'as you are,' with whom you talk the most openly and feel the most comfortable spending time" (p. 191).

Friendship for many adults is a relationship in progress, situational and changeable, modified and impacted by day-to-day circumstances as captured in these disclosures:

"We had a big 'falling out'. . . ."

"We used to be a lot closer than we are now. . . ."

"I wouldn't exactly call him a friend. . . ."

Friendships can be bilaterally or unilaterally strained and thus hard to quantify accurately at a particular moment, such as death, a reality which may strain interaction with other members of the friendorbit as well as with a chief mourner.

SOME FRIENDS CONSTRUCT PRAGMATIC DEFINITIONS

Some individuals consider a sexual partner a friend and would not accept a definitional exclusion. Stanley (1996) argues that sexualized friendships are becoming more common because Americans place a high value on romantic and sexual coupling. Sedaris, an American living in Paris, describes an experience in French class when a student asks how to say "boyfriend." The teacher replies, "You would just say this is my friend. It's nobody's business that it's your *boy*friend. Why does anybody need to know who you are sleeping with?"(cited in "An American Satirist in Paris," 2000, June, p. 9). Indeed, for many using English as a second language, the nuances in friendship are puzzling. What Americans generously dub "friendships," people in more structured cultures would label acquaintainships (Yager, 1999). In most friendships with the opposite sex, some potential exists for sexual attraction and involvement (Kolbenschlag, 1979). Many affairs begin as a friendship, just as many marriages begin with friendships. Indeed, a source of tension for dating couples is when one party desires that they remain "just friends."

An emerging reality further clouds the word "friend." How does a 32-year-old describe the woman her 75-year-old-father is dating, seeing, sleeping with? Often lady-*friend* is used. Those who do not value an individual's sexual orientation or the relationship may avoid *lover* or *partner* and use a pragmatic definition of friendship as in "He's my son's, ah, 'friend.'" One friend reveals a functional definition:

> My definition is based on reality, not memory. Maybe you have seen that commercial, "Have you driven a Ford lately?" Well, what have you as a friend done for me *lately*? I keep short books on friendships. The only people interested in the past are historians and antique dealers! In my book a friend is someone who has done something for me *lately*.

This individual would deride the common assertion, "We may go three or four years without seeing each other, but as friends we just start up where we left off." Yager (1999) observes that men feel a freedom to contact an old friend without any need to apologize for the lapse.

Fischer (1982) argues that too much research and theory on friendship, by allowing flimsy, imprecise definitions, rests on a weak, shifting foundation. Fischer captures the frustration of many researchers by titling his article, "What Do We Mean by 'Friend'?" Friends take the word "friend" for granted, generating the classic cliche, "She's a friend of mine. You know what I mean . . . a friend." I do not necessarily know what you mean. Perhaps you have had this conversation:

> I ran into an old friend of yours the other day.
> Oh, really, who was that?
> He said his name was Kyle?
> Kyle? Kyle . . . I don't know any Kyle. . . .
> Well, he knows you. He said you were good friends in college.
> Oh yeah, *that* Kyle. . . .

When asked to define a "friend," some people name someone—a particular someone who fulfills the expectations or roles of a friend. Stowe, Ross, Wodak, Thomas, and Larson (1993) found definition a significant barrier in examining support systems of drug users. Asked to use initials to identify their close friends, some named almost everyone they knew. Had these researchers asked, "Have you had *friends* die of an overdose?" the research would have been skewed by the lack of precise definition. The same could be true of individuals who boast, "Oh, I have lots of friends." So do I if I use your definition.

Friend can also be applied to "a mere acquaintance, or to a stranger, as a mark of goodwill or kindly condescension on the part of the speaker" (*The Oxford English Dictionary,* 1933/1978, p. 545). "Friend" can be used to reduce resistance to a request, "Hey, ol' buddy, ol' pal. How about doing a friend a little favor?" Sometimes one has to hear "friend" sounded to catch the qualifier in the voice.

GENDER INFLUENCES THE DEFINING
OF FRIEND

Gender distinctions exist both in creating and maintaining friendship (Goodman, 1998, August 2). Farrell (1975) and Wright (1982) contend that males make and keep friendships through doing—sharing experiences, such as a pick-up game of basketball, working on a car engine, or serving in a combat battalion. Females create and maintain friendships through being—spending time together and through talking. Sanders (1995, 1998) finds gender distinctions in bereavement expression. Ask a male about a friend's funeral and you may get, "Fine." Ask a woman and you get an appraisal, "The flowers were beautiful, the music was good, the casket was gorgeous."

Some individuals state, "My spouse is my best friend" (Culbertson, 1992; Smith, 1990); a challenging notion to clinicians who do not consider their spouse best friends. Spouses are more frequently identified as best friends by males than by females (Rubin, 1983; Yager, 1999). In the classic study, *The Season's of a Man's Life,* Levinson, Darrow, Klein, Levinson, and McKee (1978) observe, "Close friendship with a man or woman is rarely experienced by American men" (p. 335). To create an illusion of a friend network, many males blur distinctions between words like "friend" and "acquaintance." A male is more likely to have "friendly" relationships than friends or friends than friendships (Seneca as cited in Culbertson, 1992). Men rely generously on synonyms like "associate" or "colleague" since "men learn early that only one type of intimacy is allowed to them—male-female intimacy—and their experience confirms that intimacy necessarily leads to sex" (Culbertson, 1992, p. 91). Intimacy and sexuality are so linked in the thinking of many males, that they never become too chummy or intimate with another male. Homophobia is a significant influence in male friendships (Monroe & Baker, 1997).

Ask males, "Do you have a good friend?" Many males will answer "my wife" or name a friend from years before with whom they do not regularly interact (Culbertson, 1992). When a spouse identified as a best friend dies, a male experiences dual grief; that loss may be more troublesome because of the absence of a phalanx of male friends to offer committed support. When Goldberg (1979) queried men "Do you have a friend?," the most common response was, "No. Why? Should I?" (p. 21).

WOMEN AND FRIENDSHIP

Goodman (1998, July 6) suggests, "Friendship between women is not about the things we do together. It's about the things we talk over together. We measure closeness and distance by the intimacies shared and understood" (p. B-5). Alpert (1997) supports Goodman's perspective:

> Our women friends are the richest treasure we possess, and the importance of friendship in women's lives cannot be overemphasized. These precious, powerful relationships sustain us when everything else seems in flux; if we're lucky, our friendships may endure for decades and across thousands of miles (p. vii).

Alpert's point is illustrated in grief-themed movies such as *Steel Magnolias* and *Beaches*. If the importance of friendship among women cannot be overemphasized, the resulting grief when a friend dies cannot be underestimated. Although society has no institutionalized recognition or rituals for friendships (Allen, 1989), and friendships are neither covenantal nor contractual, some women friends do commit to something equivalent to "for better or worse, 'til death us do part." Alpert (1997) concludes that many friendships between women function like a marriage only the promise "to love and honor each other in soul and spirit, to stick by one another through thick and thin" (p. viii) is understood, not stated. Moreover, "In a very real sense, true friends commit to those they love for richer or poorer, in sickness and in health. No license is signed, no ceremony is witnessed, but the bonds of friendship are so often stronger than those which join a man and a woman together" (p. viii). Friendships may outlast marriages and relationships and sometimes must be divvied up during a divorce.

Martin and Doka (1998) challenge the generalizations that women grieve more effectively than males. They conclude women grieve more publicly and that some men "grieve in a like manner to most women" (p. 133). Friends of males and clinicians must "recognize and respect the masculine pattern of grieving as genuine, and not an artifact of the 'John Wayne' syndrome" (p. 142). This discomfort with friendship with other men compounds grief expression when a male friend dies. Hence, male body language at a visitation or ritual discloses a lot of awkward hugging and back-pounding and mumblings about "being strong." A visitation or funeral may be one of the rare opportunities for some males to touch or hug each other. Male friends regulate or "police" other friends (Walter, 1999, p. 125). Little wonder that females observing male friends conclude, "They are *not* grieving."

FRIEND AND GRIEF IN CONTEMPORARY CULTURE

In contemporary American society with its rich ethnic and cultural diversity, some individuals cannot understand or accept the constructs of friendships that others invest in and value. (This is also true in business friendships between Americans and others in a global economy.) Some cannot appreciate the ground rules for maintaining friendships. Ethnic understandings of friendship are filters through which we encounter and evaluate grief. Some heterosexual males are troubled by the more expressive public grief of gay males when friends die. Whites may have difficulty comprehending the outpouring of emotion at a black friend's funeral. Martin and Doka (2000) insist there are many ways for males or females to grieve.

Four men who became friends as teen soldiers in Chiang Kai-shek's Nationalist Chinese Army, migrated to America as middle-age bachelors, looking for a fresh start because there were no pensions for soldiers in Taiwan. The friends toiled in menial jobs in New York's Chinatown, lived together, and have shared the same half-bedroom apartment for a decade. Three of the friends are dead; only William Wong survives. A cardboard box and a tea tin in the room contain the ashes of Wong's three compatriots (Chen, 1998, p. 43) because the friend-survivor cannot afford to bury his friends. Some friends would have found a cheaper, or cruder, solution a long time ago; few friends well tolerate great inconvenience. But Wong understands friendship within a particular Asian construct that is, so far, unaltered by the American notion of expediency. He cannot dishonor or abandon his friends with an improper burial.

KEY CONCEPTS OF THIS CHAPTER

- Definitions count. If Neimeyer (1998) is correct in suggesting that grievers must be "active agents in negotiating the course of their post-lost adjustment" (p. 120) part of being proactive must be in clarifying definitions.

- The word "friend" requires a qualifier. Sometimes friend must be placed in quotations.
- Clinicians read this text and hear client's narratives through the filter of their own friendorbit and friendships. Moreover, a male clinician may have difficulty appreciating the friendship or friend-grief of a female client just as a female clinician may have difficulty evaluating a male's friendship or friendgrief (Yager, 1999).
- Friendgrief is shaped by the condition of the friendship at the time of death. An accurate pre-death assessment is critical for working with a grieving client. This is a particular friend grieving for a particular friend.
- A definition frames the parameters in which the friendship and the grief can be examined. Yager (1999) and Nardi and Sherrod (1994) identify three broad categories: "casual" friend, "close" friend, and "best" friend.
- Definition becomes critical if a funeral ritual is designated private or if ritual space limits the number of participants.
- Gender plays a role in defining friendship. Many males blur distinctions between words like "friend" and "acquaintance."

IMPLICATIONS FOR CLINICIANS

1. Clinicians bring to their professional setting their own assessments, negative and positive, and biases on death, friendship, and bereavement. Authors, researchers, clinicians, particularly grief educators and grief counselors, must put aside personally experienced self-definitions, shaped by their own friendships and friendgriefs to interact with a particular client. Just as a patient defines pain, the client defines friendgrief. How does a friendless clinician or a clinician whose only friend is a spouse hear the narrative of a particular friendgriever who has an expansive friend roster? Caltagirone (1988) insists that the "deepest realities of human life cannot be defined in intellectual terms. We can, at best, touch on them through stories" (p. 64)—stories that may require translation and reflection before response.

2. Clinicians must set aside personal prejudices and experiences to interact with a friendgriever. It may be a challenge to hear out the friendship experience of clients who radically define friendship particularly when it conflicts with the clinician's assessments and values, for example, friendships among substance abusers. Stowe, Ross, Wodak, Thomas, and Larson (1993) document the perception of some clinicians that Intravenous Drug Users neither deserve social support nor are prepared to utilize it. Although the friendship orbits of many I.D.U.s

have been as impacted by AIDS as those of gay men and they are well acquainted with friendgrief, drug users are far less likely to receive support for grief issues and unresolved friendgrief may intensify substance abuse. S. Klein (1998) is clear: "Counselors must constantly be aware of the complexity of nontraditional relationships" (p. 109).

Pilsecker (1994) wonders how clinicians can interact with the client-friendgriever without filtering their narratives of losses through a personal grief grid? How does the clinician who has never experienced the death of a friend respond to an individual grieving yet another death of a friend? How does a male hear out the narrative of a female client or a homosexual client? How do gay clinicians continue to hear out the friendgrief in a large clientele impacted by multiple losses to AIDS (Neville & Greif, 1994) or aging especially if their own friendorbits have been significantly devastated? Or when their own grief and sexuality may be disenfranchised by other clinicians (Andriote, 1999). In fact, a clinician's own friendgrief may be reactivated by a client's narrative of the loss of a friendship. Some clinicians limit the number of patients they see with AIDS-related losses. One psychiatrist admits, "There's a certain number I can tolerate without destroying my own psychological health or my relationship or my ability to work" (p. 351). Or what about an aging clinician who is threatened by the descriptions of friendgrief from a senior adult?

3. Some persons of faith do not believe any friendship is coincidental. "Much of the charm of friendship is that we do not cause it to happen. It is a gift from God" (Caltagirone, 1988, p. 11). Thus, "We never 'make' friends; we simply acknowledge what God intended for us since the beginning of time" (p. 11). Many people of faith do not believe any death is coincidental but part of God's plan (McBrien, 1995). Clinicians who do not share such a theological assessment of friendship or death, may have difficulty understanding the faith crisis that can be triggered by a person's conclusion that God dissolved the friendship by "taking my friend from me in death." Or hearing out an individual's refusal to confront the death because "We will meet again in heaven someday." Is belief in eternal life a coping mechanism? One friendgriever asked me, "Why would God go to so much trouble to bring us together, if he didn't have something longer in mind?" One friend told me, "God knew what he was doing in taking my friend."

4. Clinicians must translate and negotiate differences in definition and experience. Clinicians must translate fine nuances and shadings gleaned from the narratives of clients. The clinician must be alert to subtle shading in the use of "friend" within certain subcommunities. A clinician must hear, for example, a lesbian friendgriever's lament for a friend without assuming that narrative to be stereotypical for all lesbians

grieving friends. In the case of a gay male, the friend being grieved may also have been a former lover or partner who had become a friend.

5. Clinicians must re-enfranchise the stories and the griefs which have been dismissed, discounted, and disenfranchised by other friends and perhaps by other clinicians. This friend may be the only friend in the orbit embracing the grief; the continued engagement with grief isolates this griever from other friends. Indeed, a caustic or well meant: "You need to see someone!" may have prompted this individual seeking professional help or a support group. Stephanopoulis (1999), a high ranking presidential aide in the first Clinton administration, discloses that the suicide of his friend, Vince Foster, was a key factor in his decision to begin therapy.

Howard (1976) found that veterans experiencing friendgrief need the loss validated emotionally and not just intellectually. I suggest that reality can be true for other friendgrievers as well. The clinician may be the first to give the friend permission to grieve. In recommending participation in a support group, I note that in a group the friendgriever will not need a translator; that in a group a friend's grief is more likely to be recognized, valued, and heard out.

6. Friendship depends on who is doing the defining (Zeggelink, 1993). Clinicians must listen for critical modifiers before "friend" in the sentence, "My good/best/old friend died"? Has the adjective changed? Has the relationship been closer at a previous point? Clinicians must listen for gaps in the narratives that point to detours or estrangement or a lack of closeness at the time of death. Today's friend is tomorrow's diminished, exiled friend or ex-friend. Regrets over the diminishment or estrangement of a friendship complicate friendgrief. Guilt or self-indictment over failure to be a friend or to set aside differences in order to be present during a final illness can also complicate grief for a friend.

Friendships are fluid. Responsibility for the distancing in a relationship may be difficult to assess accurately; after all, there is no friend to challenge or amend the surviving friend's perspective. A person who throws wonderful parties, with people jostling for invitations, may find few takers for the next party should he be arrested for drugs or child molesting. E. Klein (1998) identifies the unshakeable friends who stood by Jackie Onassis through/after her divorce from Aristotle Onassis, especially when Aristotle's friends blasted Mrs. Onassis in the media as a financial opportunist.

Alpert (1997) insists that it is in such testing—and "even the closest friendships, no matter how strong, will be tested" (p. viii)—one learns the mettle of the friendship. In a crisis, one learns the identities of "true blue" or "real" friends. Some friendships emerge stronger after the testing; others are weakened. The testing for some is a long illness. In some cases, reconciliation never occurs, or time runs out when one of the friends die. Estrangement may complicate involvement in a funeral. Would Elton John have been asked to sing at Di's funeral had his rift with her after the death of their mutual friend, Gianni Versace not been settled? (Andersen, 1998). Arts (1983) is correct, "We have to miss a certain friend badly a few times before we can discover who this friend really" (p. 83) was and the place the friend filled in a friendorbit.

Some friends redecorate their lives periodically with new collections of friends as a process of moving on or socially moving up. Others acquire and discard friends like cards in a poker hand; the friend is jettisoned when no longer useful. An accurate assessment is critical for working with a grieving client. Ask, "How would you describe your friendship six months before your friend's death? at the time of your friend's death?" The grief may be for a lost intensity of friendship as well as for the death of the friend.

7. The friendorbit may have been sparse before this friend's death; this death may translate depletion of the social network. In fact, depression among senior adults who have outlived their friends, may be unsupported friendgrief. Clinicians recognize the truth in Dillard's (1999) assessment of friendship rosters: "Anyone's close world of family and friends composes a group smaller than almost all sampling errors, smaller than almost all rounding errors, a group invisible, at whose loss the world will not blink" (p. 130). The clinician may ask, "Who supports your grief for a friend? Who discounts your grief?" The friendgriever may be seeking a witness to hear out their lament rather than a "fixer" (Murphy, 1999).

8. The friend may be mourning the loss of a new level of friendship in the future. "I thought we would grow old together. . . ." or "We were just really getting to know each other." "We were planning on. . . ." Howard (1976) captures the reality of friendgrief, particularly tinted by his Vietnam experience. "Many conflicts have been resolved, time has had an effect, my understanding of events is deeper; yet experience takes its toll, and some scars are always easily reopened" (p. 122). An experience such as viewing *Saving Private Ryan* or *Beaches* or a high school reunion could reignite unfinished grief or reopen assumed finished grief for a friend.

9. One consequence of friendgrief, as expressed to White House staff by President Clinton after the death of his friend since childhood, colleague Vince Foster, "we have to pay maybe a little more attention to our friends" (Stephanopoulis, 1999, p. 185). The clinician may ask, "What positive impact on other friendships will this loss have?" The client may need to explore redefining the responsibilities in a friendship and not just define the friendship.

CHAPTER 4

Recognizing the Friendorbit

CHAPTER PREVIEW

In this chapter a sociological paradigm will be introduced to understand the dynamics of friend networks and the impact of death and loss on those systems. The principles and components of the friendorbit model will be explained and used to illustrate the dynamic nature of friendships.

Why should a clinician care about friendorbits? By understanding the dynamic nature of friendships and the variables that contribute to friend-making and tensions between friends, clinicians gain insight into a client's unique friendship network now impacted by death and in the future by the forced restructuring.

> Kinship seems to be the principal criterion for legitimacy of grief and mourning in our society and, to a lesser degree, within the helping professions (Weinbach, 1989, p. 57).

There is no such reality as an impact-less death. While this culture highly prizes individualism, people do not live or grieve in a vacuum. Rather individuals make and maintain friendships in a relational system. A friend's death diminishes all the participants in the social network by forcing some degree of reorganization. Neimeyer (1998) defines grieving as "an act of affirming or reconstructing a personal world of meaning that has been challenged by loss" (p. 7). A griever reconstructs personal and shared myths about friendship and an identity as a survivor in negotiation with those left in the friendorbit, especially those she primarily related to through the deceased. This can be a demanding task for the adolescent who survives a car crash that kills three friends—one of whom was a "best" friend.

Circle of friends has long been a description for friend networks. Lageman (1986) examined the "wider social radius" of those who attend funerals and concludes there are five distinct "circles." The first circle is family *and* "intimate" friends. The second circle includes "close" friends. The third circle is what Lageman terms "functional others" or "casual" friends and business associates. The fourth circle includes "general others" such as new friends. The fifth circle includes "marginal others" or acquaintances. Boundaries are not tight between the latter three circles as the first two. Often those in this last category are the "hidden casualties of bereavement" because their grief is so easily dismissed, "You hardly knew her." Imagine the rings of a dartboard and you can grasp Lageman's system. Nord (1997) graphs survivors in a figure he calls "circles of relationships." The phrase "inner circle" suggests intimacy. Nord argues "The intensity of loss is increased in proportion to its proximity to the center of the concentric circles of relationship" (p. 47). While Lageman and Nord influenced my early thinking, I find these concepts do not incorporate the "ebb and flow" of friendships in our fast paced mobile culture. I propose a comparison construct more dynamic and fluid and which resembles the planetary system.

Adaptation to a death requires a renewed coherence not just to the narrative of our lives, but also to the shared narrative of the friend network, the environment in which friendships take place—especially when other friends either do not recognize and sometimes minimize this grief. Some clinicians, with little personal experience with the death of a friend, impose a path for getting over the loss, "You will get over it as soon as you make some *new* friends." Just as parents who have experienced a perinatal loss cannot "replace" a child, neither can friends. Replacement is a myth (Grout & Romanoff, 2000) which complicates grief.

THE ROLE OF THE FRIEND IN A LIFE:
THE FRIENDORBIT

In *Friendgrief,* I rely on a conceptualization, developed with Gregory DeBourgh of the University of San Francisco. Borrowing from the field of astronomy, we theorize that friendships function like orbiting planets around a magnet-friend. Remove that magnet-friend and the entire orbit faces reorganization; remove key friends from the friendorbit and it is inevitably altered. Friendorbit is a metaparadigm for understanding the dynamic nature of friendship orbits, system alterations, and impoverishment resulting from a friend's or friends' death.

The friendorbit is a range or sphere of intentional acts, a path of friendship in orbit around a primary personality which invites an orbit. Friendships encircle, enclose, surround, but also exclude. By choosing to invest time and energy in a friendship with Susan, John excludes a friendship with Donna or freezes any existing relationship as an acquaintanceship.

A potential *for friendorbit exists until relationships are established (see Figure 1), declined, or terminated.* Potential also exists for moving into a tighter orbit, from a good friend to a close friend or from a close friend to best friend. Someone initially has to be friendly or act friendly to initiate exploration of potential, an act as simple as saying, "I'd like to get to know you better. Let's get together for lunch sometime." The agenda "I'd like to get to know you better" may never be stated only implied. The real idea is: I'd like to get to know you better to see *if* you have potential as a friend. Shared activities such as a lunch, attending movies, or working on a committee function are an ad hoc audition for friendship. Over time, through shared experiences and conversations,

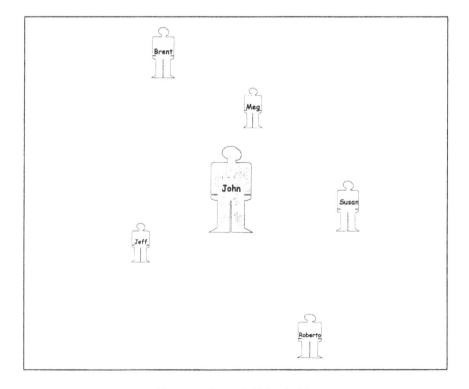

Figure 1. Potential friendorbit.

individuals get to know each other, continuously auditing the potential of the other for inclusion and placement in an existing friendorbit (close orbit, intermediate orbit, or peripheral orbit?). A friendorbit sometimes must be reconfigured to accommodate the new friend or to create a new "just us" exclusive friendorbit. Some friends in the orbit may be threatened by the introduction of a new friend into the extended orbit.

Friendships are enhanced through disclosure of personal narrative. In the early orbit formation, a friend wonders, "Can I trust the real me with this friend-to-be?" Some friends, as a form of self-protection, are reluctant to disclose fully the make-up of their friendorbit.

Figure 1 identifies John's five potential friends: Susan, Brent, Jeff, Meg, and Roberto. Through conversations, shared interests, shared experiences, and spending time together—what some young adults call "hanging out"—the orbit is tentatively initiated. In our lives are individuals who could, in time, through effort and with mutual consent, become friends and be drawn into an orbit.

Within the orbits are shared affinities. Suppose Meg and Roberto are college friends of John. They may go together to a campus event. Brent—a work friend—may not share an interest in their school related activities. When Roberto calls John and says, "Let's get together" that may well include Meg but not Susan. Or Susan may invite John to participate in a dinner party that includes Jeff but not Brent.

The tentative circle also shows that Meg is closest to John while Brent is the most distant, at the moment (see Figure 2). The nature of friendships is that proximity may change. Suppose, John and Brent are temporarily assigned to a project in Phoenix. Their circumstance-impacted friendship may blossom and expand significantly or it may be hampered by spending too much time together.

John now has five "good" friends: Brent, Susan, Jeff, Megan, and Roberto. John may consider Meg a "best" friend, Jeff a "close" friend, Roberto and Susan as "good" friends, and Brent as "just a friend" (see Figure 3).

Numerous other acquaintances—potential friends or friends in the making—interact with John. Some over time might become friends; one might become the best friend.

In time, some of those outside the existing orbits might become part of a future, revamped friendorbit with John. Friends (or one friend) may resist being drawn into closer orbit, may disinvest, or move away, sometimes into erratic orbits with only occasional interaction. Some may divert energy invested in this friendship into another friendship and friendorbit. Some decide to migrate toward the perimeter of the friendorbit and become more distant, with or without explanation (see Figure 4). "We used to be really close" is illustrated in Figure 5. One

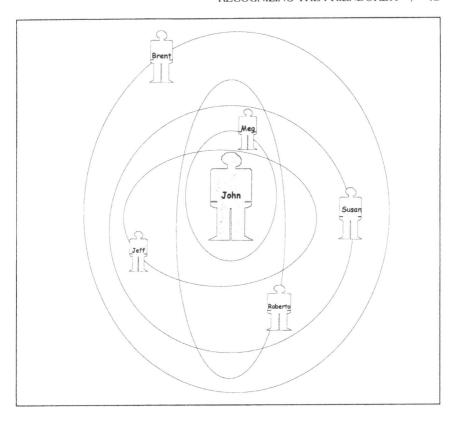

Figure 2. Tentative friendorbits (the dotted lines forming the orbit indicate tentativeness).

friend reflects, "We used up the friendship." Sometimes tension between two individuals in a friend's orbit—who are not friends of each other—may lead to distancing from the magnet friend.

A distanced friend may be kept in the address book or on the friend roster for future usefulness, favors or in case of an emergency. The friend, although out of the picture, is held in in social escrow or reserve.

Roberto has chosen to distance himself outside the orbit. However, since he was already on the fringe the impact of the distancing may not be the same as if it had been Meg who moved away. As friends mutually invest time, energy, and resources in maintaining the friendship, the orbits become tighter. With more investment of time, shared experiences, and disclosures, the individual orbit bandwidths increase and a friendship is more valued. In Figure 6, the widest band is with Sarah, although they do not current spend a lot of time together.

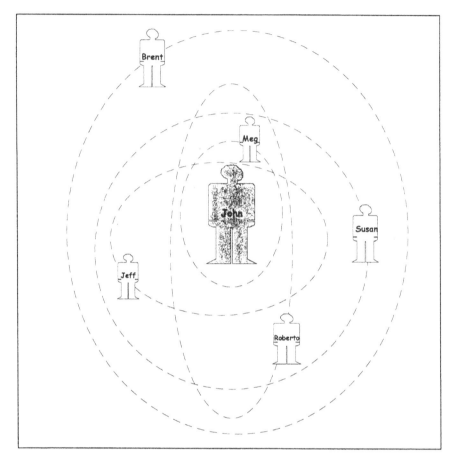

Figure 3. Orbit initiation.

Shared interests, working on a mutual project, spending lot of time together, or geographic proximity, can expand a bandorbit; stress in a relationship or perceived betrayal can shrink the bandorbit. Not all friendships are equally valued at any given moment. At the time of an unexpected death, friendships may be strained or friends may be estranged. For example, as Jackie Kennedy died, certain friends were summoned to her bedside; others were not (E. Klein, 1998). Those summoned, I would maintain, were the friends with whom she shared the widest bandwidths.

A friend's move 1,000 miles away—or only across town but out of daily contact—may shrink a bandwidth in some friendships, although

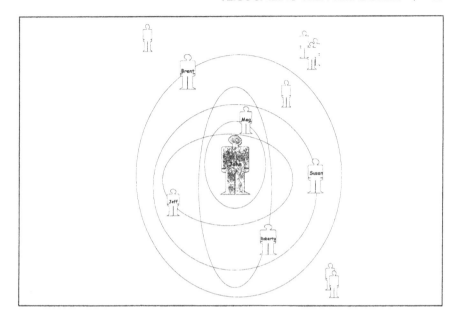

Figure 4. Acquaintances outside the friendorbit.

through e-mail and phoning some diligently seek to maintain the friendship; other friends make special periodical efforts to make quality time to be together, perhaps during holidays or around a birthday. Unless both parties invest time, resources, and effort to maintain the friendship, eventually space will open up a vacuum for a new friendship or an expanded bandwidth by another friend. Sometimes friendorbits are like a closely-cropped photo; had the full photo been seen, other individuals could have been identified in the background.

The "gravity" or valued strength of influence of the primary individual, holds the friends in orbit. If that value is reassessed, a friend will move to alter the orbit and to distance from the other. Sometimes distancing occurs as a result of a perceived slight or failure "to come through" in a crisis. One individual complains, "When my father died, this friend did not call or send a card. Nothing. And he knew. Some friend he proved to be." When estrangement occurs, neither friend assumes responsibility for the distancing. "I don't know, over time, we never saw much of each other and just drifted apart. . . ."

Others emotionally invest in friendship maintenance, so that the death of a friend or teammate from high school, two decades earlier, or a war buddy from a half century earlier, can provoke intense friendgrief. Thirty years after playing on a basketball team, through an episodically

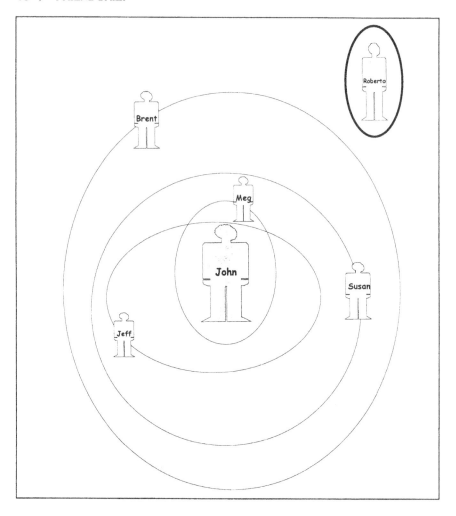

Figure 5. A distanced friend.

maintained friendship, when a teammate-friend died, a surviving friend reports the following:

> I'm beating myself up for not going to see him. He began to go downhill right before a big conference I was chairing and I was swamped with details. "Got to get up to see Bob," I thought. A couple of weeks passed and I heard he was in the I.C.U. "Got to get up there to see Bob," I reminded myself. I was planning to drive up to see him but I waited too late . . . he died. I really cared about this guy. I guess I

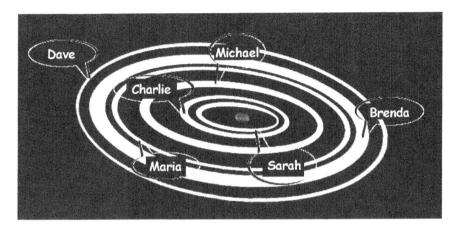

Figure 6. Friendorbit bandwidths.

was just a coward. I didn't want to see him that sick. It's not that I deliberately didn't go see him in the hospital . . . it's just that I never got around to it.

Friendorbits, although distinct and reasonably predictable, are dynamic, subject to change through benign external influences. Some friends maintain suborbits within the overall friendorbit. John, Brent, and Roberto have long invested in friendship by participating in a bowling league. In fact, John and Brent met when they were on different teams, became "friendly" competitors, then formed their own team in a new league with John's friend Roberto. Over time, Roberto and Brent became friends too. When Roberto began a new job which interfered with the league, the bowling as well as the eating-after-the-game comradery were the first casualties. Roberto and Brent/John and Roberto now have to rely on "catch-as-can" activities as opposed to a regular Friday night interaction. Another friendship in John's friendorbit (not grafted in Figure 5) was altered when a friend took a position requiring extensive travel. Time together—essential to maintaining a healthy friendship—now has to be scheduled in advance rather than the spontaneous, "Have you eaten yet? . . . Let's go grab a bite" or "Do you want to go see a movie tonight?" Spontaneity also suffers when a friend marries (Yager, 1999) or has a baby (Goodman & O'Brien, 2000) and the friendship must now include or take into consideration a third party.

Friendorbits create opportunities for interaction of varying proximity among friends. Distancing inevitably occurs in friendships due to career promotions, moves, dating, misunderstandings, marriage, divorce (Jones, 1998), remarriage, coming out, drugs, criminal activities, or mental illness. These often lead to a quiet withdraw that eventually leads to a reassessment, "We are not as close as we used to be." Sometimes a new orbiter competes for the friend's time; soon, a friend seems to have less time for an old friend although that may be disguised in excuses about work demands, family responsibilities, or stress. Some friends are possessive of shared time and are reluctant to issue a "Hey, why don't you join *us*?" invitation to another friend. Factors that disrupt the work interactions and routines alter the amount of time available for being with friends, particularly work friends. A person could continue to work for the same company but be transferred to another location or division; the loss of daily contact might redefine the friendship just as a career promotion could strain the friendship. Going back to Figure 3, suppose Brent, Meg, Susan, Jeff, and Roberto are workplace friends. What happens if Meg is downsized, takes a job with another company, is fired, or retires? Or retires *and* relocates? She is, to some degree, now out of the active friend loop.

> We used to see each other all the time when we both worked. She retired and started spending winters in Florida. Then they bought a condo, and finally just started living down there year-round. She made a whole new group of friends down there. Finally, I realized that I was talking more to the answering machine than to her. I stopped calling.

Perceptions of friendships may not be equilateral. One friend may not value the friendship as much now as at some previous point or assigns a lower priority to the friendship but never discloses the reassessment. A friendship may be carried by past memories rather than present interaction; some friends want shared multicommalities and not a singular one. For example, many war-related friendships based on war service decades ago rather than current activities, may be maintained through a once-a-year-reunion; still, the lowest common denominator in the friendship is the war experience rather than current interaction.

Some friends emotionally distance themselves without talking to the friend about it. Thus, in Figure 3 Brent might maintain the friendship with John without emotional investment because of potential payoffs in the future, say in the workplace. The friendship has deteriorated but has not ended. Actually, its continuance resembles the medical technology that keeps a patient alive on life support. The friendship, too, is being rescuitated—it is not being infused with new experiences. Even despite evidence of friendship deterioration, some friends are committed to being nice and polite and to avoid admitting that the friendship is strained or over. There may be some sense of obligation in one friend to continue, "After all she has done for me, I could not abandon her."

So, on the surface, the friendship appears intact. Brent may speak exuberantly, "Yeah, my good buddy, my pal John. . . ." John may not speak of the friendship with Brent with equal enthusiasm. If you ask Brent and John to graph the orbits and compare their assessment, the graphs might be incompatible. For individuals with sparsely-populated friendorbits, every friend counts.

The trajectories of friendorbits are impacted by major life events. Mobility, betrayal, downsizing, illness, retirement, marriage, death of a spouse, divorce, remarriage, mental illness, scandal, economic mobility, and a death in the family all challenge even the most fervent promises by friends to keep in touch. Anxious to avoid conflict and confrontation, some friends do not talk about tensions in the relationship; some walk away, sometimes in a disguised distancing—unreturned phone calls, short conversations, failure to respond to invitations, or "let me get back to you on this" answers particularly in moments and situations when a person needs a friend. A friend's insensitivity may lead to incitement and confrontation, "Where were you when I needed you?" or simmering but unverbalized resentment. In a crisis, a friend's explanation for unavailability may be heard as an excuse.

Tight and loose trajectories: tight trajectories symbolize close frequency and intimacy of contact while loose trajectories symbolize infrequent and more casual contact (see Figure 7). Illness, a change in work hours or work location, and an accompanying disinterest or inability to be available for activities, alters some friendships or may offer a convenient excuse to reassign significance to the friendship. Suppose Meg and Susan are friends (Figure 3) of each other as well as common friends of John. Suppose both are unmarried and spend lots of time together. When Susan starts seeing someone, Meg may come to feel that Susan is diverting time and energy from the friendship or is neglecting the friendship in order to invest in the romance. Overtime, Meg creates new friendships or diverts energy into other friendships. Suppose Susan breaks up and now wants to reestablish the friendship. How will Meg react?

Tight trajectories make available increased amounts of resources, contingency support, and foster strong defensive formations. "Let me know what I can do for you." Through "a friend of a friend" resources, contacts, or favors can also be arranged.

Through life events such as severe illness, institutionalization, death, friends (and therefore their individual orbits) are eliminated from the friend system (see Figure 7). Catastrophic upheaval such as civil war in Kosovo can destabilize a friendorbit as well as a complex web of interconnected friendorbits. When an earthquake struck India in 2000, an estimated 12,000 were killed. Some residents in small towns lost not just one or two friends, but a half-dozen or dozen friends. If the death of one friend can be life-shaping, how much more so the simultaneous deaths of several friends, particularly among those with only minimal previous exposure to death?

Figure 7. Missing friendorbits.

The deaths of Meg, Jeff, and Roberto are reflected in this restructured friendorbit. Current realities in the lives of Susan and Brent reduce their availability for significant interaction and friend-maintenance (thus the elongated orbit). Suppose Brent's wife is battling cancer and Brent now has major responsibilities as caregiver; time for socialization with John is significantly reduced. Thus the bandwidth will shrink unless John pitches in to support Brent in the caregiving. In that case, the bandwidth may be strengthened as the two become closer.

Friendships do not always fit into predictable or traditional patterns. Kendall Kohr, a mentally challenged adult, lived near Fire Station 23 in Kansas City, Missouri, and was teasingly called "the mayor of Independence Avenue." He often ate dinner and watched TV at the fire hall and went there when frightened during thunderstorms. Kohr, committed to keeping the neighborhood clean, was often seen walking along Independence Avenue picking up trash, particularly along the parking lots of fast-food businesses. Without hesitation, Kohr approached strangers, "Hi. Buy me a Coke?" (Heckenlively, 1999, April 2, p. B5). His family consisted of a distant cousin who lived out-of-state. Had Kendall been asked to graph his friendorbit, the orbiters would have been primarily firefighters.

After a quick read of Kohr's obituary one might predict a small funeral. Hardly. Twenty-five hundred people showed up for it! Kohr's funeral was a front page story with a large color photograph of his casket being carried into the station for the funeral; in a revised obituary the Station 23 firefighters were listed as his survivors (Bradley, 1999, March 28, pp. B-1, B-2). So many individuals wrote letters to the editor describing the impact of the death on their friendorbit, one week later, Kohr was featured on the editorial page of *The Kansas City Star* with a photo and caption, "Remembering Kendall Kohr."

Kohr's death demonstrates the timelessness of Donne's observation: No one is an island. Many people bought Cokes for Kohr and considered him a friend. Neighborhood litter these days reminds of the absence of a unique friend. Sometimes, an accurate assessment of the role of a friend cannot be determined until after death; sometimes a friendorbit cannot be graphed accurately until after a death.

The exit of friends from a friendorbit is rarely convenient or clean; the resulting disruption of a friendorbit can be harrowing and far-reaching. Decades after a friend's death, some may say, "Oh I have friends, but none like _____. I have never had another friend like____." The required integration of that absence is seldom convenient, even for those who attempt merely to make a new friend to replace the deceased friend. Friendgrief will make shambles of our efforts to curtail it or keep it tidy. Ignore it and it will go away, some assume. Sometimes, the friend-survivor will end up with the equivalent of an unhealed wound. For some, only in the pained, experienced absence, can a friendgriever appreciate the friendship. Marty (1999, August 25–September 1) captures this absence in the description of the death of his friend, historian Sidney Mead: "The stage is barer now, with Mead gone after a very long life, well lived" (p. 831).

While in England in 1999, I studied memorial tablets in Westminster Abbey, Westminster Cathedral, Bath Cathedral, and at Oxford. In examining tablets placed in the walls by friends of the deceased, I was repeatedly reminded that earlier generations knew friendgrief. William Foxcroft Jones' tablet prompted a long pause. "This tablet has been placed by friends who knew his life and work and desired that his name should not be forgotten at Oxford." At Oxford, some of his lifelong friendships were established. Two centuries later the table remains a witness to that friendorbit.

KEY CONCEPTS OF THE CHAPTER

- In this chapter the model of friendorbits was introduced as a model of understanding friendships and the influence of death in reshaping it.
- Friendships function like orbiting planets around a magnet-friend. In some cases, remove that magnet-friend and the entire orbit collapses.
- Remove key friends from the friendorbit and it is inevitably altered.
- The friendorbit is a range or sphere of intentional acts, a path of friendship in orbit around a primary personality which invites a relationship.
- Although death may seem static, the impact of the loss of a friend and the resulting changes to the friendorbit are dynamic experiences.
- Friendorbits, although distinct and reasonably predictable, are dynamic, subject to change through benign external influences.
- Friendorbits create opportunities for interaction of varying proximity among friends.
- The exit of friends from our friendorbits is rarely convenient or clean; the resulting disruption of our friendorbits can be harrowing and far-reaching.

IMPLICATIONS FOR CLINICIANS

1. The clinician may initially ask a friendgriever to sketch the friendorbit before the death and the friendorbit now altered by a friend's

or friends' deaths (using different color markers). The griever places best friends in closest orbit, close friends further away, and casual friends on the perimeters. Potential friends could be placed outside the orbits (see Figure 4). Graphing friendorbits becomes a way for a griever and the clinician to translate the wounded friendorbit of a client and the vacuum created by particular deaths. The clinician needs to know of ex-friends no longer included in the structure because these individuals would have once been vital sources of support for the grieving friend. Their absence further compounds the latest loss.

The clinician may inquire about myths regarding dying and friendship held by the client as an well as by the friendorbit. How has the friendorbit handled previous deaths? This death?

2. Some gay and lesbian persons, and persons from a dysfunctional family, deliberately and zealously maintain strict boundaries between family and friends or between sets of friends. In Figure 8 each band represents a differentiated orbit (set) of friends: i.e., work, social, and church. Sometimes, the only time friends from different orbits meet or interact is at a visitation, funeral, or memorial service. In some settings, there may be polite or nervous interaction. Strong (1994) describes conducting services for a gay man, who "chose to keep his lives

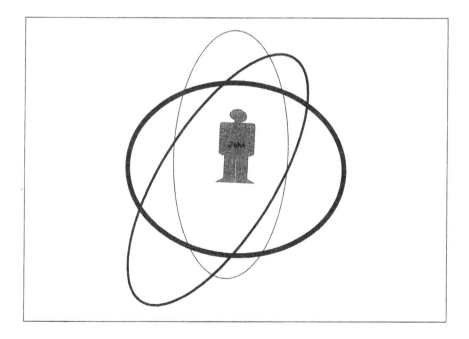

Figure 8. Differentiated orbits.

segregated. Friendships and loves, interests and attitudes, developed within each world, and he would step between them gingerly and with fear" (p. 35). Which orbit will dominate? When families do not acknowledge gay/lesbian orientation, those friends who attend services may find that the "tenor" of the service discounts both their friend's life and their own.

Some friends deliberately and zealously keep a distance between friends (or particular friends) and family; in some cases, an individual constructs a demiliatrized zone (see Figure 9). "Never the twain shall meet." Other people desire little distance between family/romantic relationships and friends; friends and family are intermeshed, and sometimes friends find themselves described as "family."

Some identify friends as "the brother/sister I never had" or "wish I had had" (see Figure 10). At my father's visitation, a neighbor of four decades told me, "Your daddy was such a good friend to me" and then broke down and wept. My father's death left that neighbor friendless.

The clinician's experience with family and friends must not interfere with hearing out the relational narratives or viewing the friendorbit graphs of those who come with radically different experiences and perspectives. For example, among some conservative evangelicals, church friends are considered family and those friendships may be more valued than biological family. Clinicians have the option of referring such people to other professionals.

3. The clinician may be the first to name the friendgrief. That naming may initially produce confusion or relief, "So I am not losing my mind!" The clinician may be the first to enfranchise the grief or to give permission to the friend to grieve. Both are essential in doing the

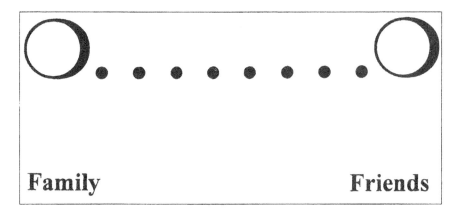

Figure 9. Maintaining distance between friendships.

Figure 10. Narrowing the gap.

demanding work of grieving for a friend. For many, a clinician's office is a safe place to do grief work. It is especially safe when tension existed between, for example, a spouse and a friend: "He never liked her or wanted me to be around her."

4. Ask how the friendorbit was recognized or ignored in the funeral rituals. How would they have preferred to be recognized?

CHAPTER 5

Being Supportive Immediately After a Friend's Death

CHAPTER PREVIEW

In this chapter we examine the ways friends support the chief mourner and family members. Historically friends have been warned that their grief must not compete with, overshadow, or complicate family grief (Sklar, 1991-92). The expectation is that friends will support—rather than receive support—motivates many friends to ignore their own grief and the needs of others in the friendorbit in order to concentrate on the needs of the family. After many deaths, friends may decide to take a break from active grieving and make themselves unavailable to offer support. Support can be challenged when lifestyle issues impact relationships.

> As the news spread around town, people began to do the only thing they could: they began to pray. Many of them did so with their hands.

> One came and sat with Mary Lou while she held Canaan and said good-bye. . . . Another came to be on the telephone in the waiting room and make the calls that spread the word. At another telephone, another friend was beginning the process of making the arrangements, the process we have all seen and dread to think about having to do (Benson, 1998, p. 135).

A friend dies. Now what? What happens in the first hours, the first day, the first week, or months after a friend's death? Whether the death has been anticipated or unanticipated, where is the authorized handbook or script that spells out what can be expected of a friend in a culture that is friendship-challenged, ritual-lite, and death-phobic? In actuality, a "close" friend on a particular day may be halfway across the country or the world. To what extent does the adjective preceding *friend* define expectations? If a friend is unavailable, does the call for support automatically transfer to the next friend on the roster? It is realistic to expect a friend to drop everything in order to offer support?

Death can be inconvenient for friends and can create havoc on schedules, priorities, commitments, as well as friendships. Death also has a way of drafting a friend with limited (or perhaps no) prior experience and saying, "Tag. You're it!" Some friends have paraphrased Prissy's words in the movie, "Gone with the Wind": "Miss Scarlett, I don't know nothing about no grieving!"

Funeral ritual etiquette focuses on the needs and wishes of the family or next of kin. I was reminded of this while researching friendgrief in a library's special collection. The librarian responded, "Why research *that*?! It is so simple: The friend is there to support the family and to stay out of their way!" That viewpoint is shared by many who have not experienced the death of a close friend. Friends are expected to meet physical, emotional, even financial needs and provide miscellaneous help and support (Fehr, 1996; House, 1981). To fail to respond is considered a serious breech of the friendship. A friend often becomes something of an emotional midwife (Hanson, 1996), emissary, or gofer— especially if the friend has had some previous experience with death and ritualing. For example, Joan Driskell wanted friends involved in her last journey. When she died, friends placed her body into a friend-made casket and placed it into a friend's pickup truck (the truck bed lined with fall foliage) for a procession to the crematory (Wood, 1999, August 1).

Commonly, when thanked, supporters often say, "That's what friends are for." A friend is expected to come through. One griever insists, "When grieving, you learn who your *real* friends are."

THE CRITICAL QUESTION:
WHO IS THE CHIEF MOURNER?

Helpfulness hinges on what Littlewood (1992) acknowledges as a key identification made at the time of death: Who is the chief mourner and who are the supportive mourners? If there are conflicting claims, whose claim prevails? Suppose a friend has a history of tension with the chief mourner. Suppose an individual was a friend of a deceased husband but not of the wife. In some cases, the de facto chief mourner and the legal chief mourner may not be the same person, especially in the case of cohabiting partners, multiple marriages with children, and when distant kin plan and control rituals. Hocker (1990) asks, " Who has a right to mourn?" then answers, "Obviously, the person who has a relationship to the deceased is the one who suffers the loss of that relationship, and the degree of intensity of that relationship is the degree to which the survivor(s) feel the loss" (p. 107). I would add this: to the degree society or a subsociety recognizes the relationship.

Suppose a husband dies. Legally the chief mourner will be the widow. The chief mourner tends to be the person(s) who stood in the closest legal and social relationship to the deceased. Once that role or privilege is determined, either implicitly or after something of a challenge or, these days, negotiated, all other mourners—especially the friends—are expected to support that chief mourner. When one funeral director was asked, "Who is the chief mourner?" he responded, "Check out the limos" (in some areas called "family cars") referring to the order: family first.

The issue can become conflicted if the deceased has been previously married or has children by different spouses or partners, when there is a large estate, or if a person is still legally married but is living with a romantic partner, say during divorce proceedings. Now who is the chief mourner? To whom does the friend offer support? Spouse or lover? Both? If the issue is confused, some friends distance themselves or limit themselves to minimal support, saying, "It's best not to get involved."

In an era of rampant family dysfunction, recognition of grieving rights becomes ticklish, sometimes requiring the skills of a career diplomat. The coverage of the males of the British royal family arriving for the funeral of Princess Diana illustrates the tension. Prince William and Prince Harry (sons) and Lord Spenser (brother) were obviously the chief mourners. But standing with them were Prince Charles (ex-husband) and Prince Philip (ex-father in law). Did not the Princes Charles and Philip, given the marital history and divorce, seem out of place? What did Diana's close friends feel seeing them sharing the limelight?

Andersen (1998) reports the intense negotiations and compromise on details between the Spencer family, the Royals, the Church of England, and the Prime Minister on details such as having Diana's friend, Elton John, sing. Prince William wanted it; the other Royals opposed it. The chief mourner's desire was honored: Elton John sang. One wonders, however, what would have been Dodi Fayed's involvement in the funeral had he—as a "special" friend—survived the crash?

THE CHIEF SUPPORTER

Just as a chief mourner emerges and is designated, so a chief supporter is recognized although some function behind the scenes. The chief supporter recruits and coordinates support for the grief mourner and communicates, interprets, or even defends the wishes of the chief mourner to other friends.

Princess Diana's confidante, Paul Burrell, was thrust into a critical behind-the-scenes role. Although Di's butler for almost a decade, Burrell had become her trusted friend. Immediately upon notification of the accident, Burrell flew to Paris, collected the personal belongings of the Princess from the hospital, then stood as a personal honor guard until Di's sisters and Charles arrived to escort the body back to England. Burrell, as something of First Friend, spent the six nights before the funeral "sitting by the coffin, reading aloud from her favorite books, telling her stories and the jokes that had made her double over with laughter." Why? Because as a friend, "I just don't want her to be alone" (Andersen, 1998, p. 249).

Burrell as friend/chief supporter, relying on Di's Christmas card list, took on the dicey responsibility for advising the royal family on which friends should be invited to the funeral—and fortunately for friends, there was a large cathedral to fill. Burrell knew Lady Diana's "real" friends. As a sign of his standing as closest friend, Burrell was the only non-Royal to attend the burial. This in-the-background manager of the details supportive friend is not uncommon.

It should be noted the wealthy have a staff of servants, aides, employees to do most of the support friends would otherwise provide. The wealthy do not show up at the palace doorstep with casseroles. Yet, this may leave friends frustrated about being supportive.

FRIENDS OFTEN SQUELCH THEIR OWN GRIEF IN ORDER TO OFFER SUPPORT

Great resentment may evolve toward a friend who fails to respond to the assumed level of friendship, who fails to "be there" or to follow through on a promise. Despite enormous social change and the increasing appreciation of friendship, many grieving friends feel excluded, overlooked, or unacknowledged. Corr (1998-99) comments, "Society often presses a griever to hold private his or her grief reaction in order not to trouble or disturb others by bringing it out into the open or expressing it in certain ways" (p. 8).

WHAT RECOGNITION CAN A FRIEND EXPECT?

What level of social support can a friend expect? Historically, strong societal norms mandated that a friend's grief not compete with, overshadow, challenge, frustrate, undermine, or complicate the family's grief (Sklar, 1991-92).

Unfortunately, this expectation encourages friends to overlook or negate their own grief to concentrate on the needs of the family of their friend. If grief was disenfranchised in previous deaths, the friend may now have no expectation of support. Self-disenfranchisement postpones and complicates reconciliation with the death. The reality can be captured by the friend who says, "Never mind me. Your loss as a family member takes precedence over my loss of *merely* a friend." As a priest, DelBene (1991) has conducted hundreds of funerals but discloses that only through his close friend Taylor's death, did he discover the needs of the grieving friends.

> Taylor's death consumed me with grief. I cried. I questioned. At first, I could not think beyond myself and my own pain. But then I began to feel guilty for being so self-absorbed. After all, Taylor's wife and children had lost even more than I had.
>
> At the funeral, Taylor's family had the support of the grieving family, which was as it should have been. But because Taylor had meant so much to me, I wanted people to tell me that they were sorry about my loss, too. I wanted to be comforted and consoled (p. 29).

The expression "blood is thicker than water" dominates social sensibility as well as corporate and governmental policies. Friends may be so busy fulfilling perceived or stated social expectations to support the family that they do not give attention to their own grief or the grief of other friends, other than a casual, "How are you holding up?" Doing offers a convenient socially-endorsed distraction from fully engaging the loss. The "stiff upper lip" or "Got to be strong for the family" mode is believed the appropriate response to the death of a friend. Thus, friends keep looking for something to do and may repeatedly remark, "I just wish there were something *more* I could do!" "Grieving, close friends may not even recognize their emotional reactions for what they are" (Sklar 1991-92, p. 109): grief needing to be honored! Only a clinician may be able to name the grief.

Delayed friendgrief is like compound interest. By the time friends get around to paying attention to the rupture in their own friendorbit, the issue is more complicated. Some friends find themselves deluged by a string of friend deaths. While elders make up 13 percent of the U.S. population, they experience approximately 73 percent of the deaths (Corr, Nabe, & Corr, 1997, p. 413). One senior adult informs me, "I spend a lot of my time going to funerals." Many elderly adults are "exposed to bereavement overload, a situation in which they do not have the time or other resources needed to grieve and mourn one significant loss effectively before another occurs. For such older persons, grief is a constant companion" (p. 421). Particularly is this so for those who live in nursing homes, assisted living, or retirement communities and will, given the size of the baby boomer consort, become a significant issue (1/3 of men and 1/2 women will spend time in a long-term care facility) (Zurakowski, 2000).

Many gays and lesbians also know about grief as a constant intrusion. One subject in Carmack's (1992) study explains, "This is cumulative. You can never finish with one before another happens. You can never truly fully process a loss; it's a dangerous thing, two or three or more happen and I haven't finished with the others" (p. 12). Nord (1998) adds, "These myriad losses are difficult to grieve contemporarily, as they occur because of their quality. They are difficult to grieve subsequently because fresh losses interrupt even the best intentioned efforts to resolve accumulated grief" (p. 217). Moreover, they are, in his experience, "a chronic reminder of previous loss" (p. 217). According to Lifton (1993), "Every death encounter is itself a reactivating of earlier 'survivals'" (p. 16). Many friendgrievers as caregivers now redirect their care to the next ill friend. Nord (1998) describes the experience of one "chronic caregiver" so impacted by his support for over 100 dying friends that when his "last" friend died, "Brian no longer had that role in anyone's life and frequently complained of feeling like he lived without any purpose in life" (p. 218). One friend's audit of the roster of friends offers insight into the need for balancing support:

> My friend and colleague from the Lifeguard Project, Bruce, died on Wednesday.... That evening, I went to the hospital to visit my friend Mark, who is in the hospital with a severe case of PCP [Pneumocystis carinii Pneumonia] ... I wonder if he'll make it.... And when I called my friend Tom today, his mom told me he's in the hospital with TB and probably won't make it this time and my ex-roommate Bobby just got out of the hospital with more problems with his KS [Kaposis Sarcoma]. Paul moved to Austin last week—but he's still healthy anyway, except for being tired a lot. And at Paul's exit party, Shawn was completely plastered when he got there. What's next? He lives on alcohol and cigarettes to avoid facing his disease. Too bad, we used to be so close. And Chad hasn't returned my calls all week so I can't help wondering if he's having problems. But nobody died this week. Yet ... there are times when HIV seems less a harsh fate than outliving all your friends (Saunier, 1966, Internet).

Reread that sentence: *Nobody died this week.* Some grievers must integrate a new grief—or anticipatory grief—the way a juggler adds an additional ball. How much grief can one person juggle? How many deaths before the person experiences grief numbing or meltdown?

Baugher (1998-99) and S. Klein (1998) point to a byproduct of protease inhibitors: a "resurrection phenomenon" whereby an individual at death's door rebounds and heads off for a dream vacation. Friends, deep in anticipatory grief, suddenly must adjust to the new reality just as other friends must accommodate the latest remission for friends with cancer or other life-threatening illnesses.

Nord (1997) and Rofes (1996) call attention to grief saturation which Rofes (1996) defines as "the limitation of our ability to mourn" (p. 5). Nord (1997) concludes, "The cumulative survivor experience is one that usually leaves a permanent psychological mark that has been called a *death imprint*" (p. 53, citing Niederland, 1971). For some friends, death is not an event but an environment (Sullivan, 1990, September 17). After so many deaths, friends may decide, no more grief and take a break from active grieving and support giving, even refusing to attend funerals. Some move to a new area of the country to create a new life and construct a new friendorbit.

Some friendorbits have been so depleted that now only acquaintances or casual untested friends compose the friendorbit. The close, intimate, "you can always count on me" friends are dead. New friends may be unsupportive because they are only somewhat aware of the grief threads running through this individual's life. One survivor explains, "If my life is like a book, no one is left who knows more than one page of it" (Nord, 1997, p. 48). Nava (1996) reports

> In the past few years, a dozen friends of mine had died from AIDS. I'd sat the watch with many of them. It sometimes seemed to me that I was living in one of those South American countries ruled by colonels, where people disappeared from the streets into the backseats of blue Fords never to be seen again. The streets were haunted with their absence and there were rips in the fabric of my reality that could not be mended by grieving or the passage of time (p. 29).

The ability to mourn is impaired in cases of disaster, such as Columbine, or the Value Jet crash in the Everglades, or the apartment building bombings in Moscow in 1999, when multiple friends die. Grief overload taxes the coping skills of friends who are simultaneously grieving multiple friend deaths. In the early days of the ritualizing, when community support may be strong, the friendgriever may be too traumatized to process the catastrophe. Other friends stumble through rituals on automatic pilot devoting constant attention to their "to do" support list.

Katz and Bartone (1998), examining the impact on one Army base when 248 soldiers were killed in the crash of a chartered jetliner in Newfoundland in 1985, note that air disasters usually involve strangers (or small groups of friends traveling together such as the French club on TWA Flight 800). In this crash, all of the dead (except for the charter's eight crew) were stationed at Fort Campbell and were members of the same battalion. One way friends coped was through the elaborate planning for the extensive rituals that took place over several months, including a visit by President Reagan. The intense, methodical preparations, although demanding, gave grief-stricken friends something to *do.* In my brief experience as a consultant on that base, I discovered that the stay-busy-supporting-the-main-grievers mind set led to a communal disengagement of friendgrief. Many soldiers said, "Grieving is something *we* do" rather than "Grieving is something I do."

Consider funeral directors who are lifelong residents in small communities or ethnic neighborhoods who must bury their friends. Limbo and Wheeler (1986) describe the functions of funeral directors as not only "preparing bodies for burial," but also serving a "greater role as *friend in grief,* to help families deal with death" (p. 119; italics mine). John and Susie Norman, funeral directors in Hope, Indiana concede, "the best and most difficult part of funeral service is serving friends" (McCormick, 1999, October, p. 142). "Most of our clients are our family, and our friends" (p. 149). One funeral director friend told me that he stopped embalming as more friends died. A funeral director in a career, might bury dozens of friends. The director/friend supports by going the extra mile to provide stellar service for a friend. Lincoln (1990) has learned:

> The quality of one's experience visiting with, discussing and arranging funerals for people one does not know is a far cry from providing for those who are close, when one is expected to keep a "stiff upper lip." However, to process the casket containing the remains of a close friend is just short of hell (pp. 159-160).

Especially when you ate lunch with that friend the day before he died. Who offers support?

DISENFRANCHISEMENT IN THE WORKPLACE

Schaller (1999) and Yager (1999) contend that the workplace is now where American adults, particularly males, build friendships. However, funeral leave policies have not kept up with that reality. Employee policies permit bereavement leave for family members but not for friends. Moreover, grief is a taboo topic in many workplaces (S. Gordon, 1997; Kemp, 1995; McNaught, 1997). So, how does a friend convince skeptical management or some colleagues that friendgrief is valid and not just a way to get off work? How does the employee answer the question, "But why do *you* need to be there?" How can friendgrievers be self-enfranchised to say, "The support I can offer is a way to pay attention to my grief for my friend." How can workplace friends—who did not know the decedent—support this friendgriever beyond a "Glad to see you are back to work?" How many will advice, "Stay busy."

SUPPORT AS ATONEMENT

Relationship quality, particularly, conflictual, is linked to "greater grief misery" (Gamino, Swell, & Easterling, 1998, p. 353). Rando (1992-93) concludes that a premorbid relationship with the decedent marked by conflict, ambivalence, or dependency is a high-risk for complicated grief. What if the estranged friend throws himself into a hyper doing-for-the-family mode to atone for the estrangement rather than confronting the issues that led to the tension, especially when the individual was unavailable during a prolonged illness? The friend may imagine the family saying, "Well it is about time you showed up!" How is that atonement or making up for absence perceived by other members of the friendorbit? Does this friend set the bar for support that other friends are expected to meet? Will other friends be judged by this friend's level of support?

FAMILIES DISENFRANCHISE FRIENDGRIEF

If the family welcomes—or at least, tolerates—the friend's (or friends') assistance, rituals may go smoothly. For every positive story of family enfranchisement of support, however, a negative story can be told. Families may perceive the presence of a close friend—to them, still an outsider—as a intruder. Family members may suspect an underlying motive for the friend's support and hospitality. During an illness, the family may have been tolerant because the deceased could override their reservations. Now the family cannot be challenged as effectively, although friends may appeal, "What would Shawn [the deceased] have wanted?"

Close friends who have had contact and who have been pillars of daily support or even just swappers of polite conversation, can be swept aside by family members. A friend's demand, to a family member, "Where were you for all these years when she/he needed you?" may be answered by silence or with a statement of simple legal reality, "We are family! We are in charge *now*."

Sometimes the family picks among support-offering friends, favoring some, ignoring others. Just before George died in the hospital, he whispered to a nurse, "Be sure to call the poker room at Harrah's Casino. The boys will want to know." George had spent a lot of time playing cards with a group of cronies three times a week. The family, however, had only contempt for these friends and had asked them not to call or visit George at the hospital. The family never gave these friends a chance to say good-bye let alone offer support.

FAILURE TO FULFILL LAST REQUESTS

Sometimes individuals' grief is complicated by a perception that they failed to follow through on a friend's last requests. One woman sobbed outside her friend's hospital room after the family had asked her to leave, saying "This is the family time." "But chaplain," she pleaded, "I promised him I would be there with him at the very end."

The friendship of Marion and Sharon was rather extraordinary. They had a do-everything-together friendship, centered primarily around church activities. Facing serious surgery, Marion gave a "just in case" letter to Sharon and mailed an identical copy to her next-of-kin, cousins in another state. After Marion died unexpectedly following the surgery, Sharon opened the letter to find Marion's wishes clearly spelled out. Sharon recalls what happened.

> Then the cousins arrived and did just about everything the opposite of what Marion had specifically stated in the letter. Marion wanted a visitation; the family did not schedule one. Marion wanted a funeral at the church—after all, she was a charter member; the family had a brief service at the grave. Marion wanted a memorial service in a couple of weeks so friends from out of state could come. The family never got around to that. Although I knew what Marion wanted I could not change their minds and they knew I had gotten the same letter they had. I was "only" a friend!

As I interviewed Sharon four years after Marion's death, she sobbed. "I felt so helpless. I could not do anything my friend wanted. My hands were tied. 'The family' was in charge! And they did not let me forget that. Marion expected me to stand up to them . . . and I didn't."

Close friends often provide emotional, physical, spiritual, even financial support during the deceased's life, especially during a prolonged illness. When the friend dies, these helpers are expected to transfer emotional and spiritual (in some instances physical or financial) support to the family. Transferred affection may be limited to the duration of the rituals or a short time thereafter. Some conclude that anything less than full, unquestioned cooperation with the chief mourner betrays the friendship. Some families do take advantage of the generosity and hospitality of friends. When one friend dared challenge a family decision by asking, "Can't we get along until John is buried?" one family member replied, "Sure we can . . . as long as you do things *our* way!"

Tension may erupt within the orbit when a friend does not come through or pick up her fair share, forcing other friends to assume more responsibility. In some cases, the decedent did not have a large friendorbit, at least at the time of death or in the immediate geographical area, so all of the assistance must come from a few friends or from one friend. Sometimes, because of realities in one's own life, a friend cannot meet the family expectations for support and feels guilty or is made to feel guilty by family members.

WHAT DEFINES EXPECTATIONS OF SUPPORT?

The expectations on a friend are primarily framed by the chief mourner's definition of friendship and previous experience with death and funeral rituals, as well as the previous grief experience of the friend-griever and the appreciation of friendship. Sometimes geography or local custom influences expectations. When one of my friends died, her family—from a small rural community—was disappointed by the lack of support from "big city" local friends. We were constantly reminded, "Back home, friends. . . ." A categorization—"casual," "close," or "best" friend—may not be mutually understood. So, when family members hear "close" friend they assume lots of support, while a close friend may be unable to meet those expectations.

A CORE OF COMMON EXPECTATIONS

Common expectations for the support of a friend vary. Kelly (2000), as a widow, developed a book to serve as a resource for friends who want to be helpful. Her title eludes to the possibility of faux pas, *Don't Ask for the Dead Man's Gold Clubs*. She paraphrases Saint Francis of Assisi—"for it is in giving, that we receive"— to suggest that by comforting friends receive a little comfort themselves. Her interviews produced the consensus that the best thing a friend can do is "to be there."

A friend may "be there" or provide support by

- calling the family on the phone or going to the primary residence upon learning of the death;
- sending flowers unless a "no flowers" decision has been made;
- donating to a designated charity in honor of the deceased friend;
- attending rituals, especially the visitation/wake and, if possible, the memorial service/funeral and the burial/scattering;
- preparing or donating food for the residence or preparing a meal for the family;
- volunteering to provide assistance: "If there is anything I can do, please call me";
- fulfilling specific family requests: "Could you go to the airport and pick up his brother?" or "Would you answer the phone for us?";
- supplying missing data: "Who was her accountant? Where did she bank?";
- sending or taking a sympathy card to the chief mourner(s).

If specifically invited by the chief mourner, a friend may offer support by

- offering advice on decisions: "What do you think we should do about. . . ?" or "You knew her. What do you think she would want for music at the funeral?";
- having a part—as defined by the family—in the funeral/memorial service or committal;
- delivering a eulogy;
- serving as an active or honorary casket/pall/urn bearer.

In recent years, the friend has come to be a passive, secondary participant unless the family specifically invites or assigns more active participation. The friend may volunteer to run errands, help with arrangements, or host out-of-town relatives. Friends do not, however, volunteer to deliver the eulogy or be a pallbearer. Volunteering for either honor may be perceived to be an infringement upon the family's freedom to choose. Some families would find such an offer intrusive. On the other hand, some families might feel obligated, especially when the friend has been helpful during a long illness, "After all he has done, how can we refuse?"

Friends may find themselves committing to immediate, short-term, and long-term support (sometimes people discover other friends have made a commitment for them). Some families initially have a large support system at the time of death and immediately following, but over time (sometimes a surprisingly brief period) support dwindles. When a family elects to have rituals in two or more cities—one where the deceased formerly lived—there may be disappointment because the friends in the latter do not meet expectations.

If the chief mourner hesitates to accept offers of support within the immediate period after a funeral, some friends "forget." A family member may restate the offer as a reminder, "Remember at the funeral home you said that if I needed help to call, well I thought of something." Some needs surface after the traditional grieving support period ends in thirty to sixty days. When the family of a friend is from out of town, sometimes a friend offers long distance support or serves as a liaison or recruits support among local friends.

SUPPORTING THROUGH SILENCE

Some people are tight-lipped about their friendships, particularly when a friend is in the public eye. In fact, silence may be a prerequisite for maintaining the friendship. Kleinfield (1999, July 24) comments on John Kennedy Jr.'s circle of young friends who were not in the public eye. Across the years Kennedy had "developed a band of fiercely loyal and discreet friends who helped create a secure zone around him" and who never hesitated to answer, "No comment" (Pooley, 1999, July 26, p. 36) to even the most persistent reporters.

Initially during the search-and-recover operations for John Kennedy Jr., friends remained unavailable to reporters; many too shaken by the loss, too respectful of the friendship to do sound bytes. But the story was too big. Reporters persisted in contacting Kennedy's friendorbit. Some friends talked to reporters from *Time,* as if somehow disclosure in certain venues was permissible. The media has enormous power to tempt those on the perimeter of a friendorbit; thus, some friends exaggerate closeness. James (1999, July 24) in *The New York Times* follows up on Peter Jennings' charge that certain "friends" of Mr. Kennedy may not have been as close as their comments on television would suggest. The fact that *The New York Times* chose to put friends in quotations is noteworthy.

Celebrity status may interfere with the friend's expression of grief. How did the friends of Dodi Fayed, Diana's "special friend," grieve? Who offered support, especially given the immediacy of his burial? How did friends of Lauren Bessette, John Kennedy's sister-in-law, offer support? How did friends of Carolyn Bessette Kennedy grieve? Sometimes in a marriage the individual friendorbits are merged into a new, expanded friendorbit. But some friends do not make that transition and remain the friend of only one partner in a her friends/his friends framework. In *The New York Times'* extensive coverage of the Kennedy funerals, (more than one full page) there was only brief mention of Carolyn—a total of 27 words to be exact–about her friend Hamilton Smith's eulogy (Kleinfeld, 1999, July 24).

Consider the experience of Kennedy friend, Diane Sawyer whose failure to appear as co-host on two mornings on ABC's "Good Morning America" created a media story of itself. Perhaps, it was speculated, she was too grief-stricken. Actually Sawyer, in the early hours after the first reports, did what friends do in such moments and rushed to be with her "longtime friend" Anthony Radziwill, Kennedy's cousin who was gravely ill with cancer (in fact, he died two weeks later). Radziwill asked her, as a friend, not to go on the air and talk about the deaths or their friendship ("Sawyer mystery solved," 1999, August 9). Sawyer supported her friends by honoring the request.

The death of Lauren Bessette would never have been national news or complicated the grief of her friends, as one news report notes, except for the fact that her brother-in-law was a Kennedy. Krista Kristtnig, a friend of Lauren, would never have been quizzed by reporters nor would her simple rebuff, "What do you think when your friend dies?" have been carried by the Associated Press and printed in newspapers around the country (Bessette sisters, 1999, July 25, p. A17). Friendship with a celebrity made her a celebrity of sorts.

NOT ALL FRIENDS ARE POSITIVE CELEBRITIES

One does not have to be famous to have grief complicated by friendship. The manner of death can turn an individual into a news blitz and create stress on a friendorbit unaccustomed to media attention. Friendgrief becomes complicated if the death becomes a media happening. Who made up the friendorbits of Eric Harris and Dylan Kiebold, shooters in the Littleton massacre? The identities of their friends fueled speculation about the possibility of others being involved. Gaidies (1999, July) writes of her experience as the drama unfolded. "My disbelief turned into sadness as I learned that John Tomlin, a boy from my church . . . died in the library that day." Then the next morning "my sadness turned to horror as I saw the name 'Dylan Klebold' flash across my television screen" (p. 54). Gaidies' friendship with Dylan's mother was immediately tested when Mrs. Klebold asked her to arrange the cremation and private memorial service for Dylan. Gaidies explains her support, "It was very important to me that I immediately tell Sue that I was there to love her and comfort her, and that I was not sitting in judgement of her" (p. 54). Moreover, she supported the Klebolds by listening to "the caring, loving side of Dylan that most people will never hear about" (p. 54).

Imagine the Klebolds' experience if they read the Associated Press accounts of a casual friend (who did Mrs. Klebold's hair after the shootings) who disclosed snippets of their conversation to the press ("Friends describe boys' parents as ordinary people," 1999, April 26). In a time of great emotional stress, an individual betrayed her position as a friend of the family. Such an act of disloyalty by one friend, may make the chief mourner distrustful of other friends.

Despite community outrage over the shootings, some friends publicly offered support by taking flowers to the doorsteps of the Klebold and Harris' families. Other friends planted a sign in the Klebold's front yard: "Tom and Sue. We love you. We're here for you. Call us" and signed their names.

It is not difficult to understand that the media and law enforcement authorities wanted to identify friends of Klebold and Harris, particularly during the time of widespread speculation on a third gunman. Not a good time to be known as a friend of either. Nevertheless both had friends whose grief was hampered by a haunting question, "How could my friend have done this?" The speedy, private funerals and burials (held under tight security) for the two gunmen denied an opportunity for their friends to participate in those rituals but also blocked those friends from openly offering (and receiving) support. Klebold's and Harris' friends grieved clandestinely—a heavy responsibility for adolescents.

GUARDING FRIENDSHIPS

Support may be complicated because some individuals zealously guard friendships and do not allow overlapping friendships. Friend A and Friend B may know something of each other's existence but do not interact. Some confine friends to clear perimeters: *work* friends, *church* friends, *neighbor* friends, etc. This is particularly true of closeted gay men and lesbians (Strong, 1994, December 13). Paradoxically, the only mingling may be at the rituals. For the friend who becomes chief supporter, by consensus or default, enlisting and trusting friends from other suborbits of the deceased, is a demanding task. How do I know this person will come through?

Moreover, there may be competition and jockeying for recognition as chief supporter. There may be "friendly" competition to see who can do the most for the family. Some friends function as gatekeepers around the chief or most prominent griever, even limiting access by other friends (Mansell, 1998). There can also be posturing, or pressuring, for acceptance of suggestions even if that requires manipulation of reality,

"Oh, we were *very* close." Some friends create tension, even havoc, if their standing is not recognized or if their advice is not taken. Individuals who rehearse a family's offenses—real or perceived—complicate the grief for other friends and may sabotage their support for the family.

POSTURING AMONG FRIENDS

Posturing commonly occurs in the friendorbits of second marriages and live-in relationships, especially when, over time, since the divorce or breakup, an ex has become a friend, or if co-parent of children. Former spouses can become "formidable friends" (Clark, 1997, p. 267); still some in the friendorbit have long memories. Andersen (1998) contends that Prince Charles had become Diana's friend; he participated in the funeral as the father of her sons *and* as a friend. Some may like an ex-now-friend more now than when a spouse or more than a current spouse or partner. Sometimes, friends from a previous marriage emerge later to offer support, compensating for support they have not offered in the remarriage.

Gays and lesbians often create strong friendships with ex-partners or rekindle friendships if they were friends before becoming lovers. Ex-lovers become part of a family of choice for many, supplementing what families of origin cannot or will not provide (Burch, 1993). It is not unusual for these friends to direct their support to a lover rather the family particularly when the family disenfranchised the relationship.

At times, the posturing resembles a card game: What beats my claim for the honor? Best friend trumps close friend; close friend trumps casual friend, and casual friend trumps acquaintance. Who decides between two best friends—especially if they are not friends with each other—or multiple close friends? Some families prefer support to be coordinated through one friend. Littlewood (1992) reminds that whoever wins the recognition as the de facto chief mourner has "few obligations other than to mourn the dead person" (p. 104). Supporters are to see that the chief mourner(s) is not distracted from mourning. Whatever the chief mourner asks—if within reason—the chief mourner gets. Some friends respond "your wish is my command." Others, from previous frustrating experience as friends offering support, qualify: "if I possibly can" or "if it is as all possible."

WOMEN FRIENDS AS SUPPORT PROVIDERS

Women face particular pressure since they are expected to be care-givers, organizers, and managers of social events in this culture. The more special the event, the more the pressure placed on the woman. One woman friendgriever recalls,

> I was too busy at the time to think about my own grief. I was so busy giving care that I could not take care of me. Some days I did not know if I was going or coming. All I could think about was Ellen and the children after Paul was killed. What did they need? Ellen was a zombie. Someone had to step in and take charge. I was that someone.

The movement of large numbers of women into the workplace has impacted their availability to offer support (Putnam, 2000). Still, many women feel constrained to meet traditional expectations while balancing job and their own family responsibilities. Some feel enormous guilt when they cannot meet their own expectations for offering support as friends, "Some friend I turned out to be." Others simply ignore their own grief to "make it happen" for the family.

WHEN THE FAMILY DOES NOT VALUE THE FRIENDSHIP

Some families do not understand how important being supportive is to a particular friend; many friends need to feel needed. Friends who have juggled busy family life priorities, social and career responsibilities as caregivers for a dying individual can feel angered when the family arrives from out of town (or now steps forward) to take charge and relegates these friends—or a particular friendgriever—to a spectator role.

Some families limit or avoid direct communication with friends; some families declare the equivalent of martial law. As one father snarled, "We do not have to explain anything to anybody!" The manner in which a request is made or support rejected, diminishes the friend. Sometimes a family (or individual family members) may create a truce with at least one friend.

Attitudes and prejudices about lifestyle may influence the decision to exclude certain friends. Whether it is cohabitation, homosexuality, substance abuse, or even religion, a family may seemingly pay back and settle previous lost arguments or disputes. Empereur (1998) notes that because of conditional love by families, individuals create and rely on "parallel families" (p. 117) of friends for emotional and crisis support. The issues become muddied, if an adult son or daughter dies without a will or preneed funeral policies. For example, rather than admit that a son or daughter is gay, family members may collude to believe that the son or daughter was negatively influenced by a particular friend or circle of friends, and thus be resistant to accepting support from those individuals. Some friends, yes; other particular friends, no! So, one family scheduled the internment at a time when the friends could not attend. Another family did not publish a death notice, in the assessment of one friend, "to get back at us." Marcia, a "discarded" friend, explains that the parents of her friend

> were very bitter. Unbelievably, they had the body removed to their choice of funeral home. Neither Bob or any of us would be told where or when the funeral would take place. We were not welcome. . . . I called every funeral home in Long Island asking when and where Alan's ceremony would be held. Finally, I located the right place. Since we knew . . . friends would be kept from the service, I showed up before the service began. Afterward, a friend and I followed the funeral procession out to the cemetery (Fishman, 1990, pp. 77-78).

Marcia arranged a second friends-oriented memorial service, escorting friends to the grave. She tried to reach out to her friend's family. Only reluctantly did the mother agree to take Marcia's phone number. By the time the mother wanted to make amends, another of the mutual friends had died and the resentment was deeply entrenched throughout the friendorbit. One shunned friend reports,

> Joan's parents were convinced that their darling little daughter would never have even experimented with drugs if she had not been influenced by us, the "damned rift-raft" as Joan's father called us. Well, that girl was wild long before she ever met us. Joan just was not strong enough to stand up to her family. The family never would admit that Joan was driven to drugs, trying to numb some awful ache in her soul. They were not interested in getting to know us. By the time Joan died, there was lots of bad blood between the family and the friends. They were convinced if Joan would have moved back to their farm in Iowa she would have "straightened up and made something of herself." If you ask her friends, a lot of us think that she had "made something of herself." I went by the apartment to take some food from the deli but you could have cut the tension as well as the ham with a knife. Her father just glared at me. They did not ask me to have a cup or coffee or anything. But at least I know that I tried to be supportive.

Sklar and Hartley (1990) insist that "the loss may be aggravated by the intentional or inadvertent inability or unwillingness of others to recognize" (p. 105) the friendship.

It may be long after the rituals that the family gains a more accurate understanding of who was close or closest to the deceased and who was not. Sometimes, only time discloses a friend's involvement in the deceased's life. Friends who do not learn of the death in time to offer early responses, may prove friendly long after the rituals.

In the first hours or day after an individual dies, many families appreciate the vital support friends offer. Notification mobilizes a friendorbit to support the chief mourner(s). Something remarkable happen when a friend asks, "What can I do to help?" or "What needs to be done?" You may have experienced that moment when a chief mourner or family member says, "Oh, thank goodness you are here."

KEY CONCEPTS OF THIS CHAPTER

- A friend is expected to offer support according to the needs of the family.
- In offering support many individuals neglect and complicate their own grief.
- Grieving friends have needs, too.
- Doing becomes a convenient socially-endorsed distraction from fully engaging with the grief following a friend's death. Guilt motivates the support of some friends.
- It is critical to know the identity of the chief mourner and the chief supporter.
- The family, an employer, other friends in the friendorbit may disenfranchise the friendgrievers' offers of support.
- A core of common expectations summarizes reasonable expectations for the support of a friend includes calling the family on the phone or going to the primary residence; sending flowers; donating to a designated charity; attending rituals; donating or preparing food; volunteering to provide assistance; responding to specific family requests; supplying missing data; sending a sympathy card.
- If the family is dysfunctional or does not recognize the friendship, offering support may be complicated.

IMPLICATIONS FOR CLINICIANS

Why should a clinician care about how friends offer support? Because some clients will avoid their own grief through support, and, sooner or later you will probably be in that position yourself. By examining the variables of support, you gain insight into the support of your clients as well as their need for support in doing their own grief work.

1. Issues that complicate and delay the grief work may come to light during counseling. The clinician can help the friendgriever reframe the

slights, whether intentional, coincidental, or assumed, whether from the family or from others in the friendorbit. Explore the extent to which the family's responses was motivated by shock or fatigue. Has the friendgriever tried to address the slights? Has the friend communicated with the family or talked with other friends? Are certain individuals in the friendorbit inflaming the issue?

2. Some friends avoid grieving by being hyper-attentive to the family. Some take the approach: "If it is to be, it's up to *me*!" Some have animosity toward certain friends who failed to be as supportive as expected. Did the friendgriever clearly give other friends opportunities to be supportive. Was the friendgriever clear in stating expectations?

3. The clinician may need to explore the griever's friendorbit. Some orbits are only held together by a key friend; if that friend dies the friendorbit may collapse or dissolve; the griever can be anxious about its continuance, especially when that friendship has great payoffs.

4. Remind the friendgriever that offering support is not limited to the period immediately following the rituals—particularly when there is a delay between death and the rituals. The friendgriever might want to drop a note, card, or letter or telephone the family to offer support. The friend offers support now with the same words, "How can I help you?

CHAPTER 6
Offering Hospitality

CHAPTER PREVIEW

In this chapter we examine the expectations for hospitality by friends. How does a friend respond if family requests, sometimes demands, are unreasonable? Rapid cultural change has significantly altered traditional expectations. Other friends in the friendorbit may not assume a reasonable share of hospitality. To what degree can offering hospitality interfere with a friend acknowledging grief? Hospitality can numb or function as an effective technique to avoid griefwork.

What roles or tasks of the friendgriever are included in the umbrella phrase, offering hospitality? Responding would be easier if there were a protocol for friends outlining exactly what "being there" includes. In a multicultural society, how can a friend avoid offending people of other world religions and cultures?

> Normal rules governing the privacy of the bereaved family are put aside, and new ones substituted during the course of the *rite de passage* that are both more and less restrictive than normal (Metcalf & Huntington, 1991, p. 205).

Fulfilling socially-defined expectations or family-shaped expectations for hospitality can be demanding on a friend and on a friendorbit. Family requests, or demands, may be excessive or unreasonable. Others in a friendorbit may fail to assume a reasonable share of hospitality. Thus, offering hospitality may interfere with friends acknowledging and creatively engaging their own grief.

The hospitality tasks of the friendgriever depend on multiple factors. Friends might respond more easily if a protocol outlined what "being there" includes. Rapid cultural change has made previous guidelines outdated, even in rural communities. Increasingly a large proportion of Americans look to the workplace, church, schools, or other voluntary associations for friends rather than among neighbors; that would also be true in a crisis (Schaller, 1999). Thus, neighbors may be only minimal suppliers of hospitality following a death (assuming the person even knows the neighbors let alone considers them friends). In the cyber age, friends may be part of the global village rather than residents of one's zip code; friends halfway across the world are unable to be part of the ad hoc groups providing hospitality. Local friends may have "only the thinnest connection with genuine friendship" (Johnson, 1999, p. 92). Instead of "Sure, what can I do to help?" the answer may be hedged, "Well, I guess I could do something" or "Let me get back to you."

THE CORE RESPONSES OF HOSPITALITY AND "BE THERENESS"

Hospitality includes three time frames: 1) Initial or "crisis" care; 2) transitional, from the time of death until a time the friend believes the principal griever should be "over it; and 3) long-term hospitality.

Initial hospitality	Transitional hospitality	Long-term hospitality

Wyse (1995) describes friends being "on call" during a final illness and in the period of initial hospitality. The ones who are "still there after the last casserole disappears" she terms "stayers." All others are "goers" off to the next crisis. "Staying is what separates acquaintances from friends" (p. 77). However, given the growing privatization of grief (Walter, 1999), friends feel less guilty "going" or withdrawing or even withholding hospitality or limiting their offers. By denying hospitality, friends may attempt to "police" the grief of a friend. True friends become important long after the death.

IDENTIFYING THE ROLES OF THE FRIENDGRIEVER

Joan describes the initial offering of hospitality in a group of friends.

The first phone call came about an hour after Joe died. "Joan, tell me what I should do. I do not want to intrude on Brenda and the family." The second call, from another member of the group came five minutes after the first, almost in identical words, "Joan, tell me what I can do. I feel like I should be doing something." The calls came from the small group of friends who had met for several years for Bible study, food, and conversation. Everyone assumed that Joan would know what to do. "Well, I tell you what I am going to do," Joan informed each caller. "I am going over there at noon and see what needs to be done." Soon after Joan's arrival, other members began arriving. Joan adds, "Joe was not just our friend's spouse, over the years he had become our friend, as well. Two hours after he died, the house was filled with friends and his absence."

Joan reports that although none of these friends knew what to do, all expressed a desire to avoid doing the wrong thing. In the absence of clear guidelines and given the passion for respecting the privacy of a friend or family member, some are at a loss to know how to offer hospitality. Long after the death, some feel guilty (or can be made to feel guilty) for failing to respond in a particular manner or on a certain timetable.

THE "TAKE CHARGE" MOMENT

The death of a friend presents a "take charge" moment. Often a friend steps into, or is assigned, the role as "hospitality manager" or coordinator. When his pal Russ died in a car wreck, Bill recognized and seized this opportunity. "I became what is called 'point man' in the military. I sized up the situation, thought about what needed to be done, and organized the response." (Mutual friends joke that Bill was more like a drill sergeant, barking out orders. "But it needed to be done and Bill was going to make sure that it got done.") Sometimes a friend assumes responsibility with little consultation with the family and very little permission-giving, particularly when family members are in shock following an unexpected or traumatic death or have also been injured. After golfer Payne Stewart was killed in 1999, a minister went to the Stewart home to try and determine who was taking charge. He soon discovered that the person who should have been in charge, Robert Fraley, Stewart's manager, had also died in the crash (Guest, 2000). Mrs. Stewart had lost not only her husband, but two close friends who in essence ran their lives in the world of professional golf.

THE FRIENDSHIP BEFORE THE DEATH SHAPES INTERACTION AFTER THE DEATH

With some friends you call ahead rather than just appear at the door; with other friends, a "my house is your house" openness prevails. Tracey Stewart comments, "My girlfriends were all here straight-away. . . and a lot of my tennis friends were here immediately" (Guest, 2000, p. 6). Hospitality following a death is an apprenticeship complete with both shining moments and possibly some glaring faux pax. One friend recounts the initial response:

> I decided that it would be easier to ask forgiveness later than to interrupt to ask permission at the moment. What was I supposed to do? Walk into the living room and say, "Could you compose yourself while I run through this list?" No. I sat in my friend's kitchen, drank a cup of coffee and thought about what had to be done. I made a list of what had to be done in the first hour, in the first six hours, what had to be done that day. I soon had a game plan. Yes, I proceeded on my own authority but you know what? It worked. Probably because I knew Jack so well and had spent so much time with his family that I just knew what he would want and what the family would want.

Kolf (1999) counsels friends, "Unless it requires a major decision, simply go quietly about the job" (p. 27). Though preferring privacy, "out of respect for the intentions of such sympathizers," the family rarely shows irritation (Metcalf & Huntington, 1991, p. 205) to acts of hospitality by friends. Schoenberg (1980) recommends the role for friends to be "presence in the immediate background" (p. 244). "A really close friend should feel free to take the initiative." However, if the friendship is not really close, "it would be best if the friend refrain from any overt action" (p. 244). Moe (1997) reports, "Help can come from very unskilled but caring people. However, this needs to be done in cooperation with the griever to keep it from becoming a further invasion upon their sense of control" (pp. 74-75). Many chief mourners later acknowledge: "I do not know what we would have done without our friends." Hospitality can lead to unspoken resentment or bruised feelings; or, for friends, a sense of a lack of appreciation or of being taken for granted. One friend says, "Whatever we do—it's never enough!"

CONFRONTING THE "NOW WHAT?" QUESTION

Joan's cadre of friends had known what to do during Joe's long illness. Prepare casseroles and salads, sit with Brenda late in the night, send encouragement cards, and inquire through brief "Wanted to see how you are doing today" calls. But death, by making their friend the first widow in the friendorbit, challenged their confidence. The mothers of these women—in a culture "dominated to a greater extent by formalized expectations and obligations" (Kahn & Antonucci, 1980, p. 260)—would have known what to do. Moreover, the large migration of women from homemaking into the workplace (Rothman, 1998) has significantly reduced the time and energy women friends have available for offering hospitality (Heller & Hindle, 1998). Nevertheless, society still expects women to be grief "magicians" and somehow to get it all done and done well.

Friendly acts of hospitality appreciated by one griever, may annoy or antagonize another. Some widows, unlike Brenda, would have preferred to be alone or with one friend rather than have a living room full of friends. Some families at the time of a death, "draw the wagons into a circle" for protection; others, welcome a close friend's knock at the door or phone call and the question, "What can I do?" Sometimes what needs to be done is relatively simple: "I need this black dress taken to the cleaners, so that I can wear it to the funeral" or more complex, "I need someone to track down her brother Ed. He is hiking somewhere in Yosemite."

FRIENDS BEARING GIFTS

Friends contribute five types of gifts: money, information, time, resources, and entitlements (Kahn & Antonucci, 1980), all of which may be needed at some point. Initially, information may be critical. Those without preneed funeral and burial plans, or who are new to a community, may ask a friend to recommend a funeral home or cemetery. Sometimes, a friend with previous grief experience offers information, makes suggestions, or puts forward a different perspective. Friends may not have answers but they can "walk" the questioner toward answers or know someone who can provide answers. For example, when Pam Moore died, her family wanted an inexpensive wood casket. When the funeral Director was reluctant to provide such a casket, a friend of the family located the casket (Moore, 1997).

When my friend Denny died, within a few hours, friends from the church arrived at his home with cleaning supplies. "We are here to tidy up the house" they whispered, although Denny's mother is known to be a meticulous housekeeper. Another friend with a car phone (in the days before cellular phones were common) arrived to help notify. Repeatedly that first day, friends stepped forward mixing resources and hospitality with condolences. At one point, a friend asked, "Have you had lunch?" No, I responded. "Then let's go grab a quick bite." When I protested that the family might need me, this person interrupted, "They will need you more tonight after other friends have had to go home."

Sometimes, front-line friends bear the brunt of irritation or anger from grieving family members; the handling of a particular detail may provoke confrontation. Offering hospitality includes navigating relational land mines. Friends coming and going in a residence may further contribute to a sense of loss of control. One friend recalls,

> It was helpful having friends around, but at times, there was no place to get away from everyone. I had to retreat to my bedroom, which, at the time, was a wreck because of the remodeling. I am a doer. I am not used to receiving hospitality. A couple of times I just snapped. I said some awful things to some friends who were just trying to be helpful. I felt so overwhelmed. I was no longer in control.

CALL THE FAMILY OR GO TO THE PRIMARY RESIDENCE

In many communities, upon notification of death, a close friend is expected to go to the residence to extend condolences and volunteer assistance. Post (1992) qualifies the expectation: "Immediately on hearing of the death, intimate friends of the deceased should go to the house of mourning and ask whether they can be of service" (p. 547). Friends often say on arrival, "I came as soon as I heard." (In some communities, casual friends are also expected to go to the residence.) African-Americans generally consider personal presence and service upon notification of death the most valued gesture of condolence (DeSpelder & Strickland, 1996).

In metropolitan areas, a phone call to the chief mourner or the residence may be preferred. Post (1992) concedes that while telephoning initial condolences is acceptable, it "may cause inconvenience by tying up the [telephone] line" (p. 548). In the cyber age, with many people having multiple phones, fax machines, and e-mail addresses, condolences and offers of support are increasingly acceptable via these mediums, particularly from friends who live out-of-town or who are away at the time of death or services. In some families, particularly immediately after the death, these expressions are preferred over a personal visit by reducing prolonged conversations or the need to repeatedly recount details of the death. Limiting phone contact reduces the number of persons (especially casual friends) with whom the chief mourner must initially interact.

The friend asks, "Would you like me to come over?" and responds according to the mourner's lead. Some friends listen closely, anticipating a reluctance to impose on or inconvenience a friend. One friend explains, "Sometimes a friend has to exercise veto power. I knew it would be hours before family members could get there. I wanted the children to see a familiar face. So I went." "I am on my way" or "I will be there as soon as I can" become valuable promises of hospitality.

Many families welcome a friend stepping forward to answer the telephone and the door. This key friend—who organizes the sympathizers—is "close enough to the immediately bereaved to be in a position to speak in their behalf on matters of protocol, yet not so close to the deceased himself as to be more properly engaged in active grieving themselves" (Sudnow, 1967, p. 156). This "gatekeeper" friend protects the family from coincidental intrusion by petition signature collectors, religious canvassers, candy sellers, and in some cases, the media. A funeral wreath once hung on the front door of the residence as a symbol of mourning and a warning to those who do not know of a death. This tradition has declined due to the fear of break-ins. (As a result of the fear of burglary, a friend extends support by staying in the residence when the family is away, especially during the rituals.)

Upon arrival, the friend generally seeks a preliminary assessment, "How is ___ [the chief mourner or this particular caller's friend] doing? What do you know so far?" In the case of a murder, suicide, or suspected foul play, the initial police investigation may delay decision making; details are tentative until the release of the body. Moreover, a death at home may require police and representatives from the coroner or public examiner's office to be present; thus, in one instance, the family and friends sat huddled for hours in a corner of the living room before the body was removed. (Crime scenes can be contaminated if friends are wandering through the house.) Friends have been kept for hours behind police lines, frustrating them as well as family members who desperately need assistance and support.

The initial assessment sets the stage for the first interaction between a friend and the chief mourner. The friend offers some words of condolence or a hug, as well as offers of practical help. Although Post (1992) suggests that it would be "immeasurably helpful to the family" if "a very close friend is willing to take charge of funeral arrangements" (p. 103), that is impractical due to the myriad of financial details involved. Funeral directors need to establish clear fiduciary responsibility, and some require a significant down payment or immediate payment. Some grievers, however, will welcome a friend accompanying them to the funeral home for the arrangements conference (Kelly, 2000).

In response to the need for someone to manage numerous details, the family may enlist one or two close friends to receive and record the flowers, calls, condolence messages, and food. Parachin (1998, March) describes the support of friends in the life of one family whose son was murdered. "Practical acts of kindness on their behalf freed the Whites to grieve, to talk with those who came to offer sympathy, to rest and to plan" (pp. 83-84). This particular family has a large circle of friends, some of whom flew to Colorado Springs upon notification. However, some families do not have large friendorbits and offers of hospitality may be limited. Moreover, after a homicide or suspected foul play, some friends may keep distance until the facts become more clearly established.

The friend-organizer (or friends taking turns in this role) may aggressively screen and record telephone calls, particularly initially. "I will tell them you called" or "I will ask her to call you back in a little while." At some point, the organizer summarizes the calls to the chief mourner or to other family members. Actually some friends and acquaintances prefer not to speak to the family, fearful of saying the wrong thing. "Oh no. Just tell them that I called and that I am thinking about them at this time." Some organizer-friends become spokespersons for the family, particularly on what the family needs and on details such as time of meals, funeral home handling the arrangements, tentative plans and times for services, preferences for flowers, etc. In cases where the deceased is famous or the death becomes newsworthy, a friend may even serve as an intermediary with the media.

Serving as the organizer can be a demanding task, particularly when another friend challenges the friend-organizer's authority or insists on talking to a family member. The friend-organizer may have to tip-toe around personalities and tensions within families and within friendorbits to diffuse potentially tense situations. However, the role has a downside. Often the organizer-friend is forced to put her own grief on hold in order to focus on the needs of the family, particularly if there is an inadequate support system. Kolf (1999) describes the "best" friendship between two of her friends, Sylvia and Charla—a friendship she envied. When Sylvia died unexpectedly, although devastated Charla

> pitched right in and took care of the children, made meals for the family and was a regular trooper. I watched with sadness, because nobody seemed to realize the depth of her *own* personal loss. They appreciated all she was doing, but she received little comfort for herself. She definitely was a forgotten griever (p. 22).

Fortunate is the organizer when friends from other friendorbits ask, "How are *you* holding up?" or "How can I help *you*?"

FRIENDS NOTIFY OTHER FRIENDS

Not everyone reads the newspapers daily or reads the obituaries, so families utilize friendship networks to get out the word of a death and details of the rituals. Friendorbits may be reactivated in crisis; individuals describe friends "coming out of the woodwork" after a death.

Notifiers must trust an individual who takes the call to forward the message. Increasingly, it is considered acceptable to leave notification of a death on an answering machine, although answering machines are not fool-proof. While writing this chapter I retrieved a message from a friend, "I hate to leave this kind of message on a machine but. . . ." As soon as I heard the tone of voice, I knew that my friend Jean had died after a long illness.

"Because we are geographically, socially, or emotionally detached from our families, they are unaware of our friends" (Deck & Folta, 1989, p. 79). At the time of death, sometimes a family or other friends do not know the full names, addresses, or phone numbers of casual friends: "She often talked about a friend named Carolyn. Do your recognize that name?" Thus, unfortunately, some friends are not notified. Although everyone assumes that *someone* called friends named Myra or Steve, actually, no one notified these friends. When there are a large number of individuals to be notified, the notifying-friend may enlist others to help, although delegation may make notification less complete or effective.

TIMING AND SOURCE OF NOTIFICATION

Friends compare notes about when and how they learned of the death. Time and method of notification indicate perceived social standing and placement in a friendorbit, especially if one is among the last to hear. The disclosure, "They [the family] called me *immediately* or *personally*" communicates a standing not experienced by the friend notified by another friend, or the friend who read about the death in the newspaper.

> People should ideally learn from someone who stood approximately in the same degree of intimacy to the deceased, and in rough order of intimacy. Some little discussion is often necessary to decide who should telephone whom, as the urgency, or lack of it, with which the close kin contact friends and relatives constitutes an evaluation of the importance of the person in the life of the deceased and in the estimation of the survivors (Metcalf & Huntington, 1991, p. 205).

Eventually the question, "Should I call _____?" surfaces. Notifying estranged friends requires diplomacy. These friends, relegated to the fringe of the friendorbit (or jettisoned from the orbit) may not learn of the death until after the rituals. At notification, some wonder, given circumstances of the friendship, would they be welcome at the rituals.

When I arrived at one friend's home, I asked for the family address book and said, "Who should I call *first*?" Admittedly, it was emotionally draining making the calls, but someone needed to spare the family the task of reporting the death to friends scattered across the country. I learned that when a healthy eighteen-year-old dies, people want details. "Was it a suicide?" one family friend asked bluntly. "Drug overdose?" another asked. The first time I was asked about suicide, I sputtered, "*Suicide!?*" Fortunately, as a friend, I was able to keep family members from having to deal with those questions. However, friends can be caught in the middle when a family wishes to conceal cause of death or details of the death.

WHEN FRIENDS ARE NOT IN
DAILY CONTACT

In large metropolitan areas friends do not always have daily contact. Those who read the obituaries with some degree of regularity, may assume others know and conclude the newspaper to be the initial or primary notifier. For six months after my mother died, my sister and I still received notes or calls, "I just heard about your mother." Trillin (1993) describes learning of a friend's suicide

> . . . I stood in my kitchen in New York early one morning—a February morning in 1991—glancing at *The New York Times*. On the obituary page, a headline over a three—or—four-inch story said, ROGER D. HANSEN, 55, PROFESSOR AND AUTHOR. Denny? I couldn't believe it. My first thought was that there were, as we had always known, other Roger Hansens. But when I started the story, it quickly became obvious that Denny was the Roger Hansen in question (p. 19).

Not every friend's death is a news story; not everyone gets an obituary or even a death notice (Marks & Piggee, 1998-99), especially in metropolitan areas where newspapers charge for these services. In Kansas City, where I live, *The Kansas City Star* provides a free basic-facts "death notice" with date of death, age, time of services, and the name of the funeral home. The death notice becomes a fee-charged obituary when any biographical information or survivors are listed; moreover, free death notices run only one day. However, even a paid obituary may not offer enough details to identify—especially with a common name like John Smith. So a casual friend asks, "Is this the John Smith *I* know?"

Notification is further complicated in large metropolitan areas. A chief mourner in Independence, Missouri, (a Kansas City suburb) might place an obituary only in the regional paper, *The Independence*

Examiner. Thus, a work friend who lives in Olathe, a suburb on the Kansas side of the metroplex, would not see the obituary in that regional newspaper, *The Olathe Daily News*. For some, the expense of multiple obituaries encourages minimal listing.

Even if a death notice is published, some have experienced so many deaths they no longer read the obituaries (Rofes, 1996). Publication of the death notice or obituary may be delayed, sometimes as a means of ensuring that services will be private. In one case, a friend died on Wednesday, but the obituary was not published until the following Monday.

In an extended circle of friends, the obituary prompted a lot of phone calls that begin, "When is the last time you saw him? How did he seem to you?" which indicates, to some degree, current intimacy in the friendship. Sometimes seeing an obituary results in calls which reestablish casual friendships, "Just saw this and didn't know if you had seen it" which may initiate a "catching up" conversation.

In some rural communities, deaths are announced on radio stations as a public service. Notification is also complicated by the mobility of the American public—15.9 percent of Americans move ever year ("Change of address? Less likely," 2000, July 12, p. A6). Moreover, a large percentage of Americans change telephone numbers, have unlisted numbers, or have disconnected numbers. Despite promises to keep in touch, friendships change or deteriorate, deliberately or unintentionally (Levinger, 1980). A person living now in another city or nation could be dead, buried, and memorialized before all of the friends are aware of the death. One "out of the loop" friend recalls:

> I was enjoying dinner with some friends with whom I used to work and we got to talking about the good old days. Someone mentioned Ken. "Wonder how he's getting along since Margaret died?" "Margaret died!" I blurted out. "When did Margaret die?" The friends looked at each other, "Oh, I'd say, what, two years ago?" Another added, "Maybe a little more than that." I sat back stunned. For them, Margaret's death was old news; for me, it was fresh. I did not stay for dessert.

In AIDS-related deaths, some families have deliberately not notified friends. With some deaths, there is no one to place the death notice. Nieves (2000, June 25) reports "More people are dying alone, with no one to arrange their funerals, settle their estates or mourn their passing" (pp. 1-12), particularly among the elderly and homeless. Derek Gordon notes that a significant number of AIDS deaths in San Francisco now involve "homeless drug addicts, many of them without friends or loved ones who would submit an obituary to the [Bay Area] *Reporter*" (cited in Kligman, 1998, August 15, p. A-9) or to the *San Francisco Chronicle*. This is true in other larger metropolitan areas as well.

Friends who are out-of-town on vacation or business may not know or know in time to change plans, contact the family, send flowers, or offer hospitality. Given the mobility of some jobs, or due to transfers and relocations, remnant friendorbits may exist in multiple locales. Since friends do not qualify for bereavement air fares, changing a ticket in order to attend rituals can be cost prohibitive.

One participant in my doctoral research disclosed his experience in coming home from vacation and retrieving a "Call me as soon as you can" message on the answering machine notifying him of a friend's death. When he called, a family member was cool to him. The family had assumed that he had chosen not to attend the services or contact them.

Some friendships have been reestablished or had tensions defused during a long illness. Clearing up unfinished business is important to many friends. The friendship between Richard Nixon and Hubert Humphrey—begun in the U.S. Senate—was strained in the 1968 presidential campaign that Nixon narrowly won. A decade passed without contact until Humphrey, dying with cancer in Minnesota, telephoned to wish Nixon a happy birthday. After the call, Nixon informed an aide, "He's only got a few days. I don't care what it takes, but I am going to the funeral. Start working on it" (Ambrose, 1991, p. 514). Since Nixon had not been in Washington, D.C. since resigning in 1974, numerous matters of protocol and practical hospitality, such as where he would stay, had to be resolved. When the White House did not offer the traditional accommodations for former presidents, Blair House, Nixon accepted the hospitality of a friend and stayed in a private home. He fretted that his presence could turn the funeral into a media circus and complicate the grief of the Humphrey family and close friends. Mrs. Muriel Humphrey assured Nixon that she would be honored to have him attend.

THE JEWISH CONDOLENCE CALL

Viewing the body is rare among Jews; there is no visitation to facilitate initial interaction among friends. The absence of embalming mandates a burial before sundown the day after the death, which can make schedule adjustments difficult for some friends. The Jewish faith structures condolence calls and visits until after burial since contact with the family or chief mourner is not expected during *aninut,* a period between the death and burial.

The family will sit *shiva,* a period following the death, (some families observe *shiva* less than a full seven days) in the primary residence of the chief mourner, and this will be the time for friends to offer condolences and support. *Nichum avelim* or comforting grievers and offering hospitality are considered a *mitzvah,* or good deed by a friend. Since Jewish chief mourners generally will not leave their residences during *shiva* and some will not talk on the phone, friends have to come to them. A friend only need say, "I am sorry." Syme (1988) comments, "That simple phrase, a touch, a hug, will mean more to the mourner than you can ever know" (p. 118).

Although many friends avoid frivolous, lighthearted conversation or humor that would detract from the active focus on mourning (Maslin, 1979), A. Klein (1998) finds a role for humor. "Like the food that the condolence callers bring to provide nourishment of the body, I believe, the things they laugh about provide nourishment for the soul" (p. xvii). Grollman (1974) summarizes this expectation, "The most important expression of condolence is your own presence at both the funeral and the house of bereavement" (p. 127). A friend's presence demonstrates "That even though individuals may die, good friends still remain" (p. 128).

IMPACT OF DIVERSITY

Magida (1996), responding to the growing religious and ethnic diversity in the United States, offers *How to Be a Perfect Stranger: A Guide to Etiquette in Other People's Religious Ceremonies* as a helpful guide for friends in navigating social interaction on special occasions. Friends, unfamiliar with the faith or cultural traditions of the deceased, may hesitate to go to a residence or funeral home to offer hospitality for fear of saying or doing something offensive. Some wish to avoid a memory-oriented residence (from happy times like dinners and parties) and prefer the controlled anonymity of a funeral home.

Friends may visit the home of the Muslim friend after the funeral or at any time during the forty days of mourning observed in Islam. When friends visit, rather than conversation, they will probably sit and listen as someone reads aloud from *The Qur'an* or to a taped reading (Magida, 1996, p. 194). Brief visits by friends to the home is considered appropriate by many Buddhists. Following the death of a Hindu, friends may visit before the *shraddha* (funeral) ceremony which takes place ten days after the death of members of the Bhrahmin caste and thirty days after the deaths of members of other castes (Magida, 1996, p. 173).

WHEN HOSPITALITY IS THWARTED BY
RELIGIOUS DIFFERENCES

In a nation that is a multicultural mix of death rituals, traditions, and social expectations, the sensitive friendgriever must be alert to fine nuances within ethnic groups. Was the deceased Cuban? Argentinian? or Mexican? That distinction could make a profound difference in grief expressions and expectations. de Paula, Lagana, and Gonzalez-Ramirez (1996) caution that diversity within an ethnic population makes sweeping generalizations about funeral ritual and grief difficult for Mexican-Americans let alone all Hispanics. Mexican-Americans who are professionals or upper middle class economically may react very differently from some in lower socioeconomic classes. Mexican-Americans who have become evangelical Protestants respond to rituals very differently from those who are devout Roman Catholics, and may refuse to participate in some of rituals. That unwillingness on the part of a friend and how that is communicated may offend the family and others in the friendorbit because it may be perceived as an inhospitable act.

The culturally-sensitive friend, particularly at a time of grief, can be gracious to the family and also help other friends who may be uncertain of the cultural particularities, especially those who question or discount the religious experiences of those outside their particular theological understandings. Some Christians believe there is only one way to salvation, through faith in Jesus Christ, everyone else goes to hell although Walter (1999) points to a decline in belief in hell. The death of a Buddhist, Hindu, Jewish, or a friend who practices New Age spirituality—even friends in mainline Protestant denomination—can be troubling because of a person's understanding of eternal life. Tension erupts when friends attempt to "correct" such pious narrow thinking (Wilcock, 1996). Some evangelical Christian friends inquire, "Was your friend *saved*?" or "*born again*" (meaning had the friend accepted Jesus Christ as "their personal Lord and Savior"—a required doctrinal confession for some). Some friends regret being unable "to lead the friend to a saving knowledge of Jesus Christ" or not having "witnessed" to them. Worden's (1991) task, finding "an appropriate place for the dead in their emotional lives" (p. 17), can be a distressing spiritual task for some friends—particularly those who believe in hell.

One friends's family was distressed that he was gay. According to their faith, after dying of AIDS-related complications, he went to hell. As I listened to their distress, I decided to disclose details of my last conversation with him, particularly his statement, "I am ready to meet God." For some family members, Karl's statement was insufficient but one sister broke into a smile and said, "then he really was a Christian. He really is with God."

It may be difficult or discomforting for some friends to hear out the questions about eternal life. But a conservative Christian friend's grief may be greatly complicated by a lack of "assurance" about their friend's salvation. Indeed, it may influence their word choice in offering condolence because they do not feel comfortable saying, "He is in a better place" or "in heaven." On occasion, I have counseled concerned friends, "We must place our friend into the hands of a God who loved him more than we did." For some that is helpful in reconciling with a friend's death.

FRIENDS SEND FLOWERS

In the days before embalming, flowers had a practical function: masking odors associated with decomposition (Grollman, 1998). In early burial processions, Greeks and Roman friends carried funeral cypress palms as symbols of grief. The early Christians preferred palm and olive branches, associating them with Jesus' palm-strewn entry into Jerusalem. Evergreen, laurel, and ivy leaves were laid on the stretcher (before the coffin/casket) as a token of the hope of immortality (Smith & Cheetham, 1875). Roman friends placed a wreath of flowers on the head as an honor comparable to a crown given to the winners of athletic competitions. The early Christians altered this practice, scattering flowers over all the body (probably to cover up bodily discharges). Today flowers cover some odors—*perceived* odors funeral directors would insist. In some cases, when the results of the embalmer's skills may be less than ideal, flowers offer a distraction.

Flowers have long been a social expression and expectation. Sending flowers gives a friend something practical to do immediately upon learning of the death. One friend explains, "It is the least I can do." Sending flowers is an act of hospitality, particularly when the friend is some distance away or when the act stimulates memories of a friend's interest in or love of flowers: "Oh, he loved Anthuriums." Before the development of the floral industry, friends, like my grandmother in her farm community, made bouquets from their own gardens or planted flowers on the grave.

CONTEMPORARY ATTITUDES ON
FLOWERS

Wolfelt (1994) identifies flowers as another "ousted symbol" like the armband or wreath on the door or women wearing black for a year. "Today we opt for the more practical but less spiritual monetary donation" (p. 9). Nevertheless, for many, flowers communicate caring when a friend cannot find words. Among the Greek Orthodox, for example, flowers may be sent by friends either to the funeral home or to the residence.

Most in the Jewish community object to flowers—although flowers may be acceptable for some Reform funerals (Magida, 1996). Others have strong personal objections to the "waste" of flowers. Friends, when uncertain of the appropriateness, call the organizer-friend or the funeral home for clarification. Many people prefer that, in lieu of flowers, contributions be sent in the name of the deceased to a synagogue, a church, a hospital, a charity, or an institution of higher learning.

For Muslims, friends often send flowers to the home of the bereaved after the funeral. Since Hindus rarely use a funeral home, the body will be at the residence. Friends may take flowers to the home of the deceased upon hearing of the death and place them at the feet of the corpse.

Potted plants or artificial plants may be preferred because they symbolize caring long after the rituals. Caring for living plants reminds the griever of a friend's love. For friends who send flowers, the decision of how much to spend on flowers may present a challenge. Flowers may be appraised not only by the family but also by friends with a competitive spirit. A floral tribute can "one-up" other friends and elicit favorable commentary, "What an unusual (etc.) arrangement" or "Look at that arrangement. I bet it cost a fortune!" To some friends, the proximity of the flowers to the casket can be perceived as a social indicator of the value the family assigns the friendship. Friends have been observed moving flowers from where a funeral home employee or family member has originally placed them.

The request, "Kindly omit flowers" eliminates a source of perceived usefulness for friends; some close friends send flowers anyway. Decision making may be more complicated for the friend when the family suggests either flowers or donations to a designated charity. By sending flowers the family (and others) immediately knows of your response; with donations to charities, it could be weeks or months before notification.

FLOWERS STIMULATE CONVERSATION

Flowers have a secondary role as conversation initiators at funeral rituals, particularly for friends from different friendorbits. An observation, "All these beautiful flowers! Pat would have loved them" may be enough to elicit a "You are right about that. How did you know Pat?" Also, the family or chief mourner may personally acknowledge your flowers, "Your flowers are beautiful. Thank you for sending them." Commenting on flowers allows for safe, unintrusive interaction with the family, with friends, and even with strangers.

Flowers dispel some discomfort at a ritual, particularly for friends with unpleasant memories from previous funerals and visitations. Focusing on the flowers or looking for those you have sent or your company or organization has sent provides a distraction.

Given the growing acceptance of direct disposal or private services, some friends send flowers to the primary residence, particularly if the deceased was known to enjoy flowers. Some friends send flowers on the anniversary of a death or on other special days. Many senior adults, who because of health or transportation limitations cannot attend a visitation or ritual, value sending flowers as a social transmission of sympathy (Euster, 1991).

FRIENDS DONATE TO A DESIGNATED CHARITY

Donating to a designated charity helps friends feel a completion of social obligation especially if they cannot attend the rituals. Giving memorial gifts provides friends "a positive mechanism for the achievement of action-oriented grief work" (Euster, 1991, p. 177).

Designated giving by friends offers a reminder of comfort and support to the bereaved family, particularly after the rituals. Gifts reconfirm friendship ties and help religious and other community programs valued by the deceased (Euster, 1991). Many friends believe memorial gifts to be a more lasting or more tangible expression of grief. One friend insists, "Flowers die but donations live on." Because of delayed notification by charities, a friend's donation may more likely be remembered. One participant in Euster's study reports that giving to a memorial on anniversaries or special days is a "living remembrance" (p. 175). Donations offer a means to express condolences for those who belatedly learn of the death. For Jewish friends, giving to a designated charity is both a *mitzvah* and a *tzedakah,* a good act done in the name of a loved one.

A family designation of a specific charity does not exclude giving in the deceased name to other charities. A friend's contribution "to any worthwhile charity is a fitting memorial to the memory of the deceased" (Grollman, 1974, p. 128). Friends, however, may be annoyed when a family designates a charity that does not reflect the interests of the deceased or which diametrically denies the interests and values of the deceased. Some not only pointedly refuse to donate, but comment on the selection to other friends and may persuade others not to give. When one friend died in a Zen Buddhist hospice, the family refused to designate the hospice for giving solely because it was operated by Buddhists. A mutual friend, impressed by that hospice's high quality care, angrily demanded, "Let's see if I have this right. It was acceptable for Buddhists to wipe your brother's butt but it is not acceptable for me to send them $50 in honor of my friend? Well, I am sending my check to the Buddhists. 'God bless 'em!'"

In some areas, friends donate toward funeral expenses or to an educational fund for the children of the deceased, particularly when this is suggested in the obituary.

FRIENDS SEND SYMPATHY CARDS OR NOTES

It is not unusual to hear a friend say, "I'm not very good with words." Thus, one early action by a friend may be to communicate caring through a condolesence card (Morgan 1994). Inadequacy at responding to death or the circumstances of a particular death, such as suicide, fuels the effort to find an appropriate card. The more intimate the friendship, the more effort invested in selecting "just the right card." Many friends are concerned as to how a family will "take" a card (Caldwell, McGee, & Pryor, 1998). Critics such as DeSpelder and Strickland (1996), charge that cards allow friends to tiptoe around death because cards use the "death talk" of euphemisms, metaphors, and sometimes slang which only heighten the distress of many friendgrievers by avoiding open acknowledgment of the friend's death. On the other hand, some friends find selecting a card to be a self-comforting process.

Friends believe that a card is "the least I can do." Not receiving a card from a friend can be perceived as a serious slight. Cards sent with only signatures may be perceived as less caring and are less appreciated (Kolf, 1999). Older adults are more likely to add a handwritten note to a sympathy card (Caldwell, McGee, & Pryor, 1998). Greeting card companies now offer sympathy cards which have the "feel" of a handwritten note through the use of script type for the card text.

Cards must be selected with attention to pictures, symbols, or content. A Christian friend should not send a card with a cross to a Jewish friend in grief, but that happens. Grollman (1993) notes that while Christian beliefs and symbols may be comforting, those who practice other faiths may be suspicious of motives, even offended. So, "Better still, send an individual letter with your personal memories as a permanent record to be read in the days and years ahead" (p. 29; Kolf, 1999). Caldwell, McGee, and Pryor (1998) support Ann Landers' advice: instead of mailing a condolence card, *take* it to the grievers.

Unfortunately, friends rarely send cards to other friends. One evidence of the disenfranchisement of friendgrief is the absence of specifically categorized sympathy cards, "On the death *of your friend*." Kolf (1999) encourages sending cards to those who have lost a best friend, noting, "These special people need your encouragement every bit as much as family members" (p. 22). I treasure a note I received after one friend's death: "I know that this is a tough time for you. Thinking of you my friend."

FRIENDS DONATE/PREPARE FOOD FOR THE RESIDENCE OR PREPARE A MEAL FOR THE FAMILY

Grievers must be fed (and sometimes housed) before, during, and perhaps, after the rituals. One initial response is preparing or arranging food for the family. In some instances, this responsibility may be spread among friends from different friendorbits. While this is still customary in "traditional communities," Pokorski (1995) laments "there aren't as many traditional communities around as there used to be" (p. 68). In some settlings, neighbors or church friends provide for a benevolence meal at the church following the services rather than meals throughout the initial bereavement period. Some are specifically for family and out-of-town guests; others are open to all the friends.

"Eat something," is physiologically valid; "eat something *with* me" is psychologically valid. Although grievers, family or friend, may protest, "How can I think about food at a time like this!" balanced meals provide strength for the physical drain of grief and a venue for friends to express hospitality, talk, and feel useful. Preparing a casserole or a meal is both a "concrete and helpful" (Searl, 1993, p. 111) response for friends. As one friend remarks, "That is something that I know how to do." DeSpelder and Strickland (1996) point out that among contemporary African-Americans, bringing prepared foods is considered a more personal gesture than donations or unprepared food because it means the friend spent time preparing. On the other hand, "Store bought has higher status" in some rural communities (Mason, 1999, p. 198). Kolf (1999) urges friends to be more original in preparing food than the traditional casseroles and desserts, pointing to a link between grief and "comfort" foods.

One friend explains, "I bake my condolences. When I do not know what to say, I bake something and take it to the family." Taking a casserole, salad, or dessert provides a rationale for even a casual friend to visit the residence, an action that otherwise might be considered intrusive: "I just wanted to drop this off and say how sorry I am." Even if the family is not receiving visitors, the food gift will be received. Receiving a food item prepared by a friend as opposed to the anonymity of something from a deli, gives the friend a chance to say a word of comfort or condolence, to hug, or to make a promise of future aid. Some friends find a particular recipe a meaningful linking object to the deceased: "She loved my banana pudding, etc."

Typically, a friend of the family records such hospitalities (Pokorski, 1995) and marks the containers so that they can be returned. Given the delicatessen business in mega supermarkets as well as the fast food restaurants offering take out, increasingly busy friends think it permissible to pick up "a bucket of something" to take to the family and thus be only minimally inconvenienced. The disposable container—when empty, throwaway/nothing to wash or return—eliminates the secondary ritual of returning a dish, bowl, or pan days or weeks after the rituals which facilitates an opportunity for initiating conversation. "How are you doing? Do you have time to talk?" A participant in my group recalls,

> I will always remember my friend walking in carrying an apple pie that she had baked. It smelled marvelous. She kept saying, "I wish I knew what to say." So, we sat down and ate pie and drank coffee. I never knew a piece of pie could taste so good. I don't remember what she said but I remember that pie.

Sometimes, the organizer-friend has to monitor the food intake of grievers (Parachin, 1998, March). Only a close friend can overcome the protest, "I'm not hungry" to insist, "You need to eat *something!*" or to ensure that the individual is not unnecessarily interrupted during a meal. Friends also notice eating habits long after the formal rituals. Many who find themselves eating alone nibble on snack foods (Fitzgerald, 1994) rather than face a table setting for one. Some even forget to eat. Caring friends express hospitality by inviting grievers to meals, weeks and months afterward and on holidays. Meals, sometimes in a favorite restaurant—or in a new restaurant to avoid the memories associated with some restaurants—provide an opportunity for friends to talk. In selecting a restaurant, friends need to pay attention to atmosphere; noisy, crowded restaurants will not be conducive to talking or venting emotions.

Friends ask grievers about plans for meals on special days such as the Fourth of July, Thanksgiving, or religious holidays like Hanukkah, Kwanza, or Christmas. "We want you to join us" may be an act of friendship remembered longer than a casserole provided after a death.

But who offers hospitality to the friendgriever? Who monitors the friendgriever's eating? In some social networks no one may know that you are grieving for a friend (Walter, 1999). It is possible to be so busy doing for or monitoring the family, that friends ignore their own grief and food intake. Thus, it might be a friend caregiver who passes out. Fortunate is the friendgriever who has a friend from another friendorbit who recognizes the need for hospitality.

SOME RELIGIOUS AND CULTURAL GUIDELINES ON FOOD

Friends must be alert to religious and cultural guidelines as well as personal preferences on food. When a Greek Orthodox dies, generally friends do not send or take food to the home. The family of the deceased "usually provides a 'mercy meal' after the funeral for relatives and friends" in a restaurant, a home, or the church hall (Magida, 1996). With Hindus, friends send fruit after the funeral. In a health-conscious, diet-restrictive culture, friends in other traditions might consider fruit a wise alternative. Sometimes well-meaning friends prepare foods loaded with sugars and starches or beverages with caffeine which are not healthy for grievers who are diabetic, have food allergies, eating disorders, or physician imposed food restrictions. A friend must also pay attention to foods that are verboten: pork for Jews and Muslims, products containing caffeine for Mormons, or any dish containing meat for strict vegetarians, or dairy products for vegans.

For Jewish grievers, by tradition, the community and friends are responsible for the first meals or in some cases, meals throughout the observance of shivah. Many Jewish commentators contend that the Jewish mourner must eat and may not skip meals because of grief (Levine, 1994). Jewish tradition insists that "At the first meal following the funeral, mourners may not eat their own food" (Shulkhan Arukh as cited in Brener, 1993, p. 101). Generally, relatives who do not live in the chief mourner's residence or close friends provide the *seudas havraah,* meals of grief. The food must be kosher. It is inappropriate to give candy, chocolates, fruit baskets, or liquor (Levine, 1994). However, if a non-Jewish friend unknowingly violates this tradition, "There is no obligation that these presents be taken back because it could offend the friends and would violate the custom that nothing is taken from the house of mourning during *shiva*" (Levine, 1994, p. 58).

MISCELLANEOUS SOCIAL GUIDELINES

So, it may be through trial and error that caring friends attempt to offer hospitality to the family and other grieving friends. In some cases there may be an unspoken element in the friend's job description, "and other duties to be defined" by the family. In my great-grandfather's day, for example, friends built the casket and dug the grave.

Hospitality offers concrete ways to "stand alongside our friends, entering their passionate struggles and trials and triumphs, feeling their pangs of pain. . . ." (L'Engle & Shaw, 1997, p. 48). In the next chapter, we take up the more subjective expressions, that leave more decision-making to the friends and leave more room for creativity and originality.

KEY CONCEPTS OF THIS CHAPTER

- Core hospitality responses are shaped by the culture, experiences with death, religious backgrounds, understandings of friendship, and hospitality.
- The growing diversity in this country and in some friendorbits makes it difficult to cite a definitive list of common expectations, particularly when no services are held or they are private.
- The loosely-accepted core of hospitality includes calling the family or going to the primary residence, notifying other friends, sending flowers or donating to a designated charity, sending or taking sympathy cards, attending rituals, and preparing and arranging food.
- Hospitality and inconvenience are influenced by the significance assigned to a friendship by the chief mourner.
- The movement of a significant number of women from homemaking into the workplace has significantly altered the time and energy available to deliver hospitality.
- After a death friends contribute these types of gifts: things, information, time, money, and entitlements (Kahn & Antonucci, 1980).
- In a multicultural society, friends, unfamiliar with the faith or cultural traditions of the deceased, although wanting to be gracious, may be reluctant to offer hospitality for fear of offending.

IMPLICATIONS FOR CLINICIANS

1. The clinician may ask, "When you learned of your friend's death, what did you initially do? What hospitality did you offer? Did you feel any sense of obligation? Did offering hospitality distract you from your own grief?"

2. The friendgriever may describe a sense of being disenfranchised by family, friends, or a gatekeeper when offering hospitality. Pursue that line of thought. Is there a way to re-frame that experience? Could the client be mistaken in evaluating the intentions of the family or doorkeeper-friends?

3. Ask if the friendgriever has donated to a charity. How did the friendgriever select that charity? Remind the friendgriever that donations honoring a friend can still be made as a "strategic social action" (Unruh, 1983, p. 349) or as a way of continuing bonds.

4. For friendgrievers who feel cheated out of opportunities to offer hospitality, explore with them ways to offer hospitality now, especially the idea of linking the hospitality to an anniversary or special day.

5. Ask, "Who recognized your grief and offered you hospitality? What acts of hospitality would you have appreciated?

CHAPTER 7

Honoring a Friend by Attending the Visitation

CHAPTER PREVIEW

An individual honors a friend by attending the rituals. Common rituals include the visitation, calling hours, or wake; the funeral or memorial service; and perhaps, the committal or scattering. What level of participation in prefuneral, funeral, and postfuneral rituals can be expected of a friend? In this chapter we examine the historic role of the visitation. The visitation may be perceived as more valuable than the funeral because it is conversation oriented while the funeral is liturgy or ritual focused. The visitation encourages interaction and dialogue not only with family but with other friends. Family and other friends assign significance to the length of time a particular friend stays. Having the wake at a funeral home, preserves the privacy of the residence for the chief mourner.

> Grief demands ritual. To die alone is bad enough, but to grieve without rituals that lift the broken heart is worse. Those whose grief is affirmed within a wider community of faith are fortunate (Woodward, 1997, September 22, p. 62).

An individual honors a friendship by attending rituals for a deceased friend. The trio of common rituals are: the visitation, calling hours, or wake; the funeral or memorial service; and the committal or scattering. This triumvirate of rituals once demanded a friend's attendance. A close friend would also attend particular rituals such as a novena among Hispanics or shiva among Jews.

Traditionally, the closeness of the friendship determines which rituals the friendgriever will participate in and attend. As private services have become more common, the chief mourner determines which rituals include or exclude friends. Whenever rituals are designated "family only," friends are denied important venues for expressing grief.

RELATIONSHIP DEFINES RITUAL PARTICIPATION

In many communities it is still considered a common courtesy to attend visitations, even if one only casually knew the deceased. Thus, if a visitation is announced in the newspaper, it is considered an open invitation to attend. These days, friends increasingly ask, Do I value this friendship enough to be go? To go out of the way to attend? Some attend only if it is convenient: "I can drop by the visitation on the way home from work or after dinner." By squeezing it in, there is an excuse for not staying long. Families may be hurt when a presumed "close" friend does not attend the wake or drops in, signs the guest books, and leaves quickly.

Friends expect their efforts to attend to be acknowledged verbally or through a card, "It was good of you to come." Friends can become irritated at a viewing if a family member discounts their friendship with the deceased: "Oh, he was *just* someone Frank worked with." According to Wallbank (1996), "the root of the anger lies in our wish for the recognition" (p. 95) of status with the deceased and the family's (and sometimes other friends') reluctance to recognize it.

THE ORIGIN OF THE WAKE

The wake began before embalming became common and was motivated by the fear of burying someone in a coma or trance. Wake rituals had two purposes: 1) to ensure that the dead were dead; and 2) to make certain they remained dead (Hatchett, 1995). Individuals were enlisted to watch the corpse closely with the hope that the friend would wake up (Foley, 1980) thus the term, "wake." Sitting with the body was not only "a mark of respect for the deceased" (p. 22) but also an act of hospitality by friends to relieve the family.

The Irish are commonly credited with bringing the tradition of the wake to America; in fact, many immigrants were "waked" before leaving Ireland because friends feared they would never see them again. However, the wake existed in other nations such as Mexico (Aguilar & Wood, 1976) and has difference expectations; in England the close kin are absent (Metcalf & Huntington, 1991).

In a time before public accommodations, if friends traveled from a distance, there was no place to stay except in the room with the corpse.

As the number of watchers increased, and to entertain themselves during the watch, the event became more upbeat; music, singing, wake games, dancing, and drinking became essentials for a "good" wake. "The livelier and more crowded the wake, the greater was the honor paid" to the deceased (Radford & Radford, 1969, p. 129). The coffin could even be used as a card table. Deceased males "would be included in the card game, toasted, or maybe a drink would be placed in his hand" (McGoldrick, 1991, p. 180) or used as a dance partner (Suilleabhain, 1967).

MacDonaugh's *Irish Life and Character,* published in 1898, encouraged friends to "crowd in to cheer up the spirits of the bereaved, to distract their thoughts from their sad loss" (cited in Metress, 1990). (Some friends still think their job is to distract others from thinking about the loss.) "The best thing one can say about a 'successful' Irish wake is that the deceased would have really enjoyed it. 'Too bad he can't be here to enjoy it with us'"(McGoldrick, 1991, p. 180). Widespread drunkenness and rowdiness at wakes in the early 20th century prompted a backlash among some Protestants, notably the Methodists (Radford & Radford, 1969) who preferred a more sedate environment. One hymn captures the perspective of Methodist friends at a visitation:

> Why do we mourn departing friends, Or shake at death's alarms?
> 'Tis but the voice that Jesus sends To call them to his arms (Watts, 1859, pp. 657-658).

One contemporary departure from historic visitations is the absence of singing. Hymnals in the 1800s contained numerous songs for dying and grieving such as "The Happy Dead"! (p. 659).

FRIENDS ATTEND THE VISITATION

Because of the intensity of the shock, especially if a sudden death, or the size of the attendance at a visitation, a chief mourner or particular family members may not remember that a friend attended, which explains why the guest book is treasured by many. The signature records attendance and nonattendance. One widow explains,

> I was in such shock at the funeral home. Only later, looking through the guest book, did I know who even came. There were longtime friends at the wake that I do not remember talking to but their signature says that they were there.

In a fast-paced, mobile society, funeral rituals are being reevaluated by many individuals (see Figure 1). Increasingly, many friends consider the funeral or memorial service "the primary death-related ritual" (Cook & Oltjenbruns, 1998, p. 129) and minimize the importance of the visitation or wake. Because of time pressures, particularly in large metropolitan communities, many friends attend either the visitation *or* the funeral. Only a committed friend would attend all of the rituals. Selwyn (1998), a physician, describes the surprise of many families that he "took time" to come to the wakes of patient-friends.

THE VISITATION

Visitations provide a venue for exchanging condolences. If living within a reasonable distance, the friend is expected to pay respects at the visitation. The visitation—calling hours in some communities—provides a social setting in which friends can meet the family as well as other friends, sometimes for the first time (Foley, 1980; Wolfelt, 1994) without feeling intrusive.

Visitations encourage interaction between friends from different friendorbits: "So you are Beth. John often talked about you." At a visitation, a friend from the bowling league meets a friend from the church. Such encounters encourage the exchange of condolences and stories about the deceased, bridge the social networks, but also give opportunities to assess the closeness of the friendship. Friends freely recall, "I remember the first time I met Harry...." Visitations provide a time of "listening to the lived experience of loss" (Gibbons, 1993, p. 597) as well as the lived experience of friendship. It gives an opportunity to speculate on life in the absence of the friend, "I don't know how we're going to get along without Harry...."

In 1950 friends attended	In 1980 friends attended	In 1995 friends attend	2010 friends will attend
Visitation & Funeral & Committal	Visitation & Funeral	Visitation or Funeral/ memorial service	? ? ?

Figure 1. Friend participation in rituals.

BIOGRAPHY WEAVING

Because the visitation is conversation focused while the funeral is liturgy or ritual focused, interaction is encouraged. In many ways, a visitation is like assembling a giant jigsaw puzzle with friends from different suborbits contributing pieces. Walter (1999) reminds

> In large-scale urban societies, we inhabit varied and non overlapping social worlds: the people I work with, commute with, play golf with, go to church with, live with are likely to be different groups. I play different roles and take on different identities in each setting. . . . (pp. 71-72).

Thus, even in a good marriage, there may be aspects of a spousal friendships that are unknown. Admittedly, once in the rural village or perhaps ethnic urban neighborhood, relational circles commonly overlapped. Not so today. So the adjective *work* friend takes on a new meaning.

The visitation encourages interaction; the funeral discourages dialogue. At the funeral, although hurried introductions may be made, there is little time for conversation, which may well suit some friends who want to avoid conversation.

The International Commission on English in the Liturgy (1990) advises, "The time immediately following death is often one of bewilderment and may involve shock or heartrending grief for the family and close friends." So, "The ministry of the Church at this time is one of gently accompanying the mourners in their initial adjustment to the fact of death and the sorrow this entails" (p. 21). This is also the "ministry" of friends. Nonreligious individuals also need to be accompanied through "great darkness of grief" (Johnson, 1999, p. 9). The visitation also facilitates initial adjustment among friends. Friends do not gather bearing answers or wisdom, but presence. This demonstration of friendship reminds friends and family of the strength of relationship: You are not alone. Despite repeated "I cannot believe it's" the visitation offers the extended friendorbit a place to confront the reality of this particular death or this latest loss in a friendorbit.

For some friends, the repeated fumbling with words is a way to try out feelings or to voice confusion or anger or air questions. Friends initiate conversations with questions such as "How are you holding up?" Friends wishing to avoid emotional assessment, focus on the details of the death: "What have you heard about the accident?" Consider a couple out for dinner with friends—killed instantly when their car is struck in a dangerous intersection. "Wrong place, wrong time," observes a friend.

"We've all got to go some time" adds a stoic friend. Another friend suggests, "That is a dangerous intersection. Been lots of accidents there. They ought to put up a light or something."

A visitation offers a forum for sense-making. At the visitation, friends exchange (in some cases for the first time learn) details and sometimes speculate on what links those details. Imagine the conversations among friends at the wake for the accident victims. One friend leads out: "I heard that the guy that hit them was speeding." Another friend follows suit with, "and his driver's license had been suspended." Another injects, "Someone said that he had been involved in another wreck a few weeks ago." This sampling of and sorting through trial or competing explanations gives a friend a safe space to begin making meaning of the death even when a friend asks, "You don't think John could have been at fault—you know, he couldn't half see." Friends speculate on the future, particularly if the deceased has young children or financial problems or was a key player in a particular project among friends or was the stable member in a circle of friends—the one who could always be counted on.

In another parlor in the same funeral home, friends of an elderly individual who died of natural causes, comment on "what a great life she lived." In this case, a life lived is evaluated in conversation rather than the circumstances of the death.

Friends also offer religious or philosophical observations or questions: "How could God let this happen to such good folks?" Some friends may feel the need to defend God. The conversation at the visitation may nervously shift from factual detail exchange and comment on causality to safer, more reflective observations, "best friend I ever had!" This cycle may be repeated as other friends arrive.

REJUVENATING THE FRIENDORBIT

Through coming together for a visitation, the friendorbit, jolted by a particular death, begins to revitalize itself (Thomas, 1987) and demonstrates resilience. A visitation offers a chance for a friend to say aloud what others may be thinking: "How are we going to get along without Kate?" particularly when Kate was the magnet that drew these friends into orbit or because of her maintenance skills, kept them in orbit. A response, "She'd want us to . . ." reminds friends that the friendorbit remains, although significantly, and permanently altered. The visitation offers an ad hoc informal group support structure for processing the reality of a friend's death. An "I just cannot believe she's gone" prompts, "Neither can I." That brief voiced expression comforts many friends: so I am not the only one feeling this loss. At a visitation, friends also recruit social support from and offer support to other friends (Neimeyer, 1998), "Now we're going to have to be there for each other."

CONFRONTING THE PROOF: A CORPSE

Before a visitation, or increasingly without a visitation, some friends have difficulty believing a friend is dead. With the growing practice of immediate cremation, limited viewings are being scheduled to accommodate a confrontation with the physical proof: the corpse. Viewing the body offers irrefutable evidence that the friend has died (Vanezis & McGee, 1999).

Acceptance may be difficult when an individual only sees the friend sporadically. Consider friends of the "snowbird" who dies in Florida in February. Consider the immigrants who are unable to go home when a friend dies (Grabowski & Frantz, 1993). Often, upon initial notification, a friend protests, "He cannot be dead!" linked with a rationale, "I just played golf with him yesterday. He looked the picture of health," or, following a suicide, "She didn't seem like she had a care in the world. Why would she kill herself?" The viewing offers friends confrontation with the unbelievable and unexplainable.

When my friend Jean died after a long battle with cancer, because of responsibilities at the hospital, I could not attend the funeral in Little Rock. Although I had talked by phone with her husband and a son, a slight trace of disbelief remained. Ten days later, driving to lunch, I slipped the audio cassette of Jean's funeral into the tape deck. Although physically driving in traffic in Kansas City, I found myself emotionally at a funeral in Arkansas. A sense of loss swept over me as that tape shattered the last remnants of my illusion. My friend Jean had died. How would I have processed her death if there had been no rituals, or no tape of the rituals or if I had avoided listening to the tape? How much easier would the grief have been for me had I encountered a casket, a visitation, *and* other grieving friends?

THE VISITATION: AN ARENA TO EMBRACE THE UNBELIEVABLE

Friends in the first millennium believed "that the presence of the dead body brought defilement to the house," to its residents (Smith & Cheetham, 1875, p. 253) as well as to anyone who came in contact with the corpse, particularly in times of plague. So, prolonged viewing and deliberately touching the body was a radical innovation of the early Christians who

> took the bodies of the saints [and all Christians were considered saints] in their open hands and in their bosoms, and closed their eyes and mouths; and they bore them away on their shoulders and laid them out; and they clung to them and embraced them; and they prepared them suitably with washing and garments (Eusebius as cited in Basilios, 1991, pp. 425-426).

Christians found precedent for this in actions in the followers of Jesus of Nazareth. It was not his family but two friends, Joseph of Arimathaea and Nicodemus, neither of whom were in the the inner circle, who, nevertheless at considerable personal and social risk, claimed and buried his body; other friends carried out the traditional preparations for the dead (John 19: 38-42). The testimony of those friends who saw him die and those who buried his body, supported claims of Jesus' resurrection; these friends insisted that he had been dead—not just in a trance. The behavior of Thomas, a close friend, who declared that unless he touched the body of Jesus, "I will not believe" [in the resurrection] (John 20: 25) was commonly cited by early Christians. For some friends, touching the casketed body is a solid encounter with reality.

The earliest visitations were in the home. The early Christians postponed burial so that friends might "come and weep and take their last look" (Smith & Cheetham, 1875, p. 253) and extend condolences to the family and to other friends who made up what was described as "the household of faith" (Galatians 6:10) or the extended friendorbit.

Thomas (1987) defines rite as "a ceremony in which behaviors, gestures and postures, words or songs uttered, and objects handled, manufactured, destroyed or consumed are supposed to possess virtues or powers or to produce specific effects" (p. 450). Some would consider the viewing to be a ceremony, admittedly informal, which produces a specific effect of pondering: "Someday I will die!"or "My friend *has* died."

OTHER PERSPECTIVES ON VIEWING THE BODY OF THE DECEASED

In this culturally diverse society, many friends are uncertain of ritual practices in other religions. At viewings for Buddhists, the friend is expected to bow slightly toward the body as a sign of respect. At a visitation for a Hindu, a friend would be expected to view the body and to "look reverently upon the body"(Magida, 1996, p. 171) without touching it. Greek Orthodox friends, "Traditionally . . . bow in front of the casket and kiss the icon or cross placed on the chest of the deceased" (Magida, 1996, p. 153). Kissing the icon is optional for friends who are not members of the Orthodox faith.

Sometimes, a visitation/wake is not held because the chief mourner (or the deceased) considers the practice archaic; some compromise with a closed casket with photos. Nevertheless, either choice impacts friends who have not seen the deceased in some time and expect a viewing as a necessary component for saying good-bye. On the other hand, some friends may say, "I want to remember him as he was when I last saw him" or "as she was before she got sick."

Some families choose direct disposal with a delayed memorial service. The wording, "Memorial services will be held at a later date," or similar words in the death notice may be misunderstood by friends (Irion, 1996, February) particularly those on the edge of the friendorbit who perceive the decision as an exclusion and a deliberate disenfranchisement of their grief. Many who lost friends early in the AIDS epidemic, were denied the visitation experience because families were stigmatized by the death (Lamendola & Wells, 1991; Oerlmans-Bunn, 1998). Walter (1999) points out that the family denied themselves the chance to create a "common biography" with the deceased's friends. Some of the stories of gay friends might have comforted the family. Friends can be distressed to learn, or assume, that the decision not to have a visitation was to cut costs.

THE CHOICE FOR CREMATION'S IMPACT ON THE VISITATION

For some, cremation means, at least from some experiences, no viewing or services. Bob Batson (in Kelley, 1997, March) reports that at one time "if a family wanted cremation, they got direct disposition" (p. 9). Today's funeral planners have a range of options including a visitation before the cremation. Because the growing choice of cremation impacts casket sales, many funeral directors have traditionally discouraged cremation. The Aurora Casket Company challenges such thinking, "Many of these families prefer the same funeral services with a cremation as with a traditional body burial—memorial services, viewing times, visitations, grave side services and burial" ("Cremation," 1997, March, p. 3). It does not have to be either/or but increasingly, both/and.

The growing public acceptance of cremation (Raether, 1997, November) challenges those friends who object on religious grounds. In 1996, the percentage of cremations to total deaths in the United States increased to 21.25 percent (Raether, 1997, November, p. 77) although some states and metropolitan communities have a significantly higher percentage of cremation: for example, Indianapolis, has a higher cremation ratio than the state of Indiana. Kelley (1997, March) finds a growth in cremation in resort and retirement communities. "With a national population that is increasingly more mobile, cremation will be a logical choice" (p. 9). Although the South has far fewer cremations than the western U.S., that will change as more people relocate from areas where cremation is common (Kelley, 1997). Cremation alters the traditional window of 24 to 72 hours for completing rituals. With cremation, a memorial service can be delayed to accommodate the schedules of certain friends and family members.

PREVIOUS NEGATIVE EXPERIENCES

Attitudes toward visitations, particularly viewing the corpse, may have been influenced by attendance at previous visitations, particularly those perceived as negative (Rocco, 1998, March). Almost one in five persons in one study reported having had a negative experience viewing an embalmed body (Harley, 1998, June), especially in cases of trauma or physical deterioration. Others decline to view the body of a friend for personal reasons. Gene, a World War II veteran, describes his reluctance:

> At my age, I've lost too many friends, especially lately. I know I should go to the visitation to pay my respects but it drains me. Even the flower smell gets to me. At the last one, I lost it and I just bawled like a baby. So, I decided no more funerals and no more cemeteries. I go to visitations and I stand in the foyer talking to folks as they come and go. But I will not go into the parlor where the body is.

A visitation can be an important time for friends who cannot attend the funeral or memorial service due to schedule conflicts, or for friends who do not like large crowds or have health or physical limitations. If the funeral is expected to be large, they may opt for the viewing.

VISITATIONS AS REUNIONS OF FRIENDS

A visitation may take on something of the reunion atmosphere. It is not uncommon to overhear, "I have not seen you since Joe's funeral" or tease, "We have to stop meeting like this." Upon arriving at the funeral home, some immediately look for particular friends or inquire, "Is Mary here?" or nudge a friend, "Look who just walked in." Friends lament that it often takes a death to gather a social network or its remnants. Visitations can be distressing for senior adults, grieving multiple losses over a short time, which allows little time for reconciliation (Alty, 1995). Still many senior adults see going to a visitation for a friend as an obligation but not necessarily an imposition.

> A normal part of grief is in talking with friends and family about the person or object the individual is missing. The fact that there may be fewer people around with whom the older person may be able to share memories of the dead person [or who wants to hear the memories] will hinder the process of reviewing the past relationship between the deceased and the bereaved and will thus inhibit resolution (Alty, 1995, p. 35).

Visitations are an important reminder of the mystery of life. Through a visitation, grievers join hands and hearts to face that mystery jointly. Friends gather to seek a common path from the unexplainable toward the explainable. Conlon (1998) notes, "Rituals are the human way of bringing greater meaning and more profound expression to our lives" (p. 118). A visitation offers a "wonderful departure from 'head understanding' of the death" (Wolfelt, 1998, June, p. 18) to an experiential understanding. (And "wonderful" can be the right word for the interaction with friends at a visitation.)

A visitation can force the painful acknowledgment of a deteriorated friendship: "He was always calling wanting us to get together, but. . . ." As a friendship deteriorates, friends are less intimate, less self-disclosing, less open (Baxter, 1985) and certainly less available for activities or for support; other friends may have taken sides in the rift or benefitted from the dissension. Friendships deteriorate because of changes such as

- the death of a mate
- remarriage
- loss of interest in shared activities
- transportation difficulties
- moving into a nursing home
- moving away from the old neighborhood
- a divorce
- a new job
- a chronic illness
- a change of churches
- retirement.

Any of these, by reducing interaction, alter friendships and lead to a diminishing, a not- the-same ness, despite promises to "keep in touch."

One friend notes, "After Jan died and Mike remarried, we were not close anymore. He made new friends and socialized with her friends." Or "When she moved into that retirement center on the other side of town, our chats were limited to a few minutes on the phone. Since I do not drive anymore, I have no way to go see her."

A visitation is a way to bring closure to a deteriorated friendship. The significance of termination is noted in Levinger's (1980, 1983) ABCDE model of friendship; "D" stands for deterioration and "E" for ending. Levinger concedes "that deteriorated relationships can continue indefinitely" (as cited in Fehr, 1996, p. 37) because neither party wants to pull the plug or even acknowledge that things are not what they once were. The friends continue perfunctorily to send holiday cards or exchange small talk, "Hi, how are you? Nice to see you, too. Let's get together some time." Thus, some friends at visitations grieve for the friendship that once existed rather than the friend (Sullivan, 1998). Many in the friendorbit still consider it necessary for an estranged friend to "show up" at the visitation, otherwise, as Baxter (1985) points out, members of the friendorbit can respond with sanctions.

A visitation facilitates active remembering. At visitations friends prime or jar memories: "Don't you remember when Harry fell out of the boat up on Lake Butler?" Some need other friends to help them remember: "Oh, I had forgotten about that." Some friends act as censors: "Oh, don't bring that up. That's ancient history. Let's let bygones be bygones." In Neimeyer's (1998) construct, since friends share a narrative with the deceased, at wakes co-friends catch up on their lives. The visitation offers a venue, although bittersweet, for storying and memory-gathering and in some cases, for memory-embellishing or reinterpretation. In reality, a visitation is a quilting: using story and memory rather than cloth. Pitts (1998, October 26) reminds that the deceased does not have to have been a saint to merit a visitation.

> Every day, creeps, cretins and crooks are lowered into the ground accompanied by eulogies suitable for saints and we let that pass, because we understand that there's a time and place for everything and that this time and place are for decorum and respect. We understand that even creeps, cretins and crooks have family and friends who love them, and we treat their grieving as sacrosanct (p. B-5).

Gusewelle (1995, March 6) describes his experience attending the ritual for a friend with whom he had worked his entire career as something of the gathering of the tribe:

The joy of working a lifetime in one place is the closeness of the friends you make. You remember one another as you were. You value one another as you have become. The hurtful part about having such friends is that time, being savage, eventually begins to take them. On a day not long ago, more than half the friends I've ever known gathered . . . to pay respects to one of our own. We've had such reunions too often in recent years (p. B-1).

Without visitations, where and when will the friendorbit gather communally to grieve, particularly if the funeral continues, at least in urban areas, to be a schedule-driven experience? (Dissanayake, 1995). Ordinarily, families give consideration to the need of friends to mourn and to gather at a formal "leave-taking" (Cook & Oltjenbruns, 1998, p. 129). This gathering is a gift for both family and friends to receive condolences. The setting and the timing create a special moment which may evoke words, tenderness, or emotions that will not be repeated. This may be a factor motivating the increased videotaping of funerals. Perhaps visitations should also be videotaped.

When friends are denied a visitation setting or when friends do not attend, they miss out on the mutual consoling (Foley, 1980). One minister, concerned about the summer heat, urged the family to move the visitation to the air-conditioned undercroft so that friends would be more comfortable. "No!" the widow snapped. "I do not want *his* friends standing around talking. I want this over with as quickly as possible!" In that instance, because the deceased husband's friends (due to the nature of some of their shared activities) were not the widow's friends, she denied them a convenient opportunity to interact.

VISITATIONS TODAY

As other funeral rituals, the visitation is changing. Hours have been curtailed. "Friends may call 6-8 P.M. Thursday" etc. is a common inclusion in death notices today; some schedule only one hour. Some visitations immediately precede the funeral or a reception may be held afterwards. By combining the two rituals, some assume there will be better attendance, although not everyone who comes for the visitation-funeral stays for the funeral. Such innovations are concessions to the reality of busy schedules as well as widespread discomfort with death and Walter (1999) argues, the growing privatization of death.

EXPECTED ETIQUETTE AT A VISITATION

In a time-conscious society such as ours, an expectation that friends will spend considerable time at a visitation may be considered unrealistic by some friends. Emily Post (1992) validates brevity: "The visit to the funeral home need not last more than five or ten minutes. As soon as the visitor has expressed his sympathy to each member of the family, and spoken a moment or two with those he knows well, he may leave" (p. 549). In some areas, a five or ten minute visit would prompt a "Might as well not have come at all!" Such an abbreviated appearance would be considered unfriendly or insensitive.

The culture suggests—and in some subcultures mandates—an etiquette for interaction at the visitation. Friends are expected to spend time at the visitation rather than drop in, offer hurried condolences, sign the guest book, and leave. Significance is assigned to the length of time a particular friend stays. By staying through the visitation, the friend is not only available to the family but sees other friends they would otherwise have missed.

While Post (1992) considers it improper for friends to ask the family about the illness or the specifics of the cause of death, unless the family member feels "a need to talk about it" (p. 549), friends may not feel any hesitancy in asking other friends.

Metcalf and Huntington (1991) identify a strong social obligation to view the corpse; thus, in some communities this ritual is called "the viewing." Although Wolfelt (1998, June) voices concern at reports of a trend "away from viewing the body" (p. 20), in some communities, viewing and offering a specific comment on the corpse, remain the norm: "He looks like he is asleep" or "She looks twenty years younger." Initial observations about the corpse are directed to the chief mourner and then exchanged with other friends, even strangers. Observations range from "Looks better than the last time I saw her" to "he looks real good" some friends adding, "doesn't he?" to elicit agreement. Some friends find such observations deny the reality of death. When a friend from another friendorbit said, "Looks like she is asleep," another friend angrily rebutted the comment, "No! She looks *dead* to me!"

At some visitations, the chief mourner stands at or near the casket to receive guests (and comments) and may accompany a close friend to the casket, which makes its hard for a friend to avoid offering some comment. When illness has been physically devastating or death was a result of violence or trauma, the friend may compliment the work of the funeral director in facilitating an open casket. Harley (1998), a funeral director, laments that poor embalming results by colleagues has done much to discourage open-casket visitations. "A good embalmer that can give your families [and the friends] positive results is priceless. The embalming process takes the look of pain and suffering out of their loved one [or friend] and leaves them looking peaceful" (p. 5) thus, providing a favorable last memory for friends. After attending the viewing for a female friend, my mother often commented "she made such a beautiful corpse."

Compliments on how good the deceased friend looks, repeated by enough friends, commercially can have the same effect as a billboard (Harley, 1998, June) and may convince friends to choose the mortuary as well as an open casket viewing in the future.

When the casket is closed at the visitation, the friend is expected to comment on

- photo/s placed on top of or near the casket.
- the casket: "What a beautiful casket!" (Later to selected friends, "Did you see *that* casket? Wonder how much they paid for it?") and
- the flowers, "The flowers are gorgeous/lovely/beautiful, etc."

Such remarks act as warm-ups for the more difficult words of condolence and also initiate conversation between friends.

There can be anger at not being allowed "to see" the deceased friend. Osborne (2000, July/August) describes being unable to get to Michigan for a friend's visitation, but that she "took comfort" that there would be a viewing prior to the funeral. However, when she arrived at the crowded funeral home, she found that the casket had already been closed.

> I was furious and searched for the funeral director to find out why; while his explanation was plausible, I didn't want answers—I wanted to see Nancy's body. I had to make sure she was actually in the casket. I "lost it" with the funeral director and then sought out Nancy's husband to get his help in letting me have a couple of minutes alone with her body. . . . although he acknowledged my presence, he could not understand my need; the new widower just wanted to "get this over with" (p. 5).

PROTECTING THE PRIVACY OF
THE RESIDENCE

A visitation protects the privacy of the primary residence. In rural communities, the dead were laid out in the home for the visitation/wake and the funeral. Many large homes had a parlor used only for such special occasions; some homes had two front doors—one into the special parlor and one for the other parts of the house (Jackson, 1977). After a death, friends rearranged furniture in the living and dining areas to accommodate seating. Being in a home where one had experienced so many happy occasions, may have been a demanding or, at least, bittersweet emotional moment for many friends.

Urbanization prompted the development of the funeral "home" with large parlors to accommodate guests; apartments, condos, and many homes tend to be smaller in cities and less suitable for a visitation (doors, halls, and elevators were too small to easily accommodate the movement of a casket) (Raether, 1999, September). Moreover, in earlier times, some friends could not go into churches of other faiths without their minister's permission, and some people did not have church affiliations. So, the funeral homes started conducting funerals in the visitation parlors; eventually many added chapels.

A visitation facilitated by detached funeral home professionals can be more controlled. For example, so many friends came the first night of my dad's visitation—people I had not seen in years—that the wake ran long. Finally my sister slipped up to me and whispered, "They [the mortuary employees] want to close." That night, all across the parlor, groups of my dad's friends talked about him and in some cases, renewed friendships with friends who had retired from the company and rarely see each other. Many friends linked their condolences to a story, "I remember the time your father . . . ." At the visitation I learned things about my dad from his pals that I had never known and will long treasure. Baxter (1985) points out that "close" friends have accumulated more "private information" than "casual" friends, and at gatherings such as visitations disclose some of those insights. Many go away thinking, "I never knew that about my friend."

THE FRIEND'S GIFT OF PRESENCE

Grollman (1974) suggests, "The most important expression of condolence is your own presence" (p. 127). The more difficult the circumstances of the death, the more presence will be valued. One son recalls the elegant silence of one friend's presence: "An old, old friend of my dad's came by. He couldn't talk. He just put his hand to his heart and gave me a hug. That was all he needed to do" (Kelly, 2000, p. 12). One wife reports:

> Any piece of history shared about Tony was important to me. I wanted to know what his co-workers thought of him, stuff he never told me—his sense of humor, his creativity, the special qualities that

made him unique. That was a tremendous help and a record for the kids, too (as cited in Kelly, 2000, p. 24).

Still, many friends are nervous about attending a visitation, fearing that they will say the wrong thing or lose control of their emotions. Isaacs (2000) captures the reality, "Strong men squirm at the task of extending sympathy. . . . Women, who are normally more expressive, feel uncertain and often tongue-tied" (p. 11) so that a visitation "can feel like a minefield" (p. 14). Thus, friends commonly have two goals: Not to offend the chief mourner and to avoid embarrassing themselves.

Attending a visitation is more than fulfilling a social obligation; it is an opportunity to console and to be consoled. Morgan (1994) reminds that "simple communication of the feeling of caring is probably the most important thing that can be done in the first hours or days after a loss" (p. 26). Friends hear, "I am so glad that you came." By attending, friends may receive an assessment of the friendship by a family member or another friend, "You were such a good friend to her. She always spoke so highly of you." Moreover, a friend's kindnesses during a long illness may be recounted with gratitude.

At some visitations, friends string memories like popcorn chains for a Christmas tree. A friend may have puzzlement over some detail in the deceased's life that only another friend can explain: "Ask Mitch, he'll remember." "Do you remember the time he/she. . . ." which may elicit a "Do I ever!" or "I had not thought of that in years!" This process Mayne (1998) considers "re-membering"—discovering "the threads that bind them together" in order to "form a whole" (p. 125).

THE NEGATIVE SIDE OF A VISITATION

A gathering of friends has risks, one of which is low attendance. Sparsely attended visitations can be emotionally difficult for the family and friends; some friends may feel obligated to stay longer. During my apprenticeship as a funeral director, I watched families of a deceased person without large friendorbits sit alone in a parlor, while friends, conversation, and sometimes floral displays, overflowed from an adjoining parlor into the common hall. Certainly, the wake has critics such as Levine (1994) who think it should be avoided: "The wake is often reduced to the level of a social gathering, where the family must suffer long hours of trivial chatter in the face of their grief" (p. 37). As a result, the family must face the funeral and committal exhausted by the visitations. Such criticism has been one factor in the shortening of visitation hours. When my father died, the family received friends at the funeral home all day; this proved wise since some aging friends explained, "I do not see well enough to drive at night" or "We do not get out much at night." Admittedly, the local custom of two nights of visitation made for a weary family the morning of the funeral but it accommodated the friends; a two-hour visitation would have been scandalous in my father's friendorbit.

Sometimes a friend functions as an informal host, introducing people from different social networks. In many ways, the visitation is the most friend-friendly of the rituals.

KEY CONCEPTS OF THIS CHAPTER

- One way an individual honors a friend is by attending the rituals for that friend.
- Common rituals include the visitation, calling hours, or wake; the funeral or memorial service; and the committal or scattering.
- The visitation is a historic ritual that has come to be valued more by some friends than the funeral.
- A secondary benefit of the visitation is that by having the gathering of friends at a funeral home, the privacy of the residence is preserved for the primary mourners.
- A visitation facilitated by detached funeral home professionals can be more controlled.
- Some friends—particularly those who think attendance is an obligation—prefer to attend the funeral rather than the visitation or wake, specifically because there is little time for social interaction or conversation.

IMPLICATIONS FOR CLINICIANS

1. Did the client attend the visitation? If so, ask for an evaluation. What was meaningful? Less than meaningful? What did the client experience emotionally ? If the visitation was troublesome, what could have made that ritual more friend-friendly or beneficial? If the client did not attend the visitation, why not?

2. Was avoiding the visitation an excuse to avoid the reality of death? If the client regrets not attending, how might the client construct a substitute ritual?

3. Who was the friend surprised to see at the visitation? Disappointed at not seeing? Who would the client liked to have spent more time with?

4. Was the client's attendance appreciated by the chief mourner? By other friends?

5. In cases where there was no ritual or the ritual was private and the friend was excluded, encourage this friend to explore the possibility of arranging an alternative ritual.

CHAPTER 8

Honoring a Friend by Attending the Funeral/Memorial Service and Committal

CHAPTER PREVIEW

Individuals honor friends by attending rituals. In this chapter we focus on two components of the ritual triumvirate: the funeral/memorial service and the committal. For many friends, the funeral or memorial service is the most important ritual. Attendance is an obligation, although in this culture in which death is increasingly privatized, many individuals have never attended a funeral for a peer. Mobility impacts attendance at rituals. Families may discount the need for friends to have a formal leave taking and exclude friends—or certain friends—through using the phrase "family only" or private services. The situation becomes conflicted if the family then invites certain friends to attend. Friends may be frustrated or angered by the design or themes of the funeral.

> When Larry's colleague told this story, she led the gathered congregation in remembering their husband, father, son, and friend. He was remembered—put back together—through her words, through the words of others who knew him and the words of liturgy, and through music and mutual embraces. On a certain afternoon in a certain year, a certain community, gathered just this once for just this purpose, remembered one particular man. . . . He took his place among them again, now not as flesh but as memory (Bass, 2000, pp. 115-116).

For many friends, the funeral/memorial service is the most important social or religious ritual. It is the main event. In fact, attendance at a funeral or memorial service may be considered an indicator of the deceased's standing in a community. "The church/chapel was filled" is a comforting social commentary; on the other hand, "Hardly anyone there" is perceived as an invalidation of this life by families as well as by friends. These days many discount the importance of the traditional funeral which is "perceived as empty and lacking creativity" (Wolfelt, 1994) although the growing ritual personalization challenges that.

> I myself have attended way too many of what I would term generic funerals—cookie cutter ceremonies that leave you feeling like you may as well have been at a stranger's funeral.
>
> As more and more people attend these meaningless funerals, society's opinion of the funeral ritual in general nosedives. This in turn causes people to devalue the funeral that will be held for them someday: "When I die, don't go to any trouble" (p. 7).

If such an attitude is believed to be the wishes of the deceased, the family may comply but thereby deny friends a formal leave-taking. Some friends have been angered by families who plan the briefest get-it-over-with-as-quickly-as-possible service. One mourner reflects on the small turnout for a friend's funeral:

> I thought about George Herbert's comment: "Life without a friend is death without a witness." One of the speakers at the memorial made reference to the man's remarkable penchant for friendship, yet there were few in attendance at the service or at graveside. At 83, the man had outlived his friends. Sometimes death without a witness is merely a measure of longevity. But those who live long enough to witness a friend's death want to be allowed to be part of it (Pogrebin, 1987, p. 107).

Witnessing a meaningful funeral may influence a friendgriever in planning his own funeral or persuade him not to have a funeral. Sallie Bingham (1989)—a member of a politically powerful Kentucky media family—had two brothers die in accidents. The service for the first brother was private; the funeral for the second, however, was extraordinary because of the supportive presence of so many friends.

> Friends from the big [media] world were there in numbers, bright young men who were moving into positions at newspapers all over the country. They seemed very young to me as they moved about slowly in the heavy rain. They were horribly shocked that Worth had died, as though they, too, believed in immortality (p. 359).

How good a friend does the deceased have to be for an individual to attend the funeral? To rearrange a schedule in order to attend, not just for a few hours but for a day or two?

Many friends have never been to a funeral for a peer; some have only attended funerals for elderly or extended family members. One famous musician scheduled to sing at his friend's funeral, stunned the funeral director by asking, "Tell me what to do. I've never been to a funeral before. What if I start crying while I am singing?"

WHEN THE FAMILY EXCLUDES FRIENDS

The chief mourner may amend or ignore the deceased's own wishes, written or verbalized, to exclude friends from attending a funeral or burial. This is legally facilitated by using the phrase, "private services only" (or some variation) in the newspaper obituary or death notice. One funeral director finds "disturbing social overtones" (Rocco, 1998, March, p. 73) in the trend because the task of turning away a friend falls generally upon the funeral director rather than family members. The fallout for that decision may have public relations and economic consequences for the funeral home. Increasingly, the courts are being asked to define—admittedly after the fact—who may be excluded/included in private funeral services.

In 1997, a mother of an adult descendent, after the service was disrupted by unruly friends of the deceased, successfully sued the funeral home/cemetery for not providing private services for her daughter. An appellate court upheld the lower court's decision that the cemetery had failed to honor "an oral contract . . . to exclude uninvited guests" (Rocco, 1998, March, p. 73). Generally, courts allow the family to be the final definer of friendship. One attorney who specializes in mortuary law comments, "The law views funeral homes as private businesses" rather than retail stores so they "can prohibit uninvited guests" (Rocco, 1998, March, p. 73) even close friends of the deceased. "Society grants virtually no grief rights to survivor-friends" (Sklar, 1991-92, p. 110). This can be seen in seating arrangements at some funerals where the family sits on a "family pew" or in an alcove called "the family room."

Litigation over right-to-die influences right-to-grieve litigation. Rocco (1998, March) cautions funeral directors to negotiate their intentions carefully so that there will be no misunderstanding that could lead to unpleasant confrontations, ill will, bad press, or litigation. "In my opinion a general invitation to services through a paid death notice opens services to all, including the unwanted guests" (p. 73) and those a family dismisses as "so-called" friends.

WHEN ESTRANGED FRIENDS SHOW UP

At some funerals, one overhears, "What is he doing here?" particularly when an estranged friend arrives. A sudden death leaves friends who have unfinished business in socially and psychologically awkward spots—both with the family and the extended friendorbit. This is reflected in the strained friendship between Sarah Ferguson and Princess Diana. Fergie, vacationing in Italy at the time of the accident, tried to charter a plane to fly to Diane's side but Di died before arrangements could be completed.

> Inconsolable, she also had to cope with the sad truth that she and Diana never repaired their rift. "Whatever happened between us," she said as she wept, "I always thought of her as my best friend and I always loved her." At times she was my only friend in the Royal Family, the only one I could talk to (Andersen, 1998, p. 224).

The Duchess, as a friend, and her children, as cousins of the princes, attended the funeral. However, in similar strained relationships, funeral directors have been instructed to ask estranged friends to leave a funeral; when the ritual is in a church or house of worship, clergy or church officials have been asked to exclude certain friends.

Estrangement with the deceased or other friends influences the decision to attend. Lyndon Johnson refused to attend the funeral of Hubert Humphrey, his long time friend who had served as his Vice President, after learning that he would had to have to sit next to his political nemesis, Richard Nixon (Solberg, 1984). Joan Rivers (1997), whose husband committed suicide, accepted her husband's best friend's decision not to attend the funeral.

> Of course, even when you are clear about your needs, people sometimes won't come through for you because of their own needs or feelings. Edgar's best friend, Tom Pileggi, didn't come to the memorial service, and I understood and accepted his reason. Edgar had promised Tom that he wouldn't do anything foolish and Tom had promised, "If you do, I won't come to your funeral." I had to respect Tom being a man of his word (p. 89).

Not all family members would expect a friend to keep such a threat. Friends may find themselves caught in a "damned if you go, damned if you don't" reality. Sometimes, family rifts challenge the loyalty of friends and impact attendance. When Houston oil tycoon, J. Howard Marshall, died at ninety, two funerals were held; one arranged by his 28-year-old third wife, and the other, arranged by his son from his first marriage and Marshall's first wife. One reporter covering the first funeral noted, that of the 30 mourners at the funeral, "Conspicuously absent was anyone who appeared to have known Marshall during his first 89 years" (Maier & Calkins, 1995, August 21, p. 41). In fact, longtime friends stayed away to support Marshall's son (and supported him in the protracted battle over the sizeable estate). Given the number of multiple marriages and dysfunctional families, clinicians must appreciate the pressures on friends to take sides in family tensions, some of which are played out or escalated in funerals.

Although Tom Pendergrass had once ruled Kansas City as a political boss, after serving time in prison for graft, he was a social outcast and a particular liability to the new Vice President of the United States, Harry S Truman. So when Pendergast died in 1945, speculation focused on whether Truman would attend his friend's funeral. Upon his arrival in Kansas City for the service, reporters quizzed him on the political fallout from his decision. Truman responded, "He was always my friend and I have always been his" (Ferrell, 1994, p. 174). Three decades later, Truman reminisces about the experience:

> You should have heard the squawks. Headlines in the newspapers and editorials and I don't know what all. And they said some very mean things, but I didn't care. I couldn't have done anything else. What kind of man . . . wouldn't go to his friend's funeral because he'd be criticized for it? (Miller, 1974, p. 196).

WHO IS IN CHARGE?

A friend might question funeral plans, initially with the family or through an appeal to a specific family member perceived as sympathetic or influential; a close friend might approach the funeral director to express grievances. Even a fervent "But my friend wanted . . ." or "had asked me to . . ." or "had promised me" will be met with, "I'm sorry. There is nothing I can do. It is up to the family." The funeral director's responsibility is to those paying for the services.

The legal rule of thumb is clear: "American jurisprudence awards limited rights and duties to family members in order to give the decedent a suitable burial" (Rocco, 1998, March, p. 70). The family right includes the ability to amend or ignore the deceased's wishes—even wishes stated in writing or pre-need arrangements, once assumed to be legally binding. Rocco concedes that funeral directors can no longer guarantee the deceased's wishes will be honored just as the expressed wishes on DNR [Do Not Resuscitate] may be circumvented by a family member. Rocco observes, "our instincts [as funeral directors] often tell us to respond to the person who steps forward to control (and hopefully pay) for the funeral arrangements" (p. 70).

EFFECTIVE RITUALS DEMAND A CLEAR
SENSE OF AUTHORITY

Funeral directors want a clear line of responsibility, generally based on financial responsibility and rituals unmarred by unpleasant incidents. Saunders (1997, October) sums up the issue, "As funeral directors our position is to serve the families as they see fit. We abide by their decisions" (p. 50).

By the time Curt died of complications from AIDS, his huge friendorbit had worked efficiently around the clock as caregivers; the absentee family never had to hire private duty nurses and he was able to die at home. However, in the arrangements conference, Curt's father informed the funeral director, "I do not want any of that 'damned gay stuff' going on around here! I do not want those friends' degenerate lifestyle rubbed in my family's face during the funeral." The funeral director chose not to ask what "damned gay stuff" included. But there were tense moments during the visitation and funeral; at the grave the family sat under the tent—the friends stood outside.

A cohabiting partner or de facto spouse may also become an obstacle to the smooth funeral. Kimberly, Jim's partner ("friend" as the family insisted on dismissing her) was not invited to sit with the family, a decision which elevated the tension as friends arrived at the funeral home. Some friends appealed without success to the funeral director to resolve the slight. Many struggled to be gracious when offering condolences to family members. Fortunately, one friend asked how she was getting to the cemetery—the family had no intention of including her in "the family car." This friend, who had not planned to go to the committal, served as her chauffeur.

A perceived slight—repeatedly rehearsed and embellished—may block friendgrievers from fully experiencing the ritual or from doing reflective griefwork afterward. The slight snowballs with each repetition. For example, for months after designer Gianni Versace's death in 1997, Elton John, his close friend, expressed annoyance that

Versace's partner, Antonio D'Amico, was not acknowledged at the funeral (Roshan, 1997, December 15).

WHEN "FAMILY ONLY" SERVICES ARE NOT LIMITED TO THE FAMILY

The decision by some families to have "family only" private services excludes and often offends friends. The situation becomes more conflicted if the family invites certain friends to attend. This can become an issue when a celebrity, public figure, or a person whose death receives significant media attention, dies and the funeral site only has limited seating; all friends cannot be invited. Or what happens to friends when what otherwise would be an intimate funeral turns into a media event because of the circumstances of the death, such as the Littleton shootings. Consider the funeral of Isaiah Shoels covered live by CNN and attended by 5,000 "mourners." Had Shoels not been killed at Littleton High School—had he died in an automobile accident—how many would have attended the funeral? (Funeral: Last victim laid to rest, 1999, April 30). How might the funeral been experienced by friends without the media presence and the intrusive presence of so many self-defined friends?

Friends have also been irritated when the family elects immediate cremation and no services. Such decisions, although prerogatives of a family, according to the courts and funeral practice, complicate the grief of friends (Rocco, 1998, March) by eliminating a venue in which the death can be communally acknowledged and support and comfort exchanged (Wolfelt, 1994).

WHEN THE FUNERAL DIRECTOR IS CAUGHT IN THE MIDDLE

Conflicted family vs. friends issues demand the attention and diplomatic skills of funeral directors. One funeral director with wide practical experience as an informal referee between the interests of family and the interests of friends, protests, "We're not trained to be social workers or therapists!" Limbo and Wheeler (1986) describe funeral directors as having "a technical expertise in preparing bodies for burial, but their greater role is as *a friend in grief* to help families deal with death" (italics mine; p. 119). But who is a friend in grief to the friends?

In the stress of grief, and particularly with a sudden or unexpected death, in the limited time frame for decision making, families make choices that overlook friends but may, nevertheless, be perceived as an intentional slight. Even a delayed, "I didn't even think about that at the time" is little consolation to some friends. "Close friends who attempt to participate in funeral arrangements are likely to be denied access to plans" (Sklar, 1991-92, p. 115).

ATTENDED A GOOD FUNERAL LATELY?

Some friends have, in reality or in their own perspective, impossible schedules. That, in itself, offers a convenient excuse for not attending. The Study of American Attitudes Toward Ritualization and Memorialization reported a significant decease in the number of respondents who had attended a funeral in the last two years—70 percent in 1995, as compared to 79 percent five years earlier (Daniels, 1996, February, p. 7). Daniels suggests, "If the results indicate a trend, perhaps consideration needs to be given to changing the hours of funeral services so that working people will be more able to attend" (p. 8). In some communities, funerals are now scheduled in late afternoon or in the evening to encourage attendance by friends, especially if the body has been cremated. Scheduling a visitation and funeral "back to back" is believed to encourage friends to attend.

Casual friends may wonder if they should attend. I was surprised by the wording in one obituary: "All of Jim's friends are welcome to attend the funeral." Although friends once received formal invitations to funerals—generally, a pair of gloves—formal invitations are only issued now to friends for the funerals of celebrities such as Frank Sinatra and John Kennedy, Jr. According to Post (1992) the published obituary serves as a de facto invitation.

> If the hour and location of the service are printed in the paper, that is considered an invitation to attend. It is entirely up to you to decide whether you knew the deceased or family well enough to wish to be at his funeral. But it is certainly heartless not to go to the public funeral of a person with whom you have been closely associated in business or some other interest, to whose house you have often been invited, or whose family are your friends (p. 550).

HOW MOBILITY IMPACTS FUNERAL ATTENDANCE OF FRIENDS

One factor impacting funeral attendance is the mobility of those who compose friendorbits. Although I have a large number of friends, they are scattered all across the United States and Europe. So a funeral for me would be a sparsely attended event, limited primarily to friends in my Kansas City friendorbit. When the friendorbit is scattered, some opt for an immediate cremation/burial with family only or private services; some postpone a memorial service until out-of-town guests or more individuals can attend (Fitzgerald, 1994). Casual friends, however, may not feel as comfortable at a smaller, intimate ritual as they would at a public funeral. Funerals in a public space and with a suggested time framework offer a degree of anonymity some friends prefer.

Some friends conclude that attendance at a ritual is "the least I can do" as a friend. In rural communities, ethnic communities, and in small-town America there may be greater expectations for attendance and notice paid to attendance at funerals. Barrett (1999, March 16) suggests that among African-Americans, not to "show up" is to show disrespect for the deceased and for the family. One friend explains her decision to attend a friend's funeral:

> I was there to affirm the life and death of my friend; to acknowledge the suffering that infused his whole being, and his ultimate protest against the world and its emptiness; to say to his family, "In my limited way, I stand with you in your bewildered suffering" (Close, 1969, pp. 82-83).

Friends who cannot attend because of distance or schedule conflicts may be creative in personalizing ritualing. When actor River Phoenix died, his friends Jonathan and Kate Pryce, filming in London, went to a chapel at the same time as the funeral ("A Brief Life," 1994, March).

Sometimes funeral attendance in another culture can be complicated. When Anwar Sadat was assassinated, his friend, former president Jimmy Carter wanted to attend as a friend and private citizen, but the White House pressured him into being part of an official U.S. delegation which included former presidents Nixon and Ford. Arriving in Cairo, he discovered that Mrs. Carter could not attend the funeral since under Egyptian Islamic customs only males attend. So Rosalyn stayed with Mrs. Jihan Sadat during the rituals. Others in the official party noticed the distinctly warmer reception given Carter by Mrs. Sadat and her son who consider the Carters personal friends while the other former presidents, were *political* friends (Carter, 1982).

WHEN FUNERAL ATTENDANCE IS MISLEADING

Friends present at rituals may present a false assessment of future support. Relatives and friends from out of town, noting the attendance, could assume that there will be adequate support for family from close friends in the local friendorbit. Goldberg, Comstock, and Harlow (1988) studied 1,144 widows and conclude that those who have few friends or who do not feel close to their children "could be at increased odds of having emotional problems following the death of their spouses" (p. S207). Some adult children have falsely concluded, based on the turnout for a funeral, "Mom will be all right . . . she has so many friends back there."

THE RELIGIOUS CONTENT OF
A FUNERAL

As late as the sixties, some people were reluctant to go to churches other than their own denomination or tradition, even for funerals— a factor that led to holding funerals in funeral home chapels. In 1999, when Cardinal Basil Hume died in London, his close friend Jonathan Sacks, the chief rabbi of England, could not attend the funeral because it was a Christian service held in the Westminster Cathedral; he watched on closed circuit television in the Cardinal's residence (Combe, 1999, June 30).

Some friends who would not describe themselves as religious, are frustrated by the design of the funeral, particularly when a minister described as "an eternal evangelist" (Rodabough, 1981-82) sees the funeral as an opportunity for evangelism. Imhoff (1993) reacts to a colleague's "God-awful funeral" by saying, "Preacher, you do not speak of the Tom Friz that I knew" (p. 145).

For some friends, funerals resurrect old personal tensions with organized religion. Trillin (1993) and friends were annoyed by the "High Episcopalian service" for a friend, Mike Dodge. One fumed at the impersonalization, "The departed could have been a stockbroker" rather than a popular Maine humorist. "Even as we grumbled, however, I acknowledge that Mike, who was an eccentric but not a rebel, had a traditionalist side that would have been horrified at anything other than a proper Episcopalian funeral" (p. 29).

On the other hand, attending a "good" funeral influences people's thoughts about their own funerals. Former U.S. Senator Barry Goldwater was so impressed by a friend's funeral that he exuberantly informed the celebrant afterwards, "Father Carl, I want you to know that the Episcopal Church always did a damned good funeral." So, at Goldwater's funeral Father Carlozzi states, "This one's for you, Barry" ("One 'damned good funeral' for Goldwater," 1998, June 4, p. 3A).

UNACKNOWLEDGED REALITIES

Some funerals or memorial services are efforts to re-write the life script of the deceased. Thus the absentee father becomes the caring father. Individuals sometimes have difficulty reconciling the friend they knew with the person being ritualized. Sometimes friends must experience the family reconstructing or re-scripting of the deceased to reflect and protect the family's image and project the family values. Jane reacted angrily when her friend, Ted, died.

> Ted became an Episcopalian after he moved here. He loved the music, especially the organ. Sometimes he would go and sit reading in the nave while the organist practiced. After he moved here, everything about him changed, especially his relationship with God. Although he was not exactly estranged from his family, they were not close. I assumed that Ted's funeral would be at Saint Mark's. Wrong! His family, members of a fundamentalist church, insisted that the funeral be at the funeral home with their minister. It was all I could do to sit there through the wheezing of the Hammond organ and the hellfire-and-brimstone-you-will-reap-what-you-sow homily. If you ask me, Ted's funeral got hijacked by the family. Once or twice I thought Ted might come out of that casket (he had quite the temper!) and say, "Wait just a minute!"

Re-scripting has been particularly hurtful on friends at funerals for gay men and lesbians—when the family was clearly in control and was unwilling to acknowledge the sexual realities of a daughter or son. Even a family that is passively tolerant of a son or daughter's sexual orientation, may want a "sanitized" ritual (particularly back in their home town). Chan (1996), an Asian American lesbian, describes the funeral of her friend, Cindy.

> Although her lover and ex-lovers were all there, there was no direct reference to her being a lesbian, to being a proud, beautiful Asian American lesbian, one of the few I have ever met and the one whom I have loved as a friend, as a sister in our gay Asian family. I struggled with whether I should say something, to cross the line Cindy's friends were all carefully dancing around, all of us respecting her family's presence and silence. . . . I swallowed the lump in my throat and remained silent (pp. 270-271).

Such silence leads friends to feel the real individual was not honored in the ritual. This has led some to organize a second memorial or alternative ritual in which sexual orientation and relationships could be openly acknowledged.

RITUAL OVERLOAD

Multiple losses, particularly unmourned losses, become the raw resources for what Kastenbaum (1969) labels "bereavement overload" (p. 57), an "overwhelming grief precipitated by the occurrence of multiple losses with little allowance for separate grieving time" (Garrett, 1987, p. 8). Many friends experience "ritual overload." The griever cannot "do" another funeral or memorial service. Some friendgrievers are ritually numb and go through another funeral on automatic pilot refusing to be actively present. Others, as a way of keeping grief in check, refuse to attend rituals—except for a really close friend. One male, way too familiar with death for his age, responds bluntly, "I don't do funerals anymore!" Attending too many funerals and rituals without finding ways to process the grief aggressively and creatively drains the spirit. I was stunned when my mother did not attend her best friend's funeral. Some friends review each death and decide, "I'll attend if its convenient" (S. Klein, 1998).

The decision not to attend a ritual—even when motivated by "compassionate detachment" (S. Klein, 1998, p. 51)—angers other friends and may complicate their friendgrief. The anger or holding an unverbalized resentment by Friend A—or even the restating of that anger to others ("Can you believe he didn't even show up!") interferes with or distracts from grieving Friend B. The absence at Friend A's ritual diminishes expectations of support: "He probably won't show up for mine either. Some friend he is—or was!"

THE COMMITTAL, INTERNMENT, INURNMENT, OR SCATTERING

The third ritual is the committal, internment, inurnment, or scattering. The funeral procession from the church or funeral home to the cemetery was once considered an indicator of the deceased's standing in a community. In the days before automobiles, the number of persons walking in the procession was a significant indicator; later, the longer the motor procession, the greater the prominence. Today, in some Asian-American funerals, friends who cannot attend send their limousines or cars to be in the procession (Chin, 1995). Until recently, custom demanded that pedestrians pause and drivers stop or pull off the road as an act of respect. Now urban sprawl and congested traffic flow challenge the custom to the point that what Lynch (1997) calls "our shiny black parades" (p. 110) are less honored and respected (Anderson, 1996, March 13) if not obsolete, except in small towns and a few inner-city neighborhoods. Newspapers such as *The Atlanta Constitution* often include the processional's starting point in the obituary: "Family and friends will assemble at 174 Thompson Road . . . at 12:00 noon" ("Family-Placed Death Notices," 1998, April 1, p. B7).

Some friends find the committal to be the most emotionally demanding of the rituals because it forces the friends to confront the brutal finality of death. One friend comments on his decision not to go to the cemetery.

> My wife and I end it at the chapel or the funeral home. We don't go to the cemetery. I tell people it's because at my age, I don't drive so good anymore, especially in a funeral procession going through those stop lights. But the truth is, I drive better than most of my friends. It's just an excuse I've created to get out of going.

Jerry Kramer, a friend of the legendary football coach, Vince Lombardi, captures the finality.

> At the cemetery in New Jersey, I stood close to the coffin and kept waiting for something to happen. Now he's gonna come out, I was thinking. Enough of this. I waited and waited, and the short ceremony was ended, and the family got up and left, and some guy next to me was clicking away with a camera, and I wanted to chew his head off, and all the people began to leave, and I waited, waited for something to happen, waited for someone to tell me the joke was over.
>
> Soon, some workmen came, and they put some dirty, ugly, rusty hooks on the four corners of the coffin, and they started to lower it into the ground. They got about halfway and I turned away. I couldn't watch it go down. I walked away. To me, he'll never be gone or buried (Kramer, 1970, p. 107).

Some friends use the committal to make promises to the deceased or to themselves. Ralph Abernathy (1989), longtime friend and trusted aide of Martin Luther King, Jr., recalls, "At that moment I bade him a silent good-bye and turned my back to the grave, determined to make his spirit live in the army and marching orders he had left behind" (p. 464).

Some friends find the vulnerability too threatening. DelBene (1991) discloses experiencing the finality at a friend's grave.

At the graveside, one of my clergy friends came up and put his arms around me. "You and Taylor were good friends, weren't you?" he said. "Yes," I replied. "We were." That was all it took. With my friend holding me in his arms and offering the comfort I needed, sobs came from the depths of my heart (pp. 29-30).

"GO TO THE HOLE IN THE GROUND"

Despite the artificial grass hiding the dirt, the committal poignantly "symbolizes the separation that the death has created" (Wolfelt, 1994, p. 50). Some friends will not go to the committal and will never visit the grave. One friend explains "I just do not like cemeteries. They give me the heeby-jeebies. Besides, John is not there. I am not real sure where he is . . . but he's *not* there. Why go?"

For many Jews, the covering of the casket is essential; friends may shovel dirt onto the casket after it is lowered into the ground. At the conclusion of the burial ritual, the friends form two lines through which the family will pass to return to "house of mourning" (the primary residence). As the mourners walk by, friends call out: "May God comfort you along with all the mourners of Zion and Jerusalem" (Syme, 1988, p. 113).

In communities where witnessing the closing is traditional, some friends leave during or after the committal prayer. In fact, a slight pause may be taken to accommodate those who do not wish to see or hear the closing of the grave. One griever describes the experience:

> Now I know what it feels like to stand at an open grave and say goodbye, to throw a handful of dirt onto a box that contains the wasted remains of someone I loved. I now know the common sorrow of outliving those I love. They can't be touched; yet I continue to feel them. No more can they speak to me; yet I still hear them. Even though they are gone, I continue to love them (Valdiserri, 1994, p. 75).

Lynch (1997) as a funeral director, encourages friends not to cop out on the committal:

> "And you should see it to the very end. Avoid the temptation of tidy leavetaking in a room, a cemetery chapel, at the foot of the altar. None of that. Don't dodge it because of the weather. We've fished and watched football in worse conditions. It won't take long. Go to the hole in the ground. Stand over it. Look into it. Wonder. And be cold. But stay until it's over. Until it is done" (Lynch, 1997, p. 197).

When Barbara Boggs, mayor of Princeton, New Jersey, died at age fifty-one, it seemed that the entire town turned out for the seasoned politician's funeral. Large numbers of friends walked in a candlelight procession from the church to the cemetery. But after the family left, five of Barbara's oldest friends stayed. Theroux (1990) recalls, "We surrounded the coffin as it descended, placed our hands upon the top and, reclaiming the hymn, 'Tantrum Ergo' from our memories, we sang our old friend into the earth" (p. C5). That's friendship!

SOME INDIVIDUALS OUTLIVE ALL THEIR FRIENDS

Thomas Nelson, pastor of the First Presbyterian Church in Independence, Missouri, faced a challenge that blustery winter day in 1965. No one had come to the funeral home to pay respects; no one had come to the cemetery. Nelson and the funeral director concluded that the aged veteran probably had no friends left, so do the committal and get out of the cold. But they decided to wait until the announced time for the service. Just before 2 P.M. they noticed a car enter that section of the cemetery.

> I recognized the car immediately. I knew it was Mr. Truman's car. The Secret Service man got out and stood in his position and Mr. Truman walked over to the bier, and I was amazed. I went ahead with the committal. Snow was still in the air, cold. . . . After I had my benediction, I said, "Mr. President, why are you here? It's cold and bitter. Did you know this gentleman?" And he [Truman] said, "Pastor, I never forget a friend." And I was just speechless. This was the President of the United States (cited in McCullough, 1992, p. 985).

Imagine the ramifications had they preceded with the committal and had President Truman arrived to find his friend already buried.

To ensure that no veteran is buried without witness in Arlington National Cemetery, The Arlington Ladies, a group of volunteers, represent the military. Suellen Lansell; who attends for the Air Force, has never forgotten the internment of one veteran, a man had lived out his final years at the U.S. Soldiers' and Airmen's Home in Washington, D.C. That cold winter day, an elderly friend from the retirement home watched from the curb. Lansell invited him to join her at the grave, but he refused because "he was not family" (Cannon, 1995, November 11, p. 2A). Friends absent for rituals for veterans will accelerate due to two factors: First, as the number of World War II veterans dying reaches 250,000 a year and as space limitations in national cemeteries require that some veterans be buried some distance from their homes (Borlik, 1999, Winter/Spring, p. 3).

SCATTERING OF CREMAINS

Generally, the scattering of cremains is a private experience. Even when the scattering is public, a dispute over the final disposition of ashes may prompt a delay that inconveniences friends; delays can last for years. Sometimes friends are asked to do the scattering or a portion of the scattering. The protocol for inurnment is similar to that of the burial: a family's decides for an event scheduled later with specific invitations to those the family, or chief mourner, wishes to attend. A friend may be asked to carry the urn; its' light weight makes it possible for a friend who might have been excluded as a pallbearer to serve.

RITUALS AS A "DRESS REHEARSAL"

Funerals and committals for a friend can be something of a wake-up call on immortality or what Wolfelt (1998, June) identifies as a "dress rehearsal" (p. 22). In a death-denying culture, who wants to be reminded: someday *me*? No one wants to wonder: will I be the last to die in the friendorbit? Which of my friends will not attend? One friendgriever casts a skeptical eye on rituals:

> After my 40th memorial service, I decided to stop going. By this time, of course, they'd become only slightly less festive than Sunday tea-dances. No somber colors. Everyone will be cheerful. Balloons are a must, darling. Music. Dancing. . . . (K. Poe cited in S. Klein, 1998, p. 52).

Carmack (1992) finds participation in the rituals—even those which produce personalized anguish—a positive balance between engagement and detachment, particularly when facing an onslaught or escalation of death among peers. The decision to choose to attend a memorial service of "an especially good friend" is a healthy sign of "functional engagement" (Carmack, p. 12) with the loss. One man who has attended many rituals, especially for someone his age, describes the mental gymnastics he relies on to get through yet another ritual for a friend:

> The first time a friend dies, you think: "Thank goodness it's not me." The second time you wonder: "Why not me?" And the third time you say: "When am I next?" With the others that follow, you don't ask questions and more and more just hope that it [death] will pass your door (van der Boom, 1991, December 5, p. 273).

Nevertheless, some feel "saturated, overextended and burned out" (Carmack, 1992, p. 12) by the accumulated mourning for friends. These friend-survivors are emotionally unable to attend a funeral ritual even though attendance might help other friends. At some AIDS-related rituals and at some rituals for senior adults, friendgrievers have all but openly speculated, "Wonder who will be next?" Rofes (1996) described his own numbing due to the unrelenting assault on his friendorbit: "I only went to 'required' funerals, stopped reading *The New York Times'* obituaries, and refused to attend movies or plays that dealt with AIDS" (p. 56). Rofes adds, "Hiding from grief has become common practice for gay men [some would argue most men, (Staudacher, 1991)]. "We fear that if we open up, we will never stop crying" (Rofes, 1996, p. 79).

Some people even avoid sick friends as part of the distancing process. One widow in a Grief Gathering demands, "Where were his friends while he was sick? Oh they all showed up at the funeral but what good could they do for him then? He needed them during those long stays in the hospital." Vilma Bansky, a silent film star in the 1920s died, angry that none of her friends had visited during her long illness, ordered that there be no services and no public announcement of her death. Eighteen months later her attorney finally disclosed her death ("Passages," 1992, December 20).

CONCLUSION

Once a friend was expected to attend the trio of rituals: visitation, funeral, and committal. Now it is a choice of one of the three; sometimes, none. Some friends—particularly those who consider attendance as an obligation—prefer to attend the funeral rather than the visitation or wake because there is little time for social interaction or conversation. In urban settings, in large funeral homes which may be conducting multiple services and with concerns for scheduling mortuary personnel and equipment, the prescribed time schedule limits or prevents conversation. Certainly, friends gather in small groups briefly in the parking lot, particularly if they are not going to the cemetery. Many urban cemeteries discourage the practice of lingering around the grave site due the "allocation of workload among the cemetery's personnel and a desire not to risk upsetting mourners" with closing of the grave (Corr, Nabe, & Corr, 1997, p. 288). Historically, in many rural cemeteries, friends once dug the grave and closed the grave while others witnessed it.

Donne's classic words may be amended, "any [friend]'s death diminishes me" (as cited in Platt, 1989, p. 30). Many friends have said, mumbled, shouted, whispered, or thought at rituals "and *this* death particularly diminishes me!" Attending the rituals is costly—but not attending, I believe, is even more costly.

KEY CONCEPTS OF THIS CHAPTER

- The ritual offers friends a public place to try out responses to the unbelievable loss of a friend and to be aware of responses of others in the friendorbit.
- Not all rituals adequately facilitate the grief of friends; some friends go away angered, annoyed, or disappointed by elements of the ritual.
- Friends attend rituals. Today the question is "Which rituals?" These days, rituals are considered to be multiple choice: one of the above.
- A friend is diminished when there is no adequate ritual to honor the deceased and when a friend's grief is un/underrecognized.
- A friendorbit is also impacted when there is no adequate ritual to honor a member's death.
- The decision by some families to have "family only" private graveside services excludes and offends friends. The situation becomes more conflicted if the family invites only certain friends to attend.
- If the hour and location of the service are printed in the paper, that is considered an invitation to attend.
- Poor rituals complicate grief for friends.
- Some friends find the committal to be the most emotionally demanding ritual.

IMPLICATIONS FOR CLINICIANS

Hayslip, Ragow-O'Brien, and Guarnaccia (1998-99) suggest that rituals may be easier for those who anticipate or expect the death because the friends' support system may already be operative at the time of death; with a sudden death, friends have to wait for the support to be activated.

1. How did the client make the decision to attend or not attend the funeral? the committal? What did the client emotionally experience by attending? When the death of a friend or loved one is sudden, ritual participation may be undermined by shock or anger (Hayslip, Ragow-O'Brien, & Guarnaccia, 1998-99). Attendance at rituals is not universally beneficial. How will this ritual experience influence attendance at future rituals for close friends? Or casual friends' rituals? If a particular ritual is troublesome, what could have made that ritual more friend-friendly or beneficial?

2. If the client says that she was too busy to attend a ritual or offers another explanation, listen closely. Is that reality or a convenient excuse to avoid the reality of death? If the client now regrets not attending, explore ways to make up the ritual deficit.

3. Clinicians may inquire as to how the absent friend expressed their grief through "individual mourning practices" (Grabowski & Frantz, 1993, p. 282). Ask: What have you done to give your grief its voice? What might you yet do?

4. The clinician must carefully ponder the placement of assumed vs. realistic proximity. After the friend's death, the clinician may need to help the friendgriever reassess her orbit in the restructured friendorbit, particularly when the friend argues that her grief was not recognized or appreciated by other friends or when encounters at the ritual resurrected old disagreements or tensions within the friendorbit. The film, *The Big Chill,* might be a helpful resource.

5. How has attending funerals of friends shaped the rituals the client desires? How will friends be involved? Why? Have these been planned in consideration of friends' needs? Have these plans been placed in writing, identified in preneed documents, or communicated with friends and family?

6. In cases where there was no ritual or the ritual was private and the friend was excluded, explore the possibility of arranging an alternative ritual for this friend. How can the client now construct a ritual to honor the life of the deceased friend?

7. Not all clinicians support attending rituals. Silverman (2000, July/August) is clear that friends have "no obligation to attend" funerals (p. 174). Some clinicians have been negatively influenced by the rituals they have attended. Grabowski and Frantz (1993) note, "Findings indicate that for both Latinos and Anglos participation in a funeral ritual has no significant impact on grief intensity" (p. 282). A clinician's beliefs about rituals—pro or con—must not be imposed upon the client.

8. Finally, given the multiculturalism and the number of immigrants, some friends in this country may grieve for specific ritual customs of their country that have been abandoned by friends in this culture (Markides, 1981). How might that lost opportunity be celebrated now?

CHAPTER 9

Praying in Friendgrief

CHAPTER PREVIEW

Prayer and *praying* carry a great deal of emotional and spiritual baggage, particularly when linked to grief and bereavement. This chapter will examine how prayer functions as a continuing bond for individuals who pray for deceased friends, for others bereaved in the friendorbit, and for grace to reconcile with the loss. The inability to pray after a friend's death or a feeling that one's prayers are ineffective may be an issue for some clients. Clinicians must be acquainted with diversity in prayer mediums.

> If thou shouldst never see my face again,
> Pray for my soul. More things are wrought by prayer
> Than this world dreams of. Wherefore, let thy voice
> Rise like a fountain for me night and day,
> For what are men better than sheep or goats
> That nourish a blind life within the brain,
> If, knowing God, they lift not hands of prayer
> Both for themselves and those who call them friend?"
> (Tennyson lines 414-421, p. 429 in Hill, 1971, p. 428)

Friends pray in anticipation of death, at the time of death, after the death, and, in some traditions, such as among some Japanese-Americans, for 33 to 50 years after the death (Klass & Goss, 1998, p. 14). Buddhists chant prayers for 49 days believed essential to the well-being and reincarnation of the deceased. Others pray for the grieving. Through prayer, grievers question, reflect, vent, and, over time, integrate a friend's death.

WHAT IS PRAYER?

Ask thirty friendgrievers to define prayer and you will receive thirty different definitions and techniques. Hence I rely on the Anglican catechism's definition: "responding to God, by thought and by deeds, with or without words" (*Book of Common Prayer*, 1979, p. 856). Prayer is a component in all world religions, although intention, occasions, and format vary. Prayer is believed to make a difference. "More things are wrought by prayer Than this world dreams of" concluded Tennyson ("The Passing of Arthur," lines 415-416 cited in Hill, 1971, p. 428). A careful reading of the citation reveals Arthur requesting friends to pray for him *after* his death.

Some grieving friends pray extemporaneously, some use prayer books, while others recite the Lord's Prayer or Kaddish. Through prayer many friends voice their grief. For over three centuries, Lutherans have sung this prayer:

> Commit thou all thy griefs
> And ways into his hands.
> God hears thy sighs and counts thy tears;
> God shall lift up thy head (Gerhardt, 1676/1994, p. 44).

In an age before modern medicine, prayer was all some friends could do (Aries, 1974; Banker, 1988). Today friends report "it was *the least* I could do" or "something I could do when nothing else was possible." Grievers may ask a friend they believe to have strong faith, "Would you say a prayer for me?" Many friendorbits have a designated pray-er for crisis times.

"MY PRAYERS DIDN'T WORK!"

For some, grief prompts an intense spiritual crisis, particularly for friends in religious traditions that discourage questioning, or that emphasize faith healing, or when the death is a result of an act of violence. Expressions of anger or confusion often alienate grievers from other friends which denies them desperately needed social support. One friend recalls:

> Church members shamed me when my friend died. The pastor's wife—who I thought was my friend—told me, in front of others, "You ought to be ashamed of yourself carrying on like this! It ain't none of your business why God took Sister Gwen home. You'd better get right with God or He will give you something to grieve about!"

Some pray their anger; others find anger blocks prayer. After a friend's death, Grumbach (1991) confesses: "I am too angry with the God I trusted to save him, to lift his affliction" (p. 57). Williams (1966) encourages such honesty. If one wants "to carry hot complaints to the very Throne," that is a "permitted absurdity." Divine wrath did not fall on Job but rather on his friends, the self-appointed comforters who attempted to distract him from his grief (as cited in Lewis, 1946/1966, p. xiii).

GOD'S WILL AND THE DEATH
OF A FRIEND

Some believe that a friend's death is an act of God. One friend-griever informed me sternly, "God is God. He can do anything he wants, whenever he wants." For some, the assertion of God's active rather than passive involvement, "God *took* my friend," complicates grief. The friend is puzzled: what kind of God would "take" a young adult or teen pal, a school chum, a golf buddy in the prime of life? Such an "explanation" has enormous power to "simultaneously complicate and facilitate the grieving process" (Doka, 1998, p. 2). While such a belief may comfort some in a religious mind set such as fundamentalism, friends who have migrated to other theological points of view but who have remained friends with the deceased and other co-grievers in the friendorbit are agitated by such a conclusion (Smith, 1998). One man explains a strained friendship with a fundamentalist friend:

> We agreed to disagree on religion and not let it affect our friendship although that was challenged when Phil, our mutual friend, was murdered. For me it is a crisis: How could God let it happen to Phil? But my friend sees it as "part of God's plan" by which he means, end of discussion. For him "God's will" explains everything.

This thought is expressed in a 16th century Lutheran burial service, "Since it has pleased almighty God to call from this life our brother . . ." (Niebergall & Lathrop, 1986, p. 126). In many Christian communities, brother/sister is a synonym for friend. The word "friend" appears commonly in Christian hymns. In fact, a relationship with Jesus may be termed a friendship (Black, 1898/1999) as captured in the popular Christian hymn, "What a *friend* we have in Jesus" (Scriven, 1855). One friendgriever concedes, "We cannot understand God's ways but some day our friend's tragic death will make sense. *Some day.*" Some believe that God will use the death of the friend "for his glory"—a common theme in the televised Columbine rituals, particularly for Cassie Bernall whose friends were told "Cassie's death was part of God's plan to bring forth witnesses out of the Columbine killings who would then win others to Christ" (Woodward, 1999, June 14, p. 64).

That assertion may comfort some Christians but alienates or angers others—particularly non-Christian friends—to whom it sounds like escapism or denial. Some take Job's assessment, "The Lord gave and the Lord took away; blessed be the name of the Lord" (Job 1:11, NRSV) and turn it into a platitude. Others avoid openly verbalizing reservations among friends. Henry Sloane Coffin, a griever and a theologian, rejects the "It was God's will" mentality:

> . . . nothing so infuriates me as the incapacity of seemingly intelligent people to get it through their heads that God doesn't go around this world with his fingers on triggers, his fist around knives, his hands on steering wheels. God is dead set against unnatural deaths . . . . The one thing that should never be said when someone dies is "It is the will of God." Never do we know enough to say that (as cited in Theroux, 1997, pp. 344-345).

In an age of great fascination with angels as guardians and protectors, some have been shaken by the untimely death of a friend. Where was their friend's guardian angel? When one friend of mine died tragically, I called a friend who has written two books on angels to ask, "Is it possible my friend had a klutz for a guardian angel?"

Grief is complicated when friends pray for a seriously ill or dying friend, but that individual dies. Some interpret the death to be an indictment of their lack of faith. One minister laments, "I prayed my guts out for my friend and he died anyway." In this case, some in the friendorbit assumed this friend's prayers should have had clout because he was clergy.

In a study of grieving mothers Braun and Berg (1994) conclude those who could not fit the loss of their child within their spiritual framework had more difficulty than those who could accept the loss as divinely ordained. I think that is true for friends, too. For some Christians, fellow church members compose a valued friendorbit more cherished or closer than other friends. They often spend many hours together and have deeply invested in friendship. Faith-based friendships are often valued more than kinship since some Christians believe that friendships are gifts from God (Black, 1898/1999; McBrien, 1995). Aelred, a twelfth-century Abbot of Rievaulx, whose teaching is still widely read, identifies friendship rather than family as the relationship that best captures God's love for humans (Boswell, 1980; Lewis, 1960; Stuart, 1992).

FRIENDGRIEF IMPACTS FUTURE PRAYER

Rupp (1988) summarizes the issue, "Grief has a way of plundering our prayer life, leaving us feeling immobile and empty" (p. 79). In grief, some question tenets of their faith previously unquestioned (Neimeyer, 1998), especially if one friend in the orbit comments, "God *could have* prevented this death." I observed this distress in three college students whose pal died on the eve of a church-sponsored ski trip; they were offered pious platitudes: "Your friend is with the Lord" and "He's skiing on the great slopes in the sky" rather than a serious engagement with their questions and pain.

Cindy watched her best friend die an agonizing death from breast cancer convinced that her friend would "beat it because of all the prayers being prayed on her behalf." The friend died. Now as Cindy accompanies another friend into what Wolfelt (1998, November-December) calls "the wilderness of the soul" (p. 15). Cindy is skeptical. "Why pray? Who am I to change God's mind? God already knows whether Sallie is going to die or live."

I have counseled persons who have been told by religious leaders that their friend died because they had not prayed with enough faith or had not used a particular formula in praying, such as ending *"in Jesus' name"* or "binding/rebuking Satan." One woman alienated friends by asking them to leave the hospital if they did not believe God was going to heal her husband. When he died, the unbelieving friends were made to feel responsible. Close friends were at a loss to know how to support their friend as a widow.

Many Christians believe, "Prayer changes things." One woman, after watching a young friend die two weeks before her wedding, modified the quotation, "No! Prayer changes *my attitude about* things that happen, especially things like Sheila's death that I do not think I will ever understand."

From the five ministers who participated in my doctoral research—and numerous clergy friends—I am reminded that clergy are not immune from questioning. One lamented, "I know what I am supposed to believe, but right now, I honestly do not know what I do believe." This anxiety was heightened because he had to deliver the homily and act as if his beliefs were unshaken. Another disclosed that if one more close friend dies, he will leave the pastorate for another career (Smith, 1993).

C. S. LEWIS: A GRIEVER'S PERSPECTIVE

C. S. Lewis, considered one of the most influential Christian theologians of the 20th century (McConnell, 1998), wrote extensively on grief. Lewis's book, *The Problem of Pain* became a literary sensation in war-shocked England, establishing the Oxford don as one who could convincingly explain pain, suffering, and loss to lay audiences. But the death of a devoted friend, Charles Williams, in 1945—a friendship Lewis insisted had grown "inward to the bone" (Lewis, 1946, 1966, p. viii)—jolted him. Although Lewis' mother had died when he was a child, he states

> This experience of loss (the greatest I have yet known) was wholly unlike what I should have expected. We now verified for ourselves what so many bereaved people have reported; the ubiquitous presence of a dead man, as if he had ceased to meet us everywhere . . . . No event has so corroborated my faith in the next world as Williams did simply by dying. When the idea of death and the idea of Williams thus met in my mind, it was the idea of death that was changed (p. xiv).

Paradoxically, much of the literature on Lewis has focused on the influence of the death of his wife, rather than the death of this friend.

THE UNEXPLAINABLE DEATH

The unexplainable, unimaginable death leaves some friends too numb to pray or too angry with God, physicians, a murderer, the person driving the other car, nurses, hospitals, or even the friend (for not wearing a seat belt or a helmet, for driving after drinking). Just as the unexpected death can interfere with the funeral (Hayslip, Ragow-O'Brien, & Guarnaccia, 1998-99), it also impacts belief and practices about prayer. I have worked with engineers and scientists—trained to find answers—dismayed by a friend's unexplainable death. After postmortem results were inconclusive, one angrily declared, "There *has* to be a reason my friend died. A thirty-two-year-old healthy man does not just drop dead playing basketball!"

FRIENDS PRAY FOR THE DEAD FRIEND

First century Christians adapted from other sources to create new funeral traditions (Meeks, 1983). Christians modified the funeral meal of the Romans into the Eucharist. They altered the custom of putting a coin in the mouth of the deceased (to pay the toll to Charon on the ferry across the river Styx), by placing a piece of the Eucharistic bread in the mouth of the deceased (Upton, 1990). They modified traditional Jewish prayers so that prayer for fast days is the oldest Christian prayer for the dead, *Commendatio Animae,* "Deliver, O Lord, the soul of thy servant . . ." (Aries, 1974, p. 98).

Many people of faith share the perspective of Anderson (1994) "Death ends a life, but it does not end a relationship" (March 3). Speaking of friends, Williamson (1994) observes, "The cord that binds us one to the other cannot be cut, surely not by death" (1994, p. 120). One World War II veteran told Brokaw (2000) "So many of my wonderful friends and old shipmates now dwell in the house of the Lord forever. As each one takes leave they seem to take a piece of me with them" (p. 140). Black (1999) insists:

> Love cannot die. Its forms may change, even its objects, but its life is the life of the universe. It is not death, but sleep; not loss, but eclipse. The love is only transfigured into something more ethereal and heavenly than ever before. Happy to have friends on earth, but happier to have friends in Heaven (pp. 76-77).

THE KADDISH

Most Jews recite Kaddish three times a day during shiva as part of a *minyan*—a group of ten. A friend's death may send a person searching through their religious tradition for assistance and support. Wieseltier (1998) explains that although he had not prayed in twenty years, when his father died he prayed the traditional Kaddish; from time to time as he prayed, he found himself also remembering friends who had died.

Joining mourners to pray Kaddish provides a rationale for friends to visit the home (to be part of the *minyan*) and to visit at meal time (to bring food). Kaddish gives permission to remember (Syme, 1988); in prayer friends may think of something to do or to offer to do. Maslin (1979) notes: "As the memory of loved ones inspires performance of such *mitzvot* [good works] as prayer, charity, and study, the dead are immortalized in the lives of those who remember them" (p. 62). Broner (1994) reports the persistence of one of her father's friends in caring for her mother, "'I promised your children I'd look in on you. Paul and I were like brothers" (p. 51).

In some synagogues, the Rabbi asks friends to pray Kaddish for persons who die without surviving family members (Wieseltier, 1998). Kaddish is also recited by friends during Sabbath services at the temple or synagogue and on special holy days like Yom Kippur during Yizkor, a memorial service (Fox & Miller, 1992). In *Siddur Sim Shalom,* the book of worship used in Conservative Judaism, Mourner's Kaddish is prefaced with these words:

In love we remember those who no longer walk this earth. We are grateful to God for these lives, for the joys we shared, and for the cherished memories that never fade. May God grant to those who mourn the strength to see beyond their sorrow, sustaining them despite their grief. May the faith that binds us to our loved ones be a continuing source of comfort . . . (Rabbinical Assembly, 1998, p. 184).

A ROMAN CATHOLIC PERSPECTIVE
ON PRAYER

Grievers in all faiths use individual *and* collective prayer: "It is extremely important to come together as friends, for in grief we need others . . ." (Stuart, 1992, p. 130). Catholic friends come together to pray, "Hail Mary, full of grace, the Lord is with thee . . . Pray for us sinners now and in the hour of our death" as well as prayers that make up the Vigil for the Deceased or the Office of the Dead. Reciting the Rosary motivates Catholic friends to gather at a particular hour rather than drifting in over the course of the wake. Through this ritual, grievers are reminded that they are part of a faith community of friends that pray.

THE ORIGINS OF PRAYERS FOR
THE DEAD

Early Christians believed the final disposition of a believer's body was a congregational matter (Caspari, 1949). Many had been rejected by their families for embracing the new faith, so friendship took on new importance as Christians embraced concepts called "the family of believers," "the household of faith" (Galatians 6: 10) or "the family of God." It may be a while before a griever feels like praying or feels that prayer has any results, so friends offer prayers for the grieving, something like a spiritual proxy (Rupp, 1988).

Initially, Christian friends gathered in the home to pray as they washed and anointed the the body with oils before wrapping it in white linen (Davies, 1986). As the body was carried to the grave, hymns and psalms were sung and prayed. Friends privately prayed for the deceased but gathered for prayer services on the third, ninth, and fortieth days after the death as well as on the year anniversary of the death. These prayers "were believed to have a beneficial effect for the dead, provided [the deceased] belong to the saved" (Caspari, 1949, p. 309) and had died in a state of grace. Since the eighth century, the church has specifically gathered to pray for all the dead on All Saints' Day (November 1) or All Souls' Day, (November 2). Hispanic Catholics also celebrate *Dias de los Muertos,* Day of the Dead on November 3.

By the Middle Ages, as church buildings became common, formal funerals evolved. Friends still prayed as they washed and prepared the body (and still do in areas without paid funeral directors). Friends prayed as they carried the corpse to the church for the formal prayers where priests received the body into the custody of the church until the funeral. Over time, as such tasks were assumed by specialists, the prayers during the preparation of the body were abandoned (Davies, 1986) although *The Order of Christian Funerals* permits "the prayerful participation" of family and friends in tasks provided by undertakers, such as preparing and laying out of the body (Sloyan, 1990) just as dressing the corpse may be carried out by Mormon friends and family.

THE EARLY CHURCH FATHERS' TEACHING ON PRAYING FOR THE DEAD

The fact that Tertullian, Cyprian, and influential early church fathers prayed for the dead (Cross & Livingstone, 1974) convinced others to follow their practice. Over time, these were incorporated into the mass, although the prayers were collective—for *all* the faithful dead rather than specific individuals. By the third century, prayer for "peace and pardon" was voiced not only for those about to receive the Eucharist but also "for those freed from the bonds of the body" (Wright, 1967, p. 672), the dead. An epitaph on the tomb of Abercius, Bishop of Hieropolis, requested the prayers of "those who understand and agree with" praying for the dead (Wright, 1967, p. 672)—a hint that not everyone agreed with the practice. Aerius, in the fourth century, was charged with heresy because he denied any efficacy and legitimacy for prayers for the dead, arguing that such prayers encouraged Christians "to live carelessly in the hope that such prayers might avail for them after death" (Atwell, 1987, p. 174). Since most believers were illiterate, they relied on the teaching and practice of the clergy. Some clergy, then and now, regard prayers for the dead primarily as expressions of gratitude for the lives of the faithful departed (McClintock & Stagg, 1891, p. 710).

Christians observed non-Christian friends periodically taking offerings to the cemeteries to honor and appease their dead. Aries (1974) suggests that the early prayers were not so much offered "to improve their stay in the shadowy realm of the underworld" (p. 146) given that day's understandings of life after death, but rather to keep them there.

In the 5th century, Augustine insisted that the practice of the early church fathers could not be ignored. Gradually, Christians came to believe "that prayer, almsgiving, and especially offering the Eucharist were efficacious for the dead" (Rutherford, 1980, p. 18)—those who died having lived a life of faith (Atwell, 1987; Marius, 1999). Augustine's perspective was shaped by grief for a close friend—a friendship he described as "sweet to me beyond all the sweetnesses of life that I had experienced" (pp. 56-57). True friendship was "not possible unless [God] bonds together those who cleave to one another by the love which 'is poured into our hearts by the Holy Spirit'" (Augustine, 1991, p. 56). More than any pope or leader, Augustine promulgated the practice of praying for the dead (Rutherford, 1980) and laid the groundwork for the doctrine of Purgatory that would intensely motivate such prayers in future centuries.

Eventually masses included the reading of the names of the faithful departed. Christians inscribed names of the dead—originally the heroes, martyrs, and bishops—on ivory tablets called *diptychs* (Banker, 1988). The lists of the dead were read after two other lists: the *universa fraternitas* of the living (starting with the current pope, bishops, kings, lords, benefactors) and the list of the saints (Aries, 1974). The names of the dead in a parish were read after the saints because it was assumed that after purgation friends were with the saints in heaven (Banker, 1988).

Praying for the dead supports the belief that the dead pray for those who are alive (Ware, 1993), and that "outstanding men of faith" act as patrons in heaven, praying "for the salvation of the living" (Pelikan, 1978, p. 33). I am an associate (oblate) of the Society of Saint John the Evangelist, an Episcopal monastic order. Our *Rule* (1997) summarizes this ancient teaching:

> In Christ we are still one with our departed brothers and we express this communion through regular prayer for them and by recalling their lives on the anniversaries of their deaths. We believe that they pray for us and that we will be reunited when Christ gathers all creation to himself . . . (Society of Saint John the Evangelist, 1997, p. 97).

Such prayers are part of what Unruh (1983) calls "strategic social action" (p. 349).

PURGATORY

The tradition of praying for the dead slowly led to the doctrine of Purgatory, a place of temporal punishment or something of a transitional "holding area" for souls not yet perfect enough for heaven. Only martyrs and church leaders such as Augustine, were good enough to be immediately received by God; all others had to undergo purifying through suffering (Boettner, 1984) in order to be made acceptable to God. (The unbaptized or those who, after baptism, commit a mortal sin or commit suicide go immediately to hell and are beyond the assistance of praying friends.)

Praying for the dead intensified due to socioeconomic influences in the 12th century. The church's teaching reflected the growth in the joy of life coupled with a newly intensified fear of death, particularly during plagues, which the church considered a judgment of God. Helping maintain ties to the dead, "Purgatory became an annex of earth and prolonged the time of life and memory" (Marius, 1999, p. 142 citing le Goff, 1987, p. 69). Suffering varied in intensity and duration, according to the guilt or impenitence of the deceased and the severity of the sins.

Certainly, dysfunctional families existed. If a widow remarried—and she had few economic resources for survival without remarrying—would a new spouse want her spending time praying for a previous spouse? After a war or plague many had no family left, so friends were expected to pray to shorten, alleviate, or even terminate the friend's purging (Boettner, 1984). So serious was the issue that one prayer book published in 1558 contained a prayer for the the dead who had been "cleane forgotten of theyr frendes" (Davies, 1970/1996, p. 413).

THE CHURCH AND FRIENDSHIP

The church exercised enormous control over friendships. Friends often pressured each other to conform to the church's teaching to avoid excommunication. After excommunication, friends had to relinquish all contact (in some contemporary religions this practice is called *shunning*). The church could deny funerals and burial space to the unrepentant. The idea of a friend lying in "unhallowed ground" was enormously discomforting.

In a day before many could read or had access to books, the Church relied on verbal descriptions of the damned to warn the living and to enlist their prayers which like indulgences and requiem masses for the dead, could limit the dead soul's time in suffering. Graphic sermons prompted even reluctant friends to pray and to pay for masses; thus, in time, friendgrief became a substantial source of revenue for many churches, priests, and monasteries. One churchman of that day jested, "When the coin in the coffer rings, a soul from purgatory springs!" (Marius, 1999, p. 135). By praying to particular saints it was believed possible to have a genuine saint as "one's 'special friend'" (Pelikan, 1978, p. 178) and patron, or a "friend in high places."

THE CONFRATERNITIES

Remembering the dead became the function of the confraternities, organizations which functioned as a burial club or guild, a forerunner of today's funeral director. The intensity of their efforts led to the conclusion by some historians that late Medieval Christianity was "a religion practiced by the living on behalf of the dead" (Collinson, 1992, p. 254). Confraternities also performed acts of helpfulness for the poor, for prisoners, and for widows, but their primary focus was burying, commemorating, and praying for the dead (McBrien, 1995). Banker (1988) notes that confraternities caught on because "one of man's primary needs is to die in the presence of other human beings and with their remembrance" (p. 1). For a fee, confraternities guaranteed remembering.

On the eve of the Reformation, thousands of confraternities functioned across Western Europe, offering enrollees a grand funeral with pomp, pall, candles (the fraternity controlled the wax and candle market in the town) as well as prayers and ritualized remembrance. Memberships were purchased with great confidence in its ability to gain divine favor (Banker, 1988), especially in an era when "the sudden death of multitudes . . . was a fact of life" (Marius, 1999, p. 10). A plague could wipe out a friendorbit, so membership offered eternal insurance.

THE PROTEST OF MARTIN LUTHER
AND THE REFORMERS

Martin Luther and others were particularly offended by the excesses of prayer for the dead. Luther launched his protest with a confident pronouncement, "The just shall live by faith" (Romans 1:17) which appealed to the hearts and minds of many who could not afford to pay continually for masses for the deceased.

Salvation was *sola gratia,* solely by grace, Luther preached, so how could good works or prayers by friends or confraternities benefit the dead? Luther denounced vigils, requiems, funeral pomp, and Purgatory as "popish abominations" (Niebergall & Lathrop, 1986) totally without influence. Among Luther's followers, at least for a period of time, burial was left up to family and friends. Toward the end of his life, Luther reconsidered his stance: "The dead are still our brothers, and have not fallen from our community by death; we still remain members of a single body; therefore it is one of the duties of 'civic neighbourliness' to accompany the dead to the grave" (p. 125). Luther advised followers: "When you have prayed once or twice, then let it be sufficient and commend them unto God" (cited in Wieseltier, 1998, p. 192).

In many areas of 17th-century Germany, for a period, there were no funerals, only silent internments—once reserved for notorious sinners and suicides (Niebergall & Lathrop, 1986). The deceased's body was carried to the grave and buried in absolute silence, without prayers, sermons, or singing; some Reformers buried their dead either late at night or at midnight. Such sterile burials (Dunlop, 1993) complicated grief among friends, particularly for those who remained loyal to Rome. Other friends were often at a loss. Had not friends died trusting them to pray for their souls? Certainly, some resolved the conflict by praying for the dead privately.

The contention of the Reformers that prayers and money did nothing for the dead—challenged not only the teachings of the church but depleted its coffers, creating a wave of financial upheaval all the way to Rome (McLean, 1996). Walter (1999) argues that the Protestants' zeal to ban "intercourse between this world and the next" (p. 47) inevitably led to a unforseen secularism. "Protestantism's reluctance to pray for the soul led to funerals that focused increasingly—in the 18th and 19th centuries—on the corpse, the coffin and the paraphernalia that went with the coffin" (p. 135) and set in motion new attitudes toward housing the dead, creating cemeteries beyond the control of the church.

CONTEMPORARY ROMAN CATHOLIC
VIEWPOINTS ON PURGATORY

Since Vatican II, belief in Purgatory has declined. One priest friend comments, "People don't seem to relate these days to Purgatory." So when friends sing at funerals—and singing is prayer—"May the angels lead you into Paradise, may the martyrs come to welcome you" (Gathering, 1994, p. 858) there is no suggested interlude in Purgatory. Although technically contradicting official doctrine, this funeral hymn comforts many contemporary Catholics who believe, "My friend has found eternal rest and *is* with God. *Now*—not in some future moment" (italics mine).

Knight (1991) argues the stance of many conservative contemporary Catholics: "We still need Purgatory . . . . If we are not ready to live the life in heaven when we die, we have to be made ready, and the prayers of other people can help us (p. 2). Knight offers his understanding in the book's title, *Purgatory—another chance to say yes . . . to God.*

Attitudes on prayer can be a divisive element in friendorbit. Protestant friends feel excluded from the Eucharist—a key part of a funeral mass for a Catholic. Strong anti-Catholic prejudice exists in some quarters of Protestant Christianity and in some cultures such as in Northern Ireland, where friendship between a Catholic and a Protestant may result in death. Some Protestants are not antagonistic toward individuals but are intolerant of specific doctrines or practices such as praying for the dead and Purgatory. Some friends will not attend the visitation if it is linked to a Rosary or a prayer vigil or they come after these rituals. For this reason, the time of Vigil/Rosary is included in the obituary.

At the funeral for one friend, the minister denounced "any notion of Purgatory" as "unbiblical." "The dead don't need our prayers!" he declared, obviously aware that Catholic friends of the deceased were present. He defends such remarks by saying that funerals are an opportunity to reach the lost; he does not consider Roman Catholics to be Christians. His sermon offended Catholic friends, some of whom felt that they had been held up to ridicule.

Former Catholics who have become Pentecostal or charismatic evangelical Christians find themselves conflicted because while they do not wish to alienate friends who are devout Roman Catholics, they do not wish to compromise their new understanding of faith. Catholics in the friendorbit may be offended by reluctance to participate in these prayer rituals.

CONTEMPORARY ROMAN CATHOLIC PRAYERS RELATED TO DEATH

Order of Saint Benedict (1989) encourages Catholics to gather for the Vigil:

> "Members of the local parish community should be encouraged to participate in the vigil as a sign of concern and support for the mourners. In many circumstances the vigil will be the first opportunity for friends, neighbors, and members of the local parish community to show their concern for the family of the deceased by gathering for prayer. The full participation by all present is to be encouraged" (p. 7).

The familiarity of the traditional words and phrases, prompts reflection by friends as well as the remembering of previous deaths, which evokes a continuing bond with the dead. During the Intercession in the Vigil for the Deceased, friends are formally recognized as the priest prays, "Lord Jesus, you bless those who mourn and are in pain. Bless N's [name of the deceased] family and friends who gather around him/her today" (*Order for Christian Funerals,* 1989, p. 14). Often a *priedieu* (kneeling bench) is placed before the casket so that friends and family may pray at times other than the Rosary or Vigil. Praying friends must balance two competing images: "the image of the person in mind as they have known him over the years" and the person in the casket. "Through that loving memory the person praying at the casket alone or with others becomes united with the deceased living after death." Prayer creates a bridge between the deceased and the friends (Foley, 1980, p. 24). Rupp (1988) encourages friends to creatively pray goodbyes on their own rather than rely on the formal prayers offered at the Rosary or Vigil. "We need more than a one-time prayer to be healed of our loss" (p. 83).

PRAYING FOR THE DEAD IN OTHER CHRISTIAN TRADITIONS

The Orthodox find no distinction between the living and the dead as Ware (1993), an Orthodox bishop, explains that Christians have a "duty" to pray for the dead, confident that such prayers benefit the dead.

> We still belong to the same family, and still have a duty to bear one another's burdens. Therefore just as Orthodox Christians here on earth pray for one another and ask for one another's prayers, so they pray also for the faithful departed and ask the faithful departed to pray for them. Death cannot sever the bond of mutual love which links the members of the Church together (p. 254).

Some Christians pray for the collective dead rather than individuals. For example, United Methodists pray at the committal:

> Eternal God, we praise you for the great company of all those who have finished their course in faith and now rest from their labor. We praise you for those dear to us whom we name in our hearts before you. Especially we praise you for [Name], whom you have graciously received into your presence. To all of these, grant your peace. Let light perpetual shine upon them" (The United Methodist Church, 1989, p. 872).

The Methodist tradition of "singing funerals" began in 1774 at the funeral of John Nelson. As the funeral procession reached Birstall, England, mourners lined the roadway for one-half mile and sang the procession to the grave (Davies, 1962/1996). Charles Wesley found the traditional funeral ritual too stifling and continuously wrote new funerals songs. Davies and Rupp (1965) comment that one is "sometimes tempted to think that a large part of Charles's time must have been taken up in writing poetical obituary" texts (p. 134). During this period, obituary poems were a common means for friends to express grief; one example of "graveyard poetry" is Gray's *Elegy on a Country Courtyard* (Walter, 1999).

In joining the Methodist movement, many lost friendships and thus bonded more intensely with new friends. Little wonder, then, that the early Methodists were organized around friendorbits called "class meetings," where they fervently sang their hope to someday be reunited in heaven with friends. Thus, early Methodist funerals were marked by joy (George, 1986) perhaps because many of Wesley's texts were sung to popular bar tunes of that day.

> Then friends shall meet again who have loved, who have loved.
> Then friends shall meet again who have loved.
> Our embraces will be sweet, At the dear Redeemer's feet,
> When we meet to part no more, who have loved, who have loved.
> When we meet to part no more, who have loved (Christ-Janer,
> Hughes, & Smith, 1980, p. 308).

Certainly not all funeral hymns of this period were pleasant; funerals were appropriate times to admonish sinners to repent.

> Then, dear young friends, a long farewell,
> We're bound to heav'n, but you to hell.
> Still God may hear us, while we pray
> And change you ere that burning day.
> Oh! turn, sinner turn (Walker, 1966, p. 263).

THE COMMUNION OF SAINTS

By reciting the Apostle's Creed, Christians profess to belief in the mystery of "the communion of saints." Christians believe that the distance between the living (the Church Militant) and the dead (the Church Triumphant) is not wide. The popular anthem "For all the saints" illustrates the theology:

> O blest communion, fellowship divine!
> *We feebly struggle, they in glory shine;*
> Yet all are one in Thee, for all are thine.
> Alleluia! Alleluia! (How, 1864/1994, p. 293; *italics mine*).

The Book of Common Prayer (1979) contains words prayed by generations of grieving friends: "Help us, God, we pray, in the midst of things we cannot understand, to believe and trust in the communion of saints, the forgiveness of sins, and the resurrection to the life everlasting" (p. 481). Many Christians find great comfort in anticipating an eventual reunion with friends, a theme reflected in Negro spirituals such as "Swing Low Sweet Chariot."

> If you get there before I do
> Coming for to carry me away;
> Tell all my friends, I'm coming too
> Coming for to carry me home (Johnson & Johnson, 1925/1969, pp. 62-63).

In my theological tradition, each week in worship we pray for deceased friends. Names of members of the congregation, who have died that week are recited while communicants say aloud names of other friends who have died. Episcopalians (and other mainline Protestants) deliberately and prayerfully remember dead family and friends on All Souls' Day.

Hearing the names spoken aloud by parishioners, I realize the extent to which one parish has been impacted by death. While writing this chapter, I attended Good Friday services at which the congregation sang, "Still in grief we mourn our dead" (Bayly, 1961), and was reminded of my friendgrief and my belief in continuing bonds. *Still in grief* sounds pathological in a culture emphasizing getting over a friend's death, but for a liturgical moment, I felt affirmed by the church for still grieving my cadre of dead friends.

FRIENDS PRAY FOR THE BEREAVED

Friends pray for a deceased friend's family and for all in a friend-orbit impacted by this death. At the 1999 funeral for Cardinal Hume, Archbishop of Westminster, the celebrant—Hume's friend—prayed: "For the family and friends of our brother George Basil, that they may be consoled in their grief by the Lord, who wept at the death of his friend Lazarus" ("The funeral rites of Cardinal George Basil Hume," June 25, 1999). Friends pray for grace and wisdom to accept this latest death, for insight into ways to remember the deceased, for reconciliation and resolution of differences and misunderstanding which arise during the dying and rituialing.

Friends go to churches or holy places to pray or light a candle as a way of expressing grief on anniversaries, birthdays, or other times of celebration (Murphy, 1999). On Gianni Versace's birthday, Elton John stopped in a church to remember his murdered friend. Visiting the Cathedral at Chartes, France, I paused to light candles for my friends, Martin, John, and Rusty as a symbolic interlude—a deliberate "time out" to remember which is "a way of overcoming the gap between past and present," (Mayne, 1998, p. 125).

PRAYER IS AN ATTITUDE

Prayer is typically thought to be a verbal exercise. Although some religious traditions distrust written prayers, grieving friends may find that when they cannot verbalize prayers, the written prayers of others are helpful. Some meditate. Victor Hugo expands the definition of prayer: "Certain thoughts are prayers. There are moments when, whatever the attitude of the body, the soul is on its knees" (as cited in Pollock & Pollock, 1996, p. 81). Through prayer, friends roam the landscape of grief.

A BUDDHIST PERSPECTIVE

Kapleau's (1998) question, "Isn't the funeral really a send-off and not a write-off?" (p. 123) summarizes the Buddhist perspective on death. Death is not an ending or annihilation. The deceased is believed to benefit from friends reading *The Tibetan Book of the Dead* over the corpse. For forty-nine days following the death, friends chant and recite sacred texts, a practice considered as important as chants during the funeral (Snelling, 1991); after this period, generally the friend is believed reincarnated as a new human being.

Chanting also helps the friendgriever. When performed "with sincerity and zest, the sounds and rhythms of chanting provide a way to circumvent the discriminating intellect and to drive home directly to the subconscious mind of the deceased the essential truths of existence" (Kapleau, 1998, p. 133). From a Buddhist viewpoint, "since the dead are not really dead, who can say that chanting and prayer at funerals and memorial services cannot help them" (p. 134) as well as friends grieving for them? Through a lifetime of contact and interaction between [friends], strong karmic bonds have been forged." These bonds of friendship are not "severed at death. In the deepest sense there is no one, nothing anywhere with whom we do not have a karmic connection" (Kapleau, 1998, p. 134).

This initial period for prayers can be extended in situations such as murder. The deceased friend cannot become a *hotoke* (or Buddha)—the desired goal—until the investigation is closed. Sometimes a Buddhist friend must inform the dead, "You are dead, you have to go away now. We regret that you have to go away, but you can't stay here any more" (Klass & Goss, 1998, p. 16).

AN ISLAMIC PERSPECTIVE ON PRAYER
FOR THE DEAD

For those who practice the Islamic faith, prayer becomes a key factor the third day after the burial, when friends and family gather at the mosque for a prayer ritual that could last several hours. A religious leader will read from *The Koran* and pray for a blessing upon the deceased; friends also pray since "the more prayers uttered for the deceased person at the time of death, and for days after that, the easier the departed one's life will be in the afterworld" (Gilanshah, 1993, p. 142). Prayer is critical during the first seven days following death. Then, forty days after the death, friends and family again gather to recite litanies in remembrance of the deceased. Whenever a deceased male's name is mentioned, the *rahimahu:* "God be merciful to him" (Glasse, 1989, p. 134) is spoken, which mirrors prayers in other religions, such as "may he rest in peace."

PRAYING AND THE NON-BELIEVER

Not all friends consider themselves religious. Brener (1993) encourages praying anyway. "Prayer does not have to be predicated on faith" (p. 154). It can also be predicated on need especially when "We are angry at God and the way in which the universe delivers its blows" (p. 154). Two Jewish proverbs underscore this belief: "A place in Heaven is reserved for those who weep, but cannot pray" (Rosten, 1972, p. 364) and "Praying can do no harm" (p. 366). Walter (1999) describes an agnostic upon seeing a close (and very religious) friend's corpse, having (and still having years later), "a powerful feeling that she is with the God he does not otherwise believe in" (p. 59). Walter suggests that others "create for themselves a spiritual imagery" (p. 59) and vocabulary in which to express grief.

PRAYING NONTRADITIONALLY

Some grievers do not find traditional liturgy and rituals friendly, particularly when the death is stigmatized or disenfranchised or when the friend feels alienated from a particular religious tradition—this a significant factor among AIDS grievers. Stuart (1992) contends that effective liturgy:

> needs to articulate and speak to the experience of those who participate in it. The unfortunate fact is that for most of its history the Church's liturgies have been written by white, middle-class men and have reflected their experience and values. Lesbian, gay and bisexual people, along with people from different races, women, children and many more have been deprived of a liturgical language to make sense of their experience (p. xv).

Because many friends attempt to make sense of experienced grief through prayer and meditation, AIDS-related griever-friendly prayer books (Glasser, 1991; Sandys, 1993; Snow, 1987) sprang up during the early years of the epidemic. Boyd (1990) added prayers for AIDS and gay-related concerns in newer editions of his prayer books. These prayers have been found valuable by friendgrievers not touched by AIDS. Substitute *cancer,* etc. for AIDS, and these prayers become applicable to any friendgrief. After experiencing the deaths of many friends, Glasser (1991) prays, "Dear God, friends with AIDS slip through my fingers faster than grains of sand and seemingly as many. I can't hold them. God, dear God, please catch them with your open hands, within your welcoming embrace, with your loving heart" (p. 129).

Friendgrievers also find comfort through meditation, in Todd Hall's words, by attempting "to make sense out of the nonsense of life" (Righter, 1998, p. 145). Every friend will have moments in which "the power of our grief catches us by surprise" (Schulman, 1998, p. 79).

Gandhi, writing from a Hindu perspective, challenges those who are skeptical of prayer's value: "Prayer is not an old woman's idle amusement. Properly understood and applied, it is the most potent instrument of action" (Merton, 1965, p. 70). Many friends find comfort when someone asks, "Is there anything I can do?" to answer, "Yes, you can pray for me."

KEY CONCEPTS OF THIS CHAPTER

- Friends pray in anticipation of death, at the time of death, after the death.
- Friends pray for the deceased friend; friends pray for the bereaved friend(s); and friends pray for grace to reconcile with the loss.
- The death of a friend causes some individuals to reassess long held beliefs, particularly about the effectiveness of prayer.

- The early Christians had great confidence in praying for the dead. In many Christian traditions this practice is still valued.
- Mourner's Kaddish is a widespread prayer form among Jews.
- Roman Catholics prayer services or the Rosary are part of their visitation practices. However, this prayer directed to the Virgin Mary is problematic for many conservative evangelical Christian friends, particularly ex-Catholics.
- Reformers, led by Martin Luther, vehemently rejected Catholic prayer practices for the dead.
- Belief in the doctrine of Purgatory motivates many individuals to pray for the souls of departed friends.
- Prayers are a way to maintain bonds with the deceased friend.
- Prayer is a component in all the world religions, although the intention and format of the prayer may vary.

IMPLICATIONS FOR CLINICIANS

1. Not every clinician is comfortable discussing prayer and religious issues with clients. Booth (1995) urges professionals to examine or reexamine beliefs about God and understandings of specific faiths. "You don't necessarily have to be able to treat every issue" (p. 65) but a clinician does need to be able to initially hear out a client's concerns. Clinicians must be cautious in referring to a minister, priest, or rabbi because not all clergy are open to "why?" questions. For the client with a strong faith perspective, the counselor must be prepared to challenge religiously masked denial.

2. Myss (1996) reminds clinicians that "Human reasoning can never answer the mysteries of our lives" (p. 89). Some friends pray, meditate, ritualize, or sing their way into answers, or into new questions, or into peace, with the questioning. Some clinicians are given the opportunity to witness and to guide the friendgriever beyond the inevitable "Why?" question. Mathewes-Green (1999) offers this insight: "The only useful question in such a time is not 'Why?' but 'What's next?' What should I do next? What should be my response to this ugly event? How can I bring the best out of it?" (p. 57).

3. Issues about prayer created by the dying and death may be linked to the larger issue of tension within a community of faith. Clients who disclose that they cannot pray may feel estranged or alienated from their religious community or shamed by religious friends. Many have reservations about God's involvement and feel enormous guilt or fear honestly expressing those reservations with other friends. The inability

to discuss doubts and questions openly with friends in a faith community may motivate the griever to seek professional help (Walter, 1999).

4. The death of a friend may provide an impetus to examine prayer forms from outside the client's tradition. Bastis (1999) offers four Buddhist meditations that friendgrievers can use.

May I be safe from inner and outer harm. May I be strong and healthy.	May I be happy and peaceful. May I take care of myself with joy.

The clinician may rephrase these or add new ones: *May I find ways to remember my friend* or *May I be at peace with my friend's passing.* Participants in groups I lead—particularly those who have served as caregivers—have found *"May I take care of myself with joy"* empowering. Vance Havner (in Zadra & Woodard, 1999) encourages all friend-grievers: "If you can't pray as you want to, pray as you can. God knows what you mean" (p. 54).

CHAPTER 10

Pallbearing a Friend

CHAPTER PREVIEW

In this chapter we examine the most historic way individuals, at least males, have demonstrated grief for friends: by carrying their friend to a final resting place. Pallbearers participate in a contemporary reenactment of an ancient drama. The movement of a corpse to final resting place has always has had great significance; society expects this act to be carried out with great solemnity, dignity, and respect. Still carrying a friend's casket can be one of life's most sobering responsibilities particularly when the death was unexpected.

> Why do we mourn departing friends?
> Or shake at death's alarms?
> Tis' but the voice that Jesus sends
> To call them to his arms.
>
> Why should we tremble to convey
> Their bodies to the tomb? (Watts, 1859, pp. 657-658)

One way an individual honors a friend is by serving as a pallbearer, whether active or honorary. In some communities either in a funeral card or through inclusion in a newspaper obituary, service as a pallbearer is publicized. Pallbearing can be emotionally demanding since the bearer is "on stage" and friends who serve as pallbearers do not have the option of skipping the trip to the cemetery. Schiedermayer (1996) describes his experience "bearing" a friend:

> The inner city turned out for the funeral
> the mayor came, the dignitaries were there
> I did help to carry you down the stairs
> your coffin was heavy, as befits royalty
> I could feel the muscles tense and pull in my low back.

I would carry you again
but only if we could put the whole thing in reverse (p. 7).

Some would explain the experience by modifying the Hollies 1969 hit, "He Ain't Heavy He's My *Friend*." Many pallbearers, especially in the case of an unexpected or violent death, would agree with Lincoln's (1990) assessment that to carry "the casket containing the remains of a close friend is just short of hell" (p. 160). I recalled those lyrics as I studied the picture on the front page of the May 21, 1998, issue of *USA Today* of six men, dressed in the traditional dark suits, white carnations on their lapels, straining to carry Frank Sinatra's casket. One man in the picture seems an unlikely pallbearer: funny man Don Rickles, a longtime Sinatra friend. That day Rickles was not dishing out caustic one liners, but was experiencing the pallbearer's strain: carrying a friend's casket is one of life's more sobering responsibilities. Many who sang the pallbearer's song that opens this chapter, experienced that intrusive awareness; in their case awareness led to trembling. Whether friends are carrying Sinatra or the body of the latest casualty of a drive-by shooting, to be a bearer is an unforgettable encounter with life; for first-timers a rude initiation.

SELECTING PALLBEARERS

Since serving as a casket/pall/urn bearer is an honor, who selects bearers? Generally, it is either the deceased—formally through pre-need arrangements or informally through conversation—or those individual(s) who assume responsibility for the arrangements. Choices may have to be modified because of changes since the pre-need arrangements were made or wishes stated; on occasion, family members veto selections. Work conflicts, illness, relocation, or finances may make serving impossible or a financial hardship. The chief mourner may have to work down down the list of friends to come up with the bearing party (the British term). The Order of the Golden Rule (1987) offers guidance on selecting pallbearers:

> Serving as a pallbearer is considered an honor and a true act of friendship. Usually those selected are people who were close to the deceased; . . . Traditionally, six pallbearers are used, however, you may choose as many as you wish. Those selected should be physically capable of lifting without injuring themselves. Honorary pallbearer status can be given to those unable to lift or attend the service (p. 4).

While selection as a pallbearer is a recognition for an investment in a friendship, in actuality, pallbearers compose a temporary work detail with a primary agenda: carrying a heavy object—a casket containing a friend. The more a friend weighs, the heavier the casket, the more the work. Carrying an equivalent weight, people may cuss, moan, groan, or joke around but not as pallbearers–the work is generally accomplished in silence. The question must be considered: Do these friends meet the traditional criteria: able to lift and were "close to the deceased."

A HISTORICAL PERSPECTIVE

Pallbearers participate in a contemporary reenacting of an ancient drama. The movement of a corpse to final resting place has always had great significance; every society expects this to be carried out with great solemnity, dignity, and respect. Egyptian bearers carried the deceased with valued possessions to the Nile and then floated the body and possessions by funeral barge across to the other shore (Stannard, 1975). Roman bearers carried the dead to tombs at night, accompanied by singers and musicians, in a festive torch-lighted procession; in fact, the word funeral is derived from the Latin, *funeralis,* "torchlight procession." (Driving with the car's headlights on in a funeral procession is a way friends symbolically continue that tradition.) The transit of a body could not be haphazard because

> a corpse was considered a defilement in both Greek and Roman traditions, laws regarding burial usually required disposition outside a city or beyond sacred limits. At Rome, all burials were outside the pomerium of the Servian wall, usually in a "burial city" (necropolis) above ground or in an underground burial chamber. Roman law and custom set the *funus* (funeral), covering all responsibilities from the time of death to the postburial ceremonies, and carried status gradations for private and public (especially state or imperial) burials (White, 1990, p. 162).

Daytime burial became common by the 4th century (Di Bernardino, 1992) influenced by the growing Christian impatience with the "noisy exhibitions of grief" traditional in Roman funerals. "The procession was limited to the corpse, its bearers, and the family and friends of the deceased" (Stannard, 1975, p. 99). A funeral procession for a Christian, particularly a martyr or leader, was "more of a triumphant march" as the friends carried the body on a stretcher with the head uncovered and elevated (Rush, 1969). Originally, friends carried the body from the residence directly to the grave. Then Christians instituted a service at a church or meeting place as an intermediate point which led to the evolution of two separate rituals: the funeral and the committal.

In a time without the hygienic protections taken for granted today, handling or touching a corpse produced some degree of stigma or social contamination (White, 1990). In ancient times, touching a dead body made a Jewish person impure for seven days. Moreover, in a plague, or when the deceased died of a communicable disease, contagion was a great concern, a risk that challenged the health of the friend-bearers and their families. Superstition and taboo were widely attached to touching or handing a corpse. To limit contamination and/or religious defilement, some enterprising friends created a reusable *feretrum* or funeral bed (Saxer, 1992). Over time, given the growing economic wealth and social status, bearers began to be compensated for the health risks. Hired bearers known as *lectarie* (Haberstein & Lamers, 1962) or *libitinarii* (White, 1990) became the forerunners of today's morticians.

THE HONOR OF BEARING A CORPSE

The early Christian bearers carried their friend's corpse on their shoulders (Haberstein & Lamers, 1962) which gave new meaning to the expression, "shouldering responsibilities." Attitudes on bearing a corpse marked one significant difference between the early Christians and their contemporaries. Christians rejected the notion of religious defilement and demonstrated this by "the holy kiss" or kissing the corpse as part of the funeral ritual.

While relatives often acted as bearers, the burial of celibate clergy prompted the use of friends; monks carried monks, priests carried priests, nuns carried nuns, even bishops could be pressed into service as bearers. For prominent persons, bishops and priests carried the body while family and friends followed (Rush, 1969). Arrangements were not left to chance. Dying persons often selected the participants for a funeral, specifically, who should carry the bier, pall, and torches (Puckle, 1926). Besides, one would not want to risk offending a friend you wanted praying for your soul's release from Purgatory.

In ancient Greece (and still in some areas of modern Greece), the unmarried dead were buried in wedding attire. Pallbearers are called "bratimia" the term used for the men of honor [best men and grooms-men] (Dansforth, 1982). In the South of France, until recently, it was customary that the pallbearers share affinities with the deceased: men carried men, women carried women, the middle-aged carried the middle-aged, and the married carried the married (Badone, 1989).

In agricultural areas of France, pallbearers compose a temporary work group or *porteurs du corps*. Ideally, the pallbearers were the closest friends and neighbors of the deceased. The bearing party was recruited by the male neighbor or friend who lived nearest the decedent. However, in recent years, with farms being converted into homes for Paris commuters, neighbors are less available. Moreover, given an aging population the friends of the deceased "are increasingly elderly and feeble and cannot be expected to undergo the emotional and physical strain of serving" (Badone, 1989, p. 80) as bearers, so males from neighboring *quartiers* are enlisted.

THE TURF OF THE PALLBEARERS

Before the development of funeral homes, the corpse was in the residence until the time of funeral or burial. In small towns, the distances for pallbearers were short. However, in the cities, due to hygienic considerations and the shortage of land, as cemeteries were developed outside a city proper (as opposed to burials inside or adjoining the church), the bearing party's work became demanding. Necessity prompted innovations such as the bier, originally little more than a stretcher (Puckle, 1926). Over time, resourceful bearers attached short legs to the stretcher. On hot days or on long processions, pallbearers would stop to rest or even change teams of bearers. Eventually, someone added wheels and the friends' work was reduced.

HOW THE BEARERS HANDLED THE CORPSE

In farming communities, bearers used a "herse," a spiked farming implement used for cultivating soil (from "herse," French for "harrow," "hearse" is derived). The herse was turned over and the wrapped body (later coffin) rested on the spikes; spikes on the edges were used as candle holders. Although helpful, this latter innovation eliminated the position of honor for friends as processional candle bearers.

Initially, weight was only a minimal factor since people were buried in light garments or shrouds. For males accustomed to strenuous physical labor, carrying a corpse was not physically demanding but could be emotionally challenging. However, the physical stamina of the bearers was tested by the tradition of "bumping." Leaving the church after the funeral, the bearers bumped the bier against the walls and against roadside crosses (common in Medieval Europe). Bumping was thought to signal "Saint Peter to open the gates of Heaven in order to receive the soul of the deceased" (Puckle, 1926, p. 124).

Other local traditions developed. In Ireland, if the funeral party passed another graveyard in route to the grave, the bearers proceeded around that cemetery three times—once for each member of the Trinity. Although cemeteries were smaller in those days, there were many cemeteries.

Weight became a factor with the development of coffins (originally for the wealthy), and after the mid-1800s, caskets. Eventually a coffin could weight as much as or more than the corpse, especially those like the early Fisk Metallic Coffin designed to deter grave robbers (Cronin, 1996) who sold bodies to medical schools for dissection. Grave robbing was a great source of anxiety for friends and families until the widespread use of the protective burial vault.

PALLBEARERS TEAMS

Due to the distance, terrain, weather conditions, and weight, teams of bearers were often used. Since a coffin did not have handles, it had to be carried on the shoulders. The casket, a later innovation, with the addition of handles, allowed bearers to carry the deceased at waist level. Handles made bearing less physically demanding and allowed more friends, particularly older males, to honor their friends by serving as bearers. (When caskets were carried on the shoulders, the pallbearers had to be of uniform height, which excluded some friends.)

In the Appalachian mountains, pallbearers inserted boards or ropes underneath the casket to make carrying easier; some, "attached the coffin to poles and put the poles on their shoulders" (Stannard, 1975, p. 101). In winter, they used sleds; occasionally, because of the terrain, bearers sat on the casket to hold it on the sled.

Carrying the casket on the shoulders is still a traditional practice in some areas and among some ethnic groups. Many Americans became familiar with the practice watching the the Welsh Guards carrying the coffin of Princess Diana. Few pallbearers are asked to shoulder such emotional (the Royal Family and the two billion watching on television) and physical strain. Although these soldiers were not friends of the princess, friends, in all probability, could not have carried such a load for such a long distance—the lead lined casket alone was estimated to weigh over 500 pounds (Raether, 1997, November).

THE ORIGIN OF THE TERM "PALL"

The term *pallbearer* traces to the *pallium,* or the long cloak Romans wore and used to cover dead soldiers on battlefields. Following the death of Saint Justin the Martyr in 165 A.D., the pall was placed over the body of all baptized believers; after the 4th century, only the bishops of Rome could wear the pallium (Noonan, 1996). Covering the face with the sheet at the time of death is a sign of respect and a reminant of the pallium. At some later point, the coffin or casket began being covered with a cloth in order to make all persons equal in the eyes of the church, at least, at the time of the funeral. The pall was stored with the bier in the vestibule as something of a visual warning of death to worshipers. Palls were commonly black (until the reforms of Vatican II) although children and women who died in childbirth were covered in white. The pall generally included a cross, an emblem, or herald (Stannard, 1975).

The term *"Memento mori"*—"Remember that thou wilt die"—was a common Medieval greeting based on a passage in the Apocrypha (Ecclesiasticus 28:6). The influential Catholic preacher, Denis the Carthusian, and numerous contemporaries often urged worshipers to think at bedtime about pallbearers, "how, in the same manner as he now lies down himself, strange hands will soon lay his body in the grave" (Haberstein & Lamers, 1962, p. 131). Thus, people gave serious thought to the selection of their pallbearers to avoid "strange hands."

In ancient times, two groups of friends were selected for the honor of moving the body. The regular bearers—sometimes called "lower bearers" or "corpse bearers" had a weightier task than those who carried the pall (Stannard, 1975). Before embalming, dry cleaning, or widespread use of the casket, "upper bearers" carried the pall high enough to cover both the casket and the "under bearers" in order to keep the cloth from touching the body (and soiling or contamination). Friends bearing the pall were forerunners of today's honorary pallbearers (Geddes, 1981). Over time, the number of friends needed was reduced "since the pall was either omitted entirely, removed before the burial procession, or arranged out of the way of the bearers" (p. 100), that is, laid on the coffin. Again innovation reduced the number of friends participating in the funeral. After the Reformation, as part of the rejection of ritual "trappings," many Protestants refused the pall.

Haberstein and Lamers (1962) offer an alternative explanation for pallbearer. "Four of the oldest or most prominent men were called the 'bearers'; another four, whose duty it was to relieve the bearers, were called 'underbearers'" (p. 355) not unlike understudies in the theater. This view is supported by Stannard (1977) who notes that in New England, during the Puritan period, the "closest associates" of the deceased took turns carrying the casket.

Today, generally only liturgical churches use the pall and the pall covers only the casket and generally is used inside the church. Thus, for many funerals the more accurate term would be casket bearers.

WHAT'S SO MAGIC ABOUT THE NUMBER SIX?

The chief mourner may have as many pallbearers as is wished. Historically, some friends and family members were excluded from serving as bearers because of health restrictions. The development of the horse/mule-drawn hearse (initially for the funerals of the wealthy), and eventually the motorized hearse, significantly reduced the physical demands on bearers; fewer were needed. Over time with this innovation, the number of active pallbearers was reduced from eight to six, again eliminating more friends from direct participation in the rituals (Stannard, 1997).

On occasion, the family could not select only six (or even eight) without offending some friends. When Puritan cleric Increase Mather was buried in 1723, twelve underbearers and six "paullholders" as well as the Lieutenant Governor, and five other leading politicians— all personal friends—carried the coffin (Geddes, 1981). Benjamin Franklin's coffin was carried by friends, while the pall was carried by the President of the State (now called the governor), the Chief Justice, the President of the Bank of Pennsylvania, and prominent friends Samuel Powell, David Rittenhouse, and William Bingham. The mourners, comprised of Franklin's family and what one historian called "a number of particular friends" (Van Doren, 1938, p. 779) followed. In 1861, 64 pallbearers were selected for famed orator and presidential candidate Stephen A. Douglas (Johannsen, 1997, p. 873). For the funeral of famed Johns Hopkins surgeon John M. T. Finner, 500 honorary pallbearers took part ("Organ music should have a 'consoling radiance'" 1969).

THE RISK OF ACCEPTING A PAIR
OF GLOVES

In times of plague or contagious illness and before the widespread acceptance of embalming, to reduce the health risk, pallbearers wore gloves. Risk to health was one reason that women, then deemed the "weaker sex," did not serve. During the colonial period, social standing in a friendorbit was recognized by receiving "a good pair of Gloves" (Geddes, 1981, p. 121) as an invitation to be a pallbearer. The gloves, of varying quality and price, gave some indication of the family's assessment of the position of the person in the friendorbit (Hammerstein & Lamers, 1962,) the best quality gloves went to the closest friends.

In Colonial New York, funerals were invitational events. Invitations—often a pair of gloves—were sent to those friends the family wished to attend. This practice is still common among the Amish

(Hostetler, 1993) where the inviters are called "leicht–ah-sager" and among celebrities such as John F. Kennedy, Jr., and Frank Sinatra. Earle (1977) records this description:

> At the appointed hour they meet at the neighboring houses or stoops until the corpse is brought out. Ten or twelve persons are appointed to take the bier altogether, and are not relieved. The clerk then desires the gentlemen (for ladies never walk to the grave, nor even attend the funeral unless a near relative), to fall into procession (p. 35).

Friends walked to and from the grave in the same order because their placement in the procession identified their significance to the deceased. After the burial, at the residence, at a post-burial meal, pallbearers and selected friends were given gifts such as spoons, bottles of wine, scarfs, rings, or handkerchiefs. So common was this tradition that one man, nearing his own death, inventorying his collection of mourning rings, counted fifty-seven funeral rings; another man passed on to heirs a quart tankard of mourning rings (Haberstein & Lamers, 1962).

Among the Dutch colonialists, twelve pallbearers carried the casket pall. After the internment, the bearers returned to the home for the distribution of tobacco and drink. Some bearers received a "Monkey spoon" so named "because the crudely executed Apostle intended for the handle resembled more the animal than the saint" (Haberstein & Lamers, 1962, p. 211).

Eventually critics charged that funeral bills, often top-heavy with excessive expenditures for strong beverages for pallbearers and friends, were impoverishing families. The scandalous costs of rewarding bearers and friends as well as feeding them and providing large qualities of alcohol (and the resulting postfuneral drunkenness and rowdiness) prompted restrictions enacted by colonial legislatures "to keep the friends of the deceased from eating and drinking the widow and orphans out of house and home" (Hammerstein & Lamers, 1962, p. 210). Although the practice declined, the phrase "eating . . . out of house and home" survives.

RECENT SOCIAL CHANGES TOWARD PALLBEARING

Since the introduction of the horse-drawn hearse, and later, the automotive hearse, in some communities, pallbearers rarely carry a friend's casket all the way to the burial plot. Moreover, with fewer funerals held in churches, the demands on bearers has been reduced. Newer funeral homes facilitate pushing a casket from a parlor/chapel to the hearse. The use of portable collapsible biers ("the church truck") eliminate much of the lifting. So, unless steps are involved, bearers push, pull, roll, or in some areas, "escort" the casket. Some funeral directors limit the actual contact between bearers and the casket to reduce liability.

Many friends self-disqualify for the honor because of medical restrictions such as avoiding lifting heavy objects. Some friends have difficulty walking. Sensitive funeral directors offer to distribute the weight to accommodate a friend's physical limitations but that means that some pallbearers have a heavier share to carry, or more than six bearers need to be used.

Social standing and friendship are easily determined. Look at an individual's distance from the casket in the procession and in seating at the rituals. Historically, the family and closest friends follow the casket (now the hearse). As part of the honor, pallbearers often ride in a limousine in front of or immediately following the hearse, while the family rides in the "family car(s)" behind the hearse (although to curtail costs, the pallbearer car is increasingly eliminated). In some communities, family and other friends remain in their cars until the casket has been placed on the lowering devise over the grave or, at least, removed from the hearse by pallbearers.

RECENT DEVELOPMENTS IN
BEARING

Women friends are increasingly serving as bearers, although one early report of women bearers is dated 1786. Still, in many minds, pallbearing is thought to be "a man's job." In 1997, traditionalists were stunned by the inclusion of female friends as pallbearers of Cardinal Joseph Bernardin of Chicago. (Because the service was widely televised, many viewers noticed the innovation.) Women pallbearers had previously gained a favorable "thumbs up" from advice columnist, Abigail Van Buren (1996, August 25). Smith (1996) reports one female bearer's perspective: "This is not some 'feminist' thing. . . . I earned my place carrying this casket in a thousand moments as his friend" (p. 66). Women friends serve as urnbearers.

Another development is hiring bearers, particularly when the deceased does not have six friends or six friends capable of physically carrying the casket even for a brief distance. Some families choose not to ask friends, perhaps because some must take off work without pay or because of schedule conflicts; some families do not want to embarrass friends or put them on the spot. Not being asked or not being able to carry can be frustrating for senior adults. Some elderly friends have strong feelings about being judged unable to serve: "The day I get too old to be a pallbearer they can just bury me as well!" (Smith, 1996, p. 68). One family resolved the issue by selecting employees of the nursing home who had functioned as friends (Fisher, 1989).

Funeral directors can supply casket bearers. Some older cemeteries, citing the lack of uniformity of level ground (due to sunken graves or tree roots) as well as liability protection, require either paid pallbearers or cemetery employees to carry the casket from the hearse to the grave. However, the use of "professional" casket bearers further relegates friends to spectator status at funerals and as Weiss (1997, September 10) charges, is another element in the overprofessionalization of death.

Some funeral directors, as a way of avoiding hurt feelings (as well as limiting things that can go wrong—which can lead to lawsuits), suggest that employees of the funeral home, rather than friends, carry the casket (Shaw, 1994), a trend illustrated in *The Kansas City Star's* coverage of the funeral of baseball legend, Mickey Mantle. A large front page picture depicts Mantle's friends walking in front of the casket with the caption: "At the end of Mickey Mantle's funeral Tuesday, pallbearers led his casket out of Lover's Lane United Methodist Church in Dallas" ("Farewell to the Mick," 1995, August 16, p. A1). Could not former Yankee teammates have just as graciously pushed their pal's casket up and down the aisle as the mortuary employees? Widely published photos, as well as video coverage, influences future decision making which excludes friends from serving as active bearers.

DIVERSITY IMPACTS THE SELECTION OF PALLBEARERS

In Appalachia no offense is taken when a friend volunteers to be a pallbearer. In other areas, volunteering would be considered pushy or intrusive, "How can we turn him down?" Originally friends carried the deceased because the family was thought to be preoccupied with grief (as if friends cannot be preoccupied with grief); increasingly less immediate relatives such as nephews, cousins, or other relatives do the bearing. Some believe pallbearing is a family responsibility. When a family has a tradition of using family as bearers, that needs to be clearly communicated to friends.

JEWISH TRADITION ON PALLBEARING

In Judaism, pallbearing is considered "a signal honor and a symbol of personal tribute for those who participate" (Lamm, 1969). Jews believe that "Handling the casket is not merely a physical activity which requires brawn; it is a personal one that demands love and respect" (pp. 59-60).

ISLAMIC CUSTOM ON PALLBEARING

Since Islamic faith forbids (in some sects, discourages) women from even going to the cemetery, four male friends or relatives carry the casket on their shoulders. As they walk the bearers chant, "*Allah Akbar*" (God is great!) and pray for blessing (Gilanshah, 1993).

HONOR AT WHAT PRICE?

Serving as a bearer can isolate a friend from support and comfort during the funeral, particularly if bearers sit together and ride together in a funeral car. Smith (1993) interviewed three adolescents friendbearers who reported that their grief was impacted by their assumption that "everyone was watching us to see who would break down first." One discloses, "I felt honored but I wish I could have sat with my girlfriend and had someone to hold my hand." Another bearer reports, "Carrying your best bud to the grave is hard but we all had to be strong . . . for each other."

Many find casket bearing more emotionally troublesome than physically. One friendbearer explains his battle for emotional control: "I focused on the flowers in front of the casket. I did not take my eyes off of them until the funeral director asked us to step forward at the end. I felt like everyone was staring at us. I felt exposed." The experience can be more stressful if the notoriety of the deceased or the circumstances of the death elicits media coverage. Bearers have "walk-on roles" in the latest "Tragedy-cam Grief TV" (Lynch, 2000, p. 193). At the funerals for two New Hampshire state troopers killed in 1997, close-up pictures (and video) of the pallbearers were published and broadcast nationwide (Rakowsky, 1997). Such an invasion of a friend's privacy can heighten a bearer's distress.

> After Lydia's funeral ended, the coffin was wheeled down the aisle, the hideous green-candled cloth folded again, and we pallbearers lifted the weight of her down the steps, and—a moment which felt like pure horror to me—into the waiting mouth of the hearse. I can

see, plainly, David's hand touching the figured surface of the coffin lid, the rose he laid on, that last touch. And then the doors were closed, and we moved away (Doty, 1996, p. 115).

"NO PREVIOUS EXPERIENCE NECESSARY"

Unfortunately, there is no preparation for serving as a pallbearer. Almost no materials are available for reflective expression before or after the ritual; there may even be little instruction on how to serve. One funeral director friend commends friend-pallbearers with a follow-up letter of appreciation:

> When a family is in sorrow, it means a great deal to know that our friends are standing by us, ready to help. In this manner you have let _____ know that you really do care about them. Your contribution, as a casket bearer, is a necessary part of the service and helped to make it complete and meaningful (Attrell, 1996, p. 1).

PALLBEARING IS NOT ALWAYS A SOMBER EXPERIENCE

Bearers may experience something resembling "gallows' humor" which break the tension. The funeral of Coke C.E.O. Roberto Goizueta was packed with friends like former President Jimmy Carter, Rosalyn Carter, Andrew Young. What went through the minds of the bearers—four business friends and two of Goizueta's sons—as they carried the casket as the Atlanta Symphony Orchestra played the Coke commercial, "I'd like to teach the world to sing . . ." (Greising, 1998). Or the minds of pallbearers of Harry Carey as they processed out of Holy Name Cathedral to "Take Me Out to the Ballgame" (Stone, 1999).

Friends may find humor or irony in the selection of pallbearers. Tilberis (1998) describes her one moment to smile during the funeral of her close friend, Princess Diana:

> . . . when the coffin was brought in, covered with the maroon and gold royal standard and borne by red-coated Welsh Guards with interlocked arms, I simply broke down. But as sometimes happens in deeply moving moments, an inappropriate thought popped into my head. The eight Welsh guards were sweating profusely under the weight of the lead-lined coffin, and I thought how amused the princess would have been, making eight beefy men suffer under her weight (p. 279).

Sometimes, because of the emotion and the tension on pallbearers to "not screw it up" something provokes laughter. Because Senator Robert Kennedy's funeral ran long in New York City, the cortege reached Arlington National Cemetery after sundown. In the darkness, bearers could not find the grave. As they wandered around, they conferred nervously:

Averill Harriman:	"Steve, do you know where you're going?"
Steve Smith:	"Well, I'm not sure."
John Siegenthaler:	"I've have a feeling we've walked too far."
Steve Smith:	"So do I. Let's stop, and you go over and ask the man where we should be."
John Sigenthaler:	"No, you go. You're the campaign manager."

Smith began laughing; soon all the bearers were laughing. Sigenthaler recalls, "I could hear Bobby laughing and saying, 'You really screwed it up—again!'" After a few moments, Smith recalls, "I distinctly heard a voice coming out of the coffin saying, 'Damn it, put me down and I'll show you the way'" (Rogers, 1993, p. 185). The bearers never forgot their experience (and their friends never let them forget either).

THE OBLIGATION TO SEE A FRIEND
BURIED "WELL"

The final destination does not matter: whether a grave, a tomb, or a scattering in the woods. Hammerstein and Lamers (1962) rightfully insist that a funeral procession transforms the disposal of the dead into a solemn ceremonial act. Being part of a funeral procession has "the power to stir" (p. 354) whether as bearers or as those who follow them. A bearer's unstated responsibility is to go all the way in order to make sure a friend is buried well. Many bearers have been surprised by the emotional intensity of the experience.

> We came to a lone birch tree, its magnificent white bark standing out among the surrounding maples. Many years before, Gretchen, her father and younger sister had discovered the tree and carved the date and their names in the bark. Someone said a prayer. Gretchen's father placed the urn in the ground below the birch. Above us, wind rustled through newly barren branches.
>
> I was among the last to leave. I emerged from the woods that day into a different world, an adult world . . . (Madigan, 1997, January, p. 69).

Historically, the bearers closed the grave; Amish pallbearers still do. But now, rarely do bearers or friends remain. Closing the grave has been turned over to cemetery employees.

Pallbearing is a front-row opportunity to witness the commemoration of a friend's life. The experience will remain in the memory although few will discuss it. By serving, many bearers have a sense of completed obligation in having been friends "to the very end" in a unique twist on the words, "'til death do us part." Some say, "he would have done the same for me." An incredible silence may prevail in the pallbearers' limousine on the ride back to a funeral home. The responsibility is ended, but the memories have only begun.

KEY CONCEPTS OF THIS CHAPTER

- Pallbearers participate in a contemporary reenacting of an ancient drama. Moving a corpse to final resting place has always had great significance; society expects this to be carried out with great solemnity, dignity, and respect.
- One way a friendship is honored is by serving as a pallbearer, whether active or honorary.
- Today bearing may be more an emotional than physical strain.
- Increasingly, bearers accompany rather than carry the casket.
- Any number of friends, male or female, can serve as bearers.
- By tradition, pallbearers must be able to lift and must be close to the deceased.
- Some believe pallbearers should be family members.

IMPLICATIONS FOR CLINICIANS

So why should a clinician be interested in bearing? Unfortunately, most friends who serve as pallbearers will never—or only reluctantly—verbalize their feelings about this act of friendship; some will only find their voice in the safe presence of a clinician. By understanding the dynamics of this experience, and by examining the variables that are altering this act from an active behavior to a primarily symbolic one, clinicians can gain insight into some of the particular stress experienced by friends who perform this honor.

1. The clinician may be the first to invite bearer-friends to translate the experience into a narrative. Clinicians may raise the issue by asking, "How did you feel? What did you think about as you carried the casket/urn? As you sat through the service? How do you feel *now* as you

recall the experience?" A clinician could jump start a conversation by asking for a response to either of these statements:

"I earned my place carrying the casket by. . . ." or
"To carry the casket of a friend is just short of hell."

If a friend sidesteps personal feelings to focus on a detail, bring the friend back to the feelings of the experience.

2. Senior adult or physically-challenged friends may have strong feelings about not being asked to serve or being unable to serve. Some may have used work responsibilities or other reasons as an excuse to avoid admitting physical limitations. Explore those limitations.

3. Among friends not included in the bearing party, there may be some anger or resentment, not only toward the family, but toward some who were chosen. "I was a much better friend than ___." Close women friends may also have negative feelings about being excluded if a casual male friend was selected. Exclusion may interfere with fully experiencing the rituals. Some may suspect that a particular family member vetoed their selection and may have unresolved feelings about that decision. The clinician may ask, "How would you confront that person? What would you want to say?"

4. Ask friendgrievers to write about the experience in a journal format, a poem beginning with the lines, "To carry the casket of a friend is . . ." or in a letter which will not be mailed or could be read at the grave.

5. For some friends, serving as bearers for a friend is a significant wake up call on the fragility of life. Explore with them any decisions that have been made as a result of the experience. Did the bearers make any promises to each other?

6. Encourage a friend to initiate a dialogue with other bearers.

7. Remind friendgrievers of the honor paid to the deceased friend by serving as bearers.

CHAPTER 11

Eulogizing a Friend

CHAPTER PREVIEW

The eulogy is a key component of the funeral or memorial service. The essential elements for a meaningful eulogy delivered by a friend are: The friend-eulogist speaks as a representative; the friend-eulogist is grieving; and the friend-eulogist and those who listen are united in a need to give accurate witness to the life of *this* particular friend. The friend-eulogist makes the service personal by stimulating the memories of the mourners; honestly remembers and affirms the deceased; and honors the character of the deceased (Searl, 1993). A eulogy by a friend creates a public opportunity for friends to promise: We will not forget you.

> I bequeath my soul to God. . . . My body to be buried obscurely.
> For my name and memory, I leave it to men's charitable speeches
> (Francis Bacon, cited in Bartlett, 1980, p. 181).

The eulogy is a key component of the funeral or memorial service. There are three elements of a meaningful eulogy: 1) The eulogist speaks with some level of permission by the family; 2) the eulogist is grieving; and 3) the eulogist and those who listen are linked in a need to applaud the life of *this* particular friend.

Many friends consider the eulogy the most memorable moment of the service for their friend. The formal public eulogy given at a funeral or memorial service is primary, but also important are the secondary or continuing eulogies which take place anytime an individual says, "I remember the time my friend . . ." or whenever the friend is praised.

WHY IS THE EULOGY IMPORTANT?

The eulogy is an important obligation of mourners and heirs (Lamm, 1969). Searl (1993), appraising modern funeral and memorial services, concludes, "The eulogy is the focal point of a funeral or memorial service" (p. 89), although many Christians insist that the minister's sermon is the focal point and some clergy consider eulogies an intrusion on their turf, fearing that the friend-eulogist will upstage their sermon or homily. Until the early 1900s, the funeral was the exclusive domain of the minister. In some congregations, it remains so.

However, some families and friends want the minister to function as something of a co-coordinator or master of ceremonies. Even in some conservative Christian settings, eulogies are the focal element of the "celebration" (an emerging grief-lite funeral), a trend Long (1997, October) laments. Rather than the great narrative of redemption and resurrection, "we tell the only holy narrative left to tell—the biography of the deceased" (p. 16). Funerals offer a once in a lifetime opportunity to thank God publically for the gift of one unique life that resulted in the creation of the friendorbit now gathered as grieving friends. The words of Yeats (1951/1974) come to mind, "and say my glory was I had such friends" (p. 318).

Hudnut-Beumler (as cited in Breslin, 1998) finds the growing personalization through the eulogy to be a reaction to staid funerals in which the deceased's name was barely mentioned or not mentioned at all. People are increasingly unwilling to allow pastors, priests, or rabbis to have "somewhat exclusive control of what goes on" (p. 3). Some friends expect everything in the funeral (prayer, reading of sacred texts, a homily) to be a warm-up to the friend-eulogist.

WHY DO FRIENDS VALUE THE EULOGY?

Bowman (1959) observes, "The important human consideration concerning funerals is the meaningfulness to the participants, particularly to those most deeply affected by the death" (p. 148). With some deaths, "those most deeply affected" comprise what Folta and Deck (1976) term "the broader population of grieving survivors" (p. 231): the friends or particular friends rather than biological kin. In fact, the eulogy may be the one place where the investment of friends and their subsequent friendgrief is recognized.

THE EULOGY AS A GIFT

"Funeral praise" although one of the oldest literary forms, is one of the least valued, perhaps, Theroux (1997) argues, because the medium is performed by amateurs. Eulogies are often composed under emotional stress in a day or two with an imposed time frame for delivery. Theroux blames friends for mediocre eulogies. "We will accept any words at all, as long as they are not mean-spirited or self-serving, and if a particularly moving or graceful tribute is delivered, we are grateful for the balm" (p. 13).

The eulogy may be the only place for a friend to participate. Since friends seldom plan funerals (Fitzgerald, 1994) rarely are they assigned more than token roles. The eulogy "isn't everything, but it's something—a chance to pay homage to your friend and to express the sorrow you feel" (p. 138). Because a eulogy is a gift to those who attend, Fitzgerald thinks friends may need to sidestep normal etiquette to volunteer to do the eulogy. The gift may unravel, however, if the eulogy "bears little relation to the real person known by the variety of mourners present" (Walter, 1999, p. 78).

THE EULOGY AS TURNING POINT

Many funeral attenders are on emotional automatic pilot until the friend-eulogist breaks in and commands attention. One funeral director suggests that the physical arrangements work against friends: "Rows of people in chairs or pews, staring at the necks of the persons in front of them waiting, hoping to hear something that directly applies to them" or that confirms their own appreciation of the deceased friend. The eulogy may move friends from passive to active listening:

> When a eulogy is given, the keenest attention of the members of the audience is devoted to identification with the dead person. After the funeral, they tell of listening for items in the narration of the life or in the characterization of the eulogy with which they were familiar, or events or loyalties which they shared with the deceased. The desire to listen to a eulogy rather than to an analysis and critical evaluation of the life that is ended, comes in part from this identification (Bowman, 1959, p. 22).

At one Greek Orthodox funeral I attended, most of the friends were unfamiliar with the liturgy. But a remarkable change occurred after the priest announced, "There are some who wish to say *a few words.*" As the first friend spoke, others slid forward on the pews and turned toward the eulogist. As the ad-hoc eulogists talked openly about their friendship with the deceased, the service took on a different emotional feel.

THE FUNCTIONS OF A EULOGY

Delivering a eulogy can be emotionally demanding. The friend-eulogist has the responsibility to paint a picture of their friend who has died; to stimulate the memories of the mourners; to honestly remember and affirm the deceased; and to honor the essential character of the deceased (Searl, 1993, p. 89) in order to help construct "a cherishable memory" (Dewey, 1988, p. 132).

Friends often preface eulogies with statements such as, "This is one of the hardest things I have ever had to do," "I am not much of a public speaker . . ." or "I just hope I can get through this. . . ." The fear of speaking in public ranks right up with the fear of the unknown (Wolmuth, 1983). Actually, the eulogist and the audience are experiencing an unknown—life without the active presence of this friend. Anticipating the pressure being placed on a friend, some dying individuals write their own eulogy and ask a friend to read it verbatim or create a eulogy around the essential ideas.

Something magical happens when an individual begins, "I want to say a few words about my friend. . . ." I have witnessed funeral sermons easily topped by a friend/eulogist, even fumbling nervously with a piece of paper, fidgeting from foot to foot, forcing the words through a lumped throat, and punctuated with tears, sighs, and abrupt silences. Ask individuals what they remember of Princess Diana's funeral. Probably not the Anglican liturgy or the royal pomp, but the eulogy spoken by her brother; probably not the organ or choral music, but the eulogy *sung* by her friend, Elton John.

In services for John Tomlin, a student killed in the Littleton, Colorado, shootings, the minister praised Tomlin's mission time in Mexico, while his pals eulogized his typical teen-age behavior (Foster, 1999, April 24). Sometimes, however, the eulogist cannot "stand and deliver." As three of Tomlin's friends stood to offer their tribute before the large local and national audience and cameras—incredible pressure on grieving teens—"Their voices trembled and their bodies shook. After a while they gave up and collapsed into each other's arms" (First funeral draws hundreds, 1999, April 24, p. 30A). For many friends, their breaking down was an eloquent eulogy all on its own. After a few moments, Brandon Sokol returned to the microphone to read from a letter he wrote while sitting in his friend's empty bedroom. Then Jacob Youngblood "squeezed a laugh out of the distraught crowd by describing

John's abiding love for Chevy trucks, especially the old one he had saved all his money to buy" (First funeral draws hundreds, 1999, April 24, p. 30A).

Wolfelt (1994) encourages such eulogies by friends. "Without a eulogy and/or other personalized means of acknowledging this particular life and death, the funeral becomes an empty, cookie-cutter formality" (p. 46). This is particularly true in faith traditions in which a funeral follows a highly prescribed ritual order, so that little variation exists between the funeral for Mary on Monday and the funeral for William on Thursday although some friends find comfort in that predictable sameness. In such rituals, the friend's eulogy is an interlude in the predictable.

In reality, there are times when a friend declines the opportunity to eulogize a friend. George Bush did so following the death of his close friend, C. Fred Chambers, writing the widow, "I hope I haven't let you down by not speaking . . ." (Bush, 1999, p. 443). Bush concluded the apology, "I'll never forget C. Fred. I will always love him—my true, ever true, best friend" (p. 443). Bush wrote in his diary that he recognized a contradiction in being able to speak at the ceremony for the sailors who died in the *Iowa* blast, but could not eulogize his own friend. "When something close and personal happens, I break up and I know it" (p. 451).

Friends remember good eulogies and want good eulogies for those they love. Wolfelt (1994) contends that because the memories "live on forever" through the eulogist's "way with words" (p. 47) or creativity, reflective listening prompts active remembering and may lead to further elaboration on the story hours, weeks, years after the service (Walter, 1999). Increasingly applause is considered an appropriate expression of agreement for a creative blend of words and memories and a job well done. Often friends request copies so they can reread and remember the experienced moment.

WHAT THE FRIEND-EULOGIST OFFERS

The eulogist invites corporate active remembering of this friend and may jump-start the exchange of memories among other friends. Friends often piggy-back onto the memories of friends. This creates a place of recognition and safety that permits friends to be with the pain of friendgrief, or as one friend recalls, "to become a mess in front of God and all of your remaining friends." A slight turn to the next person, communicates, "I remember that . . . do you?" In a moment of permitted tenderness, hands reach out for other hands and comfort is exchanged through a squeeze, a nod, a pat, a hug, or an offered tissue.

THE EULOGIST LEADS GRIEVERS IN IMPORTANT GRIEF WORK

Rando (1992-93) theorizes that one step in the accommodation of healthy grief is to "recollect and reexperience the deceased and the relationship" (p. 45). *Recollect* has a liturgical derivation. The pray-er in a service "collects" various concerns of members of the congregation into a unified whole or *collect* (coll-ek). To *re*collect is to "bring back to the level of conscious awareness; and to remind (oneself) of something temporarily forgotten" (Webster's Ninth New Collegiate Dictionary, 1983, p. 984). The eulogist can frustrate or anger friends by choosing not to remember realistically, by airbrushing memories, by spreading what White (2000) calls "mythic lacquer"; or by sticking to a family's safe script.

Even when the eulogist has a reputation as a speaker, the unplanned can occur. Eulogizing his longtime friend, David Powers, Senator Edward Kennedy regaled the audience with highlights from the Kennedy campaigns in which Powers played a key role. Friends were reminded of Bobby, Teddy, and Dave Powers singing "Heart of My Heart" on the eve of the JFK's 1958 Senate victory and at three-year-old John, Jr.'s birthday party the day of President Kennedy's funeral in 1963. Then, while reciting the lyrics, Kennedy was ambushed by the pathos of the occasion. "He stood silently for 15 seconds, fighting back tears and struggling for control" before concluding, "You were the heart of all of our hearts, Dave. We loved you and we always will" (Lehigh, 1998, April 2, p. 3). A good eulogy by a friend sets-up a public opportunity for friends to promise: We will remember you. We will not forget you.

REAL REMEMBRANCE AND MOURNING CANNOT TAKE PLACE IN UNSAFE ENVIRONMENTS

The eulogist generally has time for "a *few* words." Within minutes, the service will end and friends will be "reconnected to the common-place, the ordinary, and the everyday" (Herman, 1992, p. 236) exchanging platitudes about "life going on," "the beauty of the flowers," as well as cliches about the busyness or stress of schedules: "Too bad we only get together at times like this. . . ." Some friends never get a second safe, public moment to express grief. For others, grief will be acknowledged only with a clinician or after a few drinks with friends, or strangers.

HOW THE AUDIENCE OF FRIENDS AND FAMILY LISTENS

Friends listen for links to their own experience with the deceased and want "Oh, I remember that" or a "You are right about that!" cues. Sometimes, humor offers a welcome respite from the heaviness of mourning. At comic Henny Youngman's funeral in 1998, friends eulogized the "King of the one liner." Picking up on Youngman's infamous "Take my wife, *please*" Noach Valley quipped, "Dear God, take Henny, *please*" (Breslin, 1998, p. 3). Would anyone expect a somber eulogy for a comedian? Yet, to get away with humor in a eulogy, one must disclose the right to joke as his longtime friend, Alan King did by saying: "I knew Henny Youngman for 50 years, and until two weeks ago, he always called me 'kid'" (King, 1998, March 9, p. 52). King chose an incident with which many present could identify: "Every single day for 50 years, Henny walked into the Friars Club and said the same thing: 'I want a table near a waiter.'"

King concluded his eulogy: "Recently he [Youngman] appeared at the Friars Club in a wheelchair, and he reeled off 40 one-liners before even saying hello" (King, 1998, March 9, p. 52). Sometimes a friend skillfully uses imitation of a speech pattern to remind mourners that their friend was not Joe Anonymous! but "some kind of guy!"

The eulogist plays on and to the emotions of the gathered friends so that the audience may be laughing one minute, crying the next, as in the funeral for Sonny Bono, once straight man to Cher but who died a member of Congress. Governor Pete Wilson of California, praised Bono's work on the clean-up of Salmon Sea, calling him "California's gift." Sensitive to his friend's dry wit as well as to the presence of many attorneys and politicians, he added, "For sure, he would have looked out over [this] audience and asked, 'Who invited all of these lawyers?'" ("Bono eulogies filled with sentiment, Wit," 1998, January 10, p. A12).

EULOGIES SET THE TONE FOR FUTURE EULOGIES

After hearing a great eulogy, many friends think when I go, I want a eulogy like that! One eulogist's innovation may be widely copied. At the funeral of Harry Caray, priests cracked jokes and friends roasted the colorful baseball broadcaster not only for his "love and tireless commitment to the fans" but also his "passion for alcohol and a night at the bars" (Breslin, 1998, p. 1). The outrageous, bigger-than-life dimensions of the deceased could not easily be portrayed in a traditional Mass.

Father Jerry Boland, President of the Catholic Archdiocesan Priests Council of Chicago, contends:

> This is the direction we're moving in—to be more connected with people. That was what really struck people at Harry Caray's funeral. I think they thought some priest was going to get up there and talk about Jesus and the cross and never mention Harry. I would rather err on the side of personalizing too much than to err on the other side, where people go to a funeral and then say it could have been anybody (Breslin, 1998, p. 3).

Admittedly, Caray's widow, as chief mourner, gave eulogists great permission by saying: "Let it be a celebration." However, not all grievers appreciate levity and not all circumstances lend themselves to joviality. Boundaries set by the family may necessitate postponing the friend-friendly toasting to post-ritual informal gatherings of friends. Trillin (1993) reports that after the memorial service for a longtime friend, some grumbled about details of the service rather than confront their own pain. Trillin thinks that such grumbling after funerals and memorial services is common. "It must be natural for people feeling a loss to fasten on to some factual error in a eulogy or some way that the setting or the order of the service was inappropriate" (p. 27).

After Denny Hansen's service, a mutual friend, Tersh Boasberg opened his home to Hansen's friends for drinks, conversation, and reflection. Something—perhaps the mystery that led to their friend's suicide—brought them together seeking a closure denied them at the staid memorial service. As Trillin (1993) listened, he recalled a line from *Tender Is the Night*.

> "Well, you never knew exactly how much space you occupied in people's lives." Denny obviously occupied much more space than he could have imagined. There we were, analyzing his life with great intensity, I thought, and everybody in the room had to understand, when you looked at it realistically, that we didn't really know him (p. 60).

HONORING THE FRIENDSHIP

Sometimes friends are annoyed by a ritual imposed upon them. Dissanayake (1995) describes feeling alienated by "the bland impersonal remarks of a stranger and the irrelevant hymn we were asked to sing"

(p. 139). How could such a ritual help anyone? "I felt a sudden pang of loss, wanting to tell my dead friend about the meaninglessness of the stupid funeral I had just attended" (p. 139). The friend who had been a great listener on so many occasions was the deceased.

After a good eulogy, the friend still grieves, but in Coffin's (1997) analogy, the loss is "a clean wound" (p. 346). However, a bad eulogy prompts a "I cannot believe he got up and actually said. . . ." Kavanaugh (1972) was outraged by remarks for an alcoholic friend:

> The eulogizer told more lies than are told at a devil's convention. Virtues my friend could neither spell nor pronounce were attached to his past life. . . . As we left the chapel, the resentment and shame pervaded the crowd. Everyone needed to laugh out his embarrassment, but nobody could. . . . Friends were teased into tears when in fact they were relieved by the death of a man who had suffered too long (pp. 15-16).

Friends may be equally offended by what is left unsaid. The lack of specificity and acknowledgment, trivializes the deceased's life, and leaves friends feeling unsatisfied. Gibbs (1974) bemoans the funeral for a friend where "There was not a single mention of the name of the person who had died, and no reference to his life. In short, a generic funeral. I left the service wanting to shout, 'My friend died.' His life had meaning . . ." (p. 248).

CAPTURING A WHOLE LIFE IN A FEW MINUTES

The eulogy may be hamstrung by the limitation: *a few words.* How can a friendship be captured in "a few words"? When a family is unfamiliar with or disapproves of the friendorbit–an offer to do a eulogy may be refused, politely or gruffly. One friend was told, "We want *only* family up front. If we let you, every Tom, Dick and Harry would want to put in their two cents!" "*'Two cents!'*" the would-be eulogist fumed. "I was his best friend since we were in high school."

AFRICAN-AMERICAN TRADITION ON EULOGY

In the African-American community, the eulogy and the music, are "typically designed to provoke the release of emotions" (Hines, 1991, p. 188). Many give vent to their emotions openly and unrestrained grief is acceptable if not expected by some (Devore, 1990). Barrett (1998) contrasts differences in lower-socioeconomic and middle-class and affluent blacks. In the former, funeral services could generally be described as "emotional, traditional homegoing services" (p. 90) with the eulogist highlighting the particularness of the deceased. Mourners expect a spirited eulogy—often delivered by the minister. However, middle income blacks prefer funerals which are clearly "less emotional, more stoic, and more formal" (p. 90) and more like traditional middle class funerals. Friends from one socioeconomic level can be disappointed by the quality of the eulogy for a friend from another economic level. One black man, attending a workplace friend's funeral, complains: "It was cold to me. Cut and dried. Not much was said about my friend. I did not feel like I had been to a funeral. In my church, when we have a funeral, you leave knowing you have been to a funeral and feeling that the deceased was Somebody!"

THE JEWISH TRADITION ON EULOGY

Jewish tradition compels the eulogist "to tell the truth about the person who has died and about the loss and its emotional consequences" (Brener, 1993, p. 25). Eulogies should be *kara'ui* or balanced and appropriate (Lamm, 1969). Thus, the friend should not "grossly exaggerate, or invent, qualities that the deceased did not in fact possess. Such praise is a mockery and an effrontery to the departed" (p. 50). On the other hand, "mourners should remember that although the deceased may have been undistinguished in many ways, and lacking certain moral qualities, there is always a substratum of goodness and decency in all . . . which can be detected if properly sought" (Lamm, 1969, p. 50). While the eulogist is not sworn "to tell the truth, the whole truth, and nothing but the truth," sometimes selective narrative-making is an act of friendship or friendly kindness. Jewish tradition teaches, "It is *mitzvah* [good deed] to speak well of the dead" (Maslin, 1979, p. 56). In some conservative Jewish communities, only the rabbi offers a eulogy; family or friends supply information, insights, anecdotes to enhance the rabbi's remarks.

SPEAK NO ILL OF THE DEAD!

Crafting and delivering an effective eulogy requires serious reflection. Influencing the preparation is the strong cultural admonition: *De mortis nil nisi bonus* or "Of the dead, nothing but good" which over time evolved into an inhibiting cliche: "Do not speak ill of the dead" (Bartlett, 1980, p. 62). Brutus' infamous eulogy, "Friends, Romans, countrymen, lend me your ears; I come to bury Caesar, not to praise him" (Bartlett, 1980, p. 216) reminds friends that the eulogy is a borrowing of the ears, hearts, and memories of those attending the funeral or memorial service or wherever a eulogy is shared or re-shared, given the growing audio taping or videotaping of funeral rituals.

WHEN THE FAMILY SETS THE AGENDA

When tension exists over lifestyle issues, families may reluctantly consent to a friend giving a eulogy, but restrict what is to be said or left unsaid. Some eulogists find themselves in untenable positions. Can the eulogist remember selectively? Can the eulogist truly honor the friendship? If the eulogist challenges the family script, he offends or annoys the family. "Eulogy, with its injunction to speak only good of the dead, encourages glossing over the inevitable difficulties in relationships and the uncomfortable feelings associated with loss" (Brener, 1993, pp. 24-25) as well as realities in the life of the deceased to the point that it is not a eulogy but a carefully constructed image, which further complicates mourning (Rando, 1992-93).

Nevertheless, the family may wish to convert the deceased into a saint or exemplary family man—despite widespread awareness among friends of contradictions. Gay and lesbian friends have left funerals offended because the eulogist made no mention of the sexual orientation or volunteer work in gay organizations. One convert to Buddhism, was buried as a Baptist despite protests from friends (both Baptist and Buddhist). Some friends have teased an audience, "Lots of things that I *could* say but I won't." Brener (1993) insists that the *hesped* or funeral oration "impels us to tell the truth about the person who has died and about the loss and its emotional consequences" (p. 25) although Brener concedes, "memory is not always a friend" (p. 61).

COMPLICATED EULOGIZING

Eulogies become complicated when an individual is murdered or dies in suspicious or uncharacteristic circumstances. Some friends of Jeff Trail, one of serial killer Andrew Cunanan's friends *and* victims, refused to attend and others refused the request to "get up and say a few words about Jeff" (Orth, 1999, p. 285) fearful of negative fallout on their Navy careers.

The eulogist for David Madison, also killed by Cunanan, faced incredible pressure in Madison's hometown because police initially considered Madison an accomplice in the killing of Trail. Had Madison died in a car wreck, few in the community would have known that he was gay or that he had been a lover of Cunanan or any of the other speculations served up in the national media blitz. Some friends had a hard time reconciling the eulogist's words with reporters' speculations. A year would pass before Madison would be exonerated and his name cleared and the memory of friends repaired (Orth, 1999).

David Schwartz, a partner in a prestigious Wall Street law firm, was found dead in a seedy motel room, stabbed numerous times by a teenaged male who claimed that Schwartz had made sexual advances. Friends and colleagues faced with this secret life and the unsavory publicity quickly distanced themselves. Still sixty attorneys from the firm showed up to do the "Cravath walk"—a solemn two-by-two procession into the funeral, a tradition for every full partner who died. Jensen (1993) reports Schwartz's colleagues stymied his investigation of the killing. Some colleague-friends "who had worked closely with him for more than a decade—seemed strangely unable to remember much about him" (p. 30).

WHEN FRIENDS HAVE BEEN ESTRANGED

Eulogies can be troublesome for individuals estranged from a friend at the time of death if the family asks for the eulogy. Conflicted by the question, "How much do I tell?" the chosen eulogist may struggle with the double-bind of honesty.

> Call me "straight-as-an-arrow." I believe that marriage vows are "for better or for worse." *No* straying. When I learned that my friend, Rob was having an affair, I decided to confront him, hopefully before his wife, family, and the community found out. I took him to lunch and told him that I knew about the affair. Rob angrily jumped up from the table, knocked over a chair, slammed his fist on the table and screamed, "You self-righteous son of a bitch!" and stalked out. We never talked again. I tried many times but Rob never took my calls or returned my messages. I never told my wife what I knew. I just said that I was not socializing any more with them. About six months later he was killed in a car wreck late one night. I am sure that if I had never confronted him, I would have done the eulogy. At the funeral I sat through a flowery eulogy about what a great husband and family man Rob had been, the whole family values, blah, blah, blah. Twice, I glanced across the aisle at her—his "friend" who actually showed-up for the funeral! So, at least two mourners knew the truth. Rob had not died on the way home from a late dinner with a client. He died on the way home after being with his mistress. So, if you ask me, the eulogy was all a lie. And Saint Rob got away with it.

Some eulogists edit (to protect the deceased or the family) and may, thereby, make the experience bittersweet as the eulogy is heard and remembered through different filters of experience (Irion, 1990-91). Friends hear what they want to hear.

At one funeral the drinking and hard partying habits as well as the deceased's love of drag were the focal point of the eulogy by a close friend. Some nodded in agreement while other friends squirmed in discomfort for the family and nongay friends. To the officiant of the service, a nun, the eulogist chuckled, "And Sister, maybe some Saturday night you can tag along with us to some of his favorite bars—although you may be too tired for church the next day. Ha. Ha."

At the reception after the funeral, one friend angrily confronted the eulogist, "You idiot! Were you out of your mind? All that partying you talked about is what killed Brian!" When the eulogizer appeared incredulous, he continued, "And inviting a nun to go bar-hopping?! His family are devout Catholics! Damn if you didn't manage in ten minutes to offend every one of them. And why bring up that drag-queen crap? What about his friends from his work? They didn't need to know about that!" When the eulogist protested, "I was just being honest," the challenging friend retorted, "Oh you were that. Painfully honest!" Rando (1984) reminds would-be-eulogists that the eulogy like other elements of the funeral "involves many more people than the immediate survivors, for the funeral is a public ceremony which puts each participant in connection with her own feelings toward death and the dead she had known" (p. 186).

THE EULOGY AS A RECRUITMENT TO A CAUSE

Some eulogists encourage support of a project to which the deceased was committed. Author Ken Kesey in 1995, at the funeral of Jerry Garcia, leader of Grateful Dead, chose vernacular that the mourners would understand, "This guy is going to kick our asses if we get up there and we haven't carried the torches" (Foege, Huhn, & Hunter, 1995, p. 24).

The eulogist may not be the first choice. When former Vice President Hubert Humphrey died, the family asked his long-time friend, former President Lyndon Johnson, to deliver the eulogy. When Johnson learned that he would be seated next to Richard Nixon, he refused to attend. The family turned to Walter Mondale, Humphrey's friend and Senate colleague, and Mondale rose to the occasion: "Above all, Hubert was a man with a good heart. . . . He taught us how to hope, and how to live, how to win and how to lose, he taught us how to live, and finally, he taught us how to die" (Solberg, 1984, p. 456). Mondale's words have been incorporated into many eulogies for friends.

THE EULOGY AFFIRMS FINALITY

Through verb tense the eulogy fulfills one of Irion's (1966) goals for a funeral: to affirm finality. Some individuals request that there be no eulogy. Moreover, a private service also eliminates a eulogy by a friend or a eulogy being heard by other friends. Lamm (1969) contends, "Most people deserve a eulogy and should not be deprived of it" (p. 51). I would add that most people deserve a *good* eulogy and not just a half-hearted, get-through-it- somehow effort.

Shaw (1994) suggests the hunger for good eulogies influences the growing number of memorial services which are designed to accommodate the remarks of friends. Multiple eulogies take the pressure off one individual doing *the* eulogy. Neimeyer (1998) cautions eulogists trying to decide what to say, in light of time constraints, "Reconcile yourself to telling an incomplete story" (p. 135). Shaw (1994) urges

> . . . the tributes and remembrances shared at memorial services can be far more heartwarming for everyone gathered to celebrate this life than a formal funeral service if this has been out of context to the loved one's lifestyle. Sometimes the dearest stories are ones that make us chuckle; a tale about kindness the deceased offered to another, a favorite poem, a favorite song, or a story about his or her adoration with a hobby, sport, charity, or grandchildren (pp. 48-49).

A good anecdote in a eulogy may ignite a chain reaction of recollections, even playful repartee later at the cemetery, over a meal afterwards, or that will warm the heart days, weeks, even years later.

TELL THE TRUTH

Do some friends surrender the right to a eulogy? Were eulogies offered for Dylan Klebold and Eric Harris, the gunmen in the Littleton shootings? If so, by whom? after all a headline reports, "Closest friends were deceived" (McImse, Bartels, & Foster, 1999, April 25, p. 25AA). Sometimes the circumstances of a friend's death or the last days of a life, leave eulogists in a dilemma. How much can mourners handle? The friend-eulogist has to decide. One eulogist tried to absolve friends for not having seen the threat of a suicide.

My friend, Tom was a hard working, high stressed professional. "Pull yourself up by the bootstraps" and all of that. Worked hard to make something of himself and to provide the good life for his family. Only the best. But there were two Toms. One: The hard working, family loving, community civic leader; the other: a compulsive gambler and drug experimenter. In a moment of great financial strain, because of losses, Tom sold his soul to a loan shark. Then his business lost a key contract and went into a nose-dive. Tom went out in the woods, where we hunted for years, and shot himself. Oh, some friends tried to argue that it was an accident—after all, it was hunting season. Within twenty-four hours Tom's widow's world crumbled as she uncovered the financial mess. They were broke. Every credit card was maxed out. Tom had borrowed heavily against his life insurance and even let one policy lapse because he could not pay the premiums. Friends were stunned, then angered, to learn that he had left his family destitute but they didn't have to get up and do a eulogy. I wanted to scream, "Tom, you worthless son-of-a-bitch! How could you kill yourself? How could you leave your family in such a financial mess? How could you think your buddies would turn our backs on you?" I cannot remember how many drafts I wrote. Fifteen minutes before the service I did not know what I was going to say. That was the hardest afternoon of my life. I felt badly about my eulogy until one day at the grocery store. Tom's father saw me, grabbed me and fighting tears, said, "Thank you, thank you for what you said about my son."

EULOGY AS WITNESS

In 1989, The United Methodist Church altered its funeral liturgy to encourage more participation by friends. After the sermon, there is opportunity called "the witness" for friends "to voice their thankfulness to God for the grace they have received in the life of the deceased" (United Methodist Church, 1989, p. 874). A final witness is needed for all friends. Rofes (1996) argues the need for a witness in the HIV+ community where the question, who will survive this to remember me? is common. Rofes adds that "gay men need both public and private outlets for communal exchange and witnessing" (p. 274) and must create them, especially when the traditional vehicle of the eulogy is denied or when no services are held. Obituaries in gay periodicals often have been more eulogies than death notices, with close friends commonly identified as survivors (Andriote, 1999).

The power of the witnesses has led many families to conclude, "I am glad we had a service" and has led friends to remark, "I am glad I came." Gurley (1992, November 26) describes the funeral of a friend as "a masterpiece of solemn simplicity. There was no chamber-of-commerce-style eulogy to distract us from the awesome finality of death" (p. C-1). The eulogy reminds us of the values of the deceased and offers an opportunity for other friends to become custodians of those values and memories (Rando, 1984, p. 189), even unpleasant ones (Murphy, 1999).

SUMMARY

Eulogies, particularly those well delivered by friends, stimulate individual and communal memories. That is one reason Jewish people say, "May their memory *to us* be a blessing" as a parallel to the more common, "May she/he rest in peace." Through eulogies from various orbits of an individual's life, friends gain an integrated image (Rando, 1988). Many friends have walked away from a memorial service saying, "I never knew that about her." A good eulogist in essence says, "No wonder that you are feeling such pain. This was a great woman who left big shoes to fill. The world is going to be dull without her."

IMPLICATIONS FOR CLINICIANS

1. Poor eulogies interfere with the grieving process of friends. Lageman (1986) describes his experience at a funeral where the priest did not give opportunity for a public witness for his friend. "A portion of my own grieving process was blocked by what had not happened at the funeral" (p. 21). When the presiding clergyperson does not personally know the deceased but makes it sound as if he did, friends take exception and rehearse that resentment. Ask, "If you could change any part of the eulogy for your friend, what would it be?"

2. Clients informally eulogize or de-eulogize the friend. Clinicians must listen, sometimes between the lines for what is not said as well as for what is said. While selective memory in a public setting may be wise, at some point, the real life must be acknowledged in order for thorough grief work to be achieved. The listening clinician may be the first to hear contradictions and inconsistences or may solicit such by asking:

What was not said that should have been said?

What was said that should not have been said?

What was the most meaningful thing said?

3. Some friends are troubled when the family rejects their offer to do a eulogy. Some friends are annoyed that although given an opportunity to eulogize they did not respond at the time or in time. Some may feel embarrassed that they lost control in delivering the eulogy or that they forgot things that they intended to say.

Ask the friend to prepare another eulogy to be read to the clinician or put on video and viewed by the clinician. The clinician gives permission by suggesting, "What is it that you wish you could have said in the eulogy?" This written or audio eulogy could also be shared with selective friends in the friendorbit.

Neimeyer (1998) suggests asking the client to write a biography of the friendship rather than the friend. How did you meet? What were testing points in the friendship? What hurdles had to be overcome? What were quirks or idiosyncracies? How did you know you were appreciated by your friend? The biography, even if two or three pages, allows the friend "to take stock of the whole of [a friend's] life, to appreciate its complexities and contradictions, and especially its impact on our own" life (p. 135).

4. In some cases, the clinician's role may be to help the friend-griever, particularly if estranged from the friend at the time of death, or if offended by the family, to sort through the estrangement, in order to reconstruct the friendship and process the loss.

5. The clinician should distinguish between primary (formal) and secondary (informal) eulogies. Words of praise offered at a visitation are informal eulogies; some friends have spent time anticipating what they wanted to say to family or other friends. The clinician may encourage the friendgriever to write a eulogy, that could be mailed to or shared with selected friends or saved. For example, the family of David Madison in the year before their son was cleared of any involvement in the death of Jeff Trail, "cherished letters that poured into them from David's co-workers and friends, telling of acts of David's kindness and recalling his humor" (Orth, 1999, p. 250). The clinician may encourage the friend-griever to go to the grave or scattering site, perhaps with other friends, and read the eulogy, aloud or silently. Some friends have eulogized a friend by writing a letter to the editor of the local newspaper. Others write journal entries that give witness to the life of a friend. Stories remembered and told about friends are informal eulogies.

6. The friendgriever may want to do a *mitzvah* or good deed in honor of the friend as a eulogy. A note praising the friend and attached to a check to a charity can be a eulogy.

7. Take note of the timing. The anniversary of the death or the deceased's birthday or a special day could be a good time to do an anniversary eulogy. It may be important for the friendgriever to confront an unfinished slight or to deliberately forgive the family or chief mourner for some insensitivity.

8. Explore any strained or severed relationships with other members of the friendorbit as a result of the friendgriever acting as an emissary for the family. A friendgriever may have gotten caught in the

crossfire between family and friends and has come off looking like the bad guy. The friendgriever may have to conclude: "I did the best I could *at the time*," offer to make amends, and then to move on with life. The clinician's question, "What would you say to ___ now?" may be a healthy start for reflection.

9. The friendgriever might decide to offer some assistance to the family of his friend or to other friends now. A "I was just wondering how you were doing?" phone call leads to an opportunity to offer a moment of praise or re-eulogize the friend, "I keep thinking about what a great friend she was to me/to us. . . ."

10. In pursuing a *kara'ui* or balanced and appropriate" eulogy (Lamm, 1969), ask the friend, "What do you miss most about your friend?" And then "what do you *not* miss ?" The client may have to be persuaded that acknowledging the negatives is not disloyalty. Many friends expend a great deal of energy denying some aspects of a friend's life (drinking, temper, dishonesty). All of our stories need to be told (Murphy, 1999).

11. The clinician may want to keep on hand these resources for eulogies:

- Harris, Jill. (1999). *Remembrances and celebrations: A book of eulogies, elegies, letters and epitaphs.* New York: Pantheon Books.

- Isaacs, Florence. (2000). *My deepest sympathies: Meaningful sentiments for condolence notes and conversations.* New York: Clarkson/Potter.

- Theroux, Phyllis. (1997). *The book of eulogies: A collection of memorial tributes, poetry, essays, and letters of condolence.* New York: Scribner.

CHAPTER 12

Responding Graciously

CHAPTER PREVIEW

In the previous chapter, the common expectations for hospitality expected of friends were examined. In this chapter we turn to more subjective expressions. Friends promise future assistance, friends touch, and friends validate. Making and redeeming promises are one way to maintain the bonds of friendship. Touching, at least for many in this culture, although far more subjective, benefits the giver and the receiver. Because of cultural perspectives, the friend must be sensitive to differences and expectations. Friends are also asked to give validation to the grief decisions of the chief mourner as well as others in the friendorbit.

> When Vice President Harry Truman, hastily summoned from the Capitol, arrived, she [Eleanor Roosevelt] put her arm on his shoulder and said gently, "Harry, the President is dead." Truman was speechless for a moment and then said, 'Is there anything I can do for you?' "Is there anything *we* can do for *you*?" she returned. "For you are the one in trouble now" (Boller, 1988, p. 300).

After someone's death, every griever is, to some degree, "the one in trouble now." Friends may be even more so because their grief is underrecognized. As Harry Truman learned that day, life changes when a friend dies. How does a friend respond graciously to the chief mourner, other friends, and to himself?

THE FRIEND PROMISES FUTURE ASSISTANCE

Given the mobility of family and friends, family members and close friends may scatter across the country after the rituals (sometimes immediately after). Local friends may find their services needed more in the weeks and months after the death. Through various acts of hospitality, opportunities are created to offer not only condolences but promises of assistance: "Call me if there is anything I can do. *Anything at all.*" Through the making and keeping of promises, the bonds of friendship are strengthened; mourners are reminded that they are still part of a friendorbit (Cook & Oltjenbruns, 1998) although participation may be redefined over time. Affirmation is the reason individuals gather after a death" (Grollman, 1998). "Being there demonstrates that although someone has died, friends like you still remain. Being there is the most eloquent statement that you care" (p. 31). In reality, however, socialization patterns among friends change, sometimes radically, after a death, a process Yager (1999) labels "friend*shifts*."

Some grievers discover that what they thought was a friendship was underdeveloped (Schwartzberg, Berliner, & Jacob, 1995), shallow, or one-sided. Others discover that despite having spent time with a person, you are not emotionally close—as with workplace friends (Fan, Conner, & Villarreal, 2000). The relationship was a pragmatic acquaintanceship rather than an intimate, emotional friendship, although it may have been labeled a friendship.

In some relationships, the deceased took the lead in inviting; perhaps the deceased was the one who remembered birthdays and kept in touch. In many couples, one person (often the female) is the social manager. Lovegren (1996) suggests that wives often maintain social contacts for an aging couple; this accounts for the increased stress among older widowers. Cook and Oltjenbruns (1998) report that the death of a spouse is linked to a decline in interaction with friends by widowers but not by widows, "particularly if the widow has friends who have been widowed previously" (p. 318). Among individuals of all ages, friends are sources of entertainment, enjoyment, fun, help. Friends told one widow after her husband's suicide, "We liked the old you better. You were more fun to be around."

There are also functional friends (Hymer, 1988) who can "open doors," provide contacts, "Tell 'em I sent you" relationships. These friends are often held in escrow for times of need. These friends know the meaning of the words, "You owe me one." So, when the usefulness declines, the friendship changes. Through friends one meets others— some of whom, in time, will also become friends—others will remain on the fringe of a friendorbit as a "friend of a friend." While some proponents of convergence in relationships argue that friends' values become more similar over time, sometimes attitudes of one spouse toward a spouse in a friend couple may be politely masked. After a death some friends disclose, "I never really liked her very much but I did

like her husband, a wonderful man. Too bad he was the one that died."
Figure 1 illustrates this pattern.

A + B are active friends of C + D and have socialized for several
years. However, that relational tradition is altered by the death of any
one of the four.

The death of D changes the dynamics of the friendcouple, sometimes
radically (see Figure 2). Yager (2000) reports that people may discover
that what they thought was a network of four friends (two couples) was
in fact two friends "plus two spouses" (p. 95) and no more.

One common pattern of realignment, is that over time, the friends
of the same gender, or the original friends in these figures, A and C,
begin socializing and spending time together. Friend B becomes socially
isolated or occasionally interacts with C. In this pattern of post-death
friendships, will A + B actively or passively maintain a friendship with C
(now a widow/er) (see Figure 3)? Will they de-invest and allow the
relationship to deteriorate? Will A and C maintain a friendship? In some
instances, A + B would never allow the friendship with D to deteriorate
had D survived, because they liked D better than C; in some cases, A + B
only tolerated or acted friendly toward C because of D. In time, married
individuals will learn if shared friends or *our* friends become *my* friends.

Just as some friends have "friends of the family," they may also
have "friend of a friend." A relationship with an individual is sustained

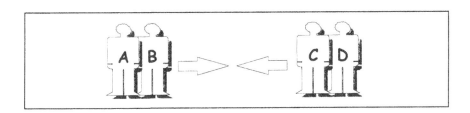

Figure 1. A two couple friendship.

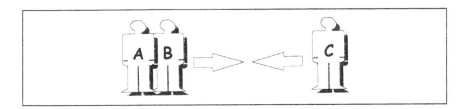

Figure 2. The death of a friend.

through a mutual friendship. In Figure 4, Friend A is "friendly" with Friend C through their shared friendship of Friend B.

If mutual friend B dies, how long will A and C continue to interact (see Figure 5)? How long before one (or both) reevaluates their "friendship" in the absence of Friend B? Thus, A and C may let the relationship slowly deteriorate, without investing the energy to end it formally or bring closure on the loss, "We just do not have much in common any more." This results in a secondary grief (A for C/ C for A) as well as the loss of anticipated sources of support.

> After Herb died it was a real problem. Herb's first wife, Kit, was a such a wonderful woman! She could light up any room and was so much fun to be with. After Kit died, Herb married right away. And this woman he married! She is loud, opinionated, interrupts you when you are talking. Changes the subject to what she wants to talk about. We went out with them some because it was good for business and we liked Herb. After Herb died, the relationship died. I suppose we said to her, "Give us a call if we can help" but to tell you the truth, I never missed being around her.

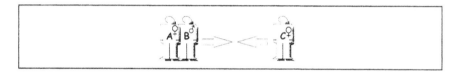

Figure 3. The realigning of friends.

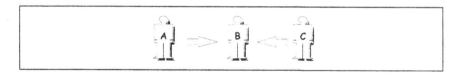

Figure 4. A friendship of three individuals.

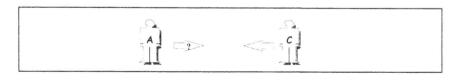

Figure 5. The death of friend B.

Realignment of friendships can be experienced through exclusion from social gatherings (L'Engle & Shaw, 1997). Some surviving spouses distance themselves from couple friends because being with them reminds them of the loss; Walter (1999) says this is particularly true of women. A widow's presence threatens some married friends: if your husband died, mine could die. Thus, "out of sight, out of mind" reduces discomfort. Yager (1999) relates the experience of calling a widow-friend to offer help. The friend responded, "Call me in a year, when no one's remembering me anymore. Right now, I am overwhelmed with visitors and attention" (p. 151).

WHEN FRIENDS FEEL GUILTY

Some friends feel guilty acknowledging, let alone confronting tension in a friendship. So, a friend may feel a sense of obligation to be gracious; promises may be grudgingly honored, not unlike I.O.U.'s. Wyse (1995) identifies two groups of friends: *stayers* (those who stay after the last casserole disappears) and *goers* (the ones who disappear).

HOW A FRIEND RESPONDS TO A PROMISE

Individuals respond to future promises with variations in enthu-siasm. For some friends, redeeming a promise is an obligation, for others an opportunity. A friend may offer—and really want to help, for example, sort through an individual's clothing or tools but the widow/friend may resist, delay that particular help. "I am not up to it today" or "This is something I need to do, alone." Some friends will not offer assistance again.

Friends, particularly those with little experience in grief, may become impatient for the friend to "to get on with life." In Walter's (1999) assessment, these friends attempt to police or regulate grievers. Some friends have a different perception of helpfulness, as in "God helps those who help themselves." Others, "just do it." One young widow described her "nightmare" when some friends came to her home during the post-funeral dinner at the church and emptied the residence of her husband's personal effects, clothes, books, and pictures. The widow's initial response upon arriving home was that she had been burglarized; she called the police. Word about the "robbery" spread quickly through the small town. Then, rather sheepishly, the friends confessed, "We thought we were doing her a favor by getting rid of his stuff. It would just be one less thing for her to have to do."

Some friends are annoyed when family members respond, "Thanks but no thanks! We're family. We take care of our own." At times, helpfulness and hospitality lead to tension with a friendgriever's partner, especially when the partner is not a close friend of the deceased: "Let the family take care of it. You have done enough!" Tension escalates when a friend uses assisting as a way of avoiding one's own friendgrief, especially after a long illness. "I have been in the caretaker mode for so long that I have trouble remembering that it's me who needs loving care now" (Lanoue, 1991, p. 67). Cook and Oltjenbruns (1998) advise friends to assist in specific practical ways.

> Grief can be such a draining experience that the bereaved may have neither the energy nor the insight to determine what others might do for them. Specific offers of assistance such as "I plan to bring a meal over" or "I would like to take the children to the park next week" put much less responsibility on the bereaved and, as a result may more easily alleviate their burden (p. 125).

FRIENDS AND POST-RITUAL REALITIES

During a long illness, some friendship interaction may have been curtailed, to the point that it is difficult to re-establish doing things together. One widow explains,

> During Carl's long illness I was at his side day and night. I cut myself off from all our friends. After he died, I soon discovered that life had gone on for them. In those three years, they made new friends. I never heard from some of our "friends"—or what I thought were friends—after the funeral.

Some friends feel more obligation to honor pledges of assistance when there are young children or financial hardship; others, however, feel more responsibility when there are not older or grown adult children to provide resources and care.

THE DANGERS OF OVER-RELIANCE

Friends can foster unhealthy codependency feelings. The caregiver friend can evolve into a care*taker* friend (Cook & Oltjenbruns, 1998) unless boundaries between caring and care-giving are understood (Bowers, 1999). Situationally learned helplessness—learned or nurtured through a prolonged illness—can motivate a chief mourner's over-reliance on friends and may tax or deplete the goodwill of the friendorbit. Some friends who "need to be needed" mothball their own grief to attend the chief mourner's needs. Here are things that signal imbalance in a friendgriever:

- thinks oneself indispensable to the chief mourner—"If I don't help her, who will?";
- worries constantly about the griever or griever issues, particularly with financial or legal matters;
- ignores personal relationships and responsibilities;
- overcommits (Cook & Oltjenbruns, 1998, p. 475);

or makes commitments beyond the scope of one's competencies and resources. Resistance may develop when a friend commits her spouse (who is a secondary friend to the chief mourner) to a particular level of involvement. "She's your friend—not mine."

Some friends encounter codependency after a friend's death but feel powerless to renegotiate boundaries, especially when there was something of a "deathbed" promise. Some individuals empower such promises with great intensity. "I *have* to follow through. I promised before he died that I would. . . ." Slow response or non-response angers friends. A woman in one of my grief groups demands,

> I would like to know just where are all the friends who stood by Bob's casket and promised to "be there" for *me*!? I have only called on them when I really needed something but they always act odd. Oh, no one says no, but there is a hesitancy, a "Well, I guess I can do that. . . ." No one has said "No" outright but no one has said a very enthusiastic, "Sure! Be right there" either. I expected more of our close friends.

Dissension in a friendorbit erupts, when friends disagree on how long it should take to get over a death (the perceived agenda of some). One friend may say repeatedly, "She should be over it *by now*!" Such statements discourage involvement by friends who may agree with the assessment, but believe a friend's role is to be supportive. Infrequent social requesters, or support rejecters, may grieve longer than those who cash in on promised help (Sprang, McNeil, & Wright, 1993). Some friendships have been strained after a friend scolds a mourner, "You have to move on! He's dead." "That's easy for you to say" one widow cut off a friend, "*Your* husband is still alive."

Misunderstandings arise between friends when promises to help are tied to advice. Some friends link continued assistance with favorable response to their advice. When Myra's husband of forty years died unexpectedly, with minimal estate planning, one friend stepped forward saying, "Just leave everything to me." Myra dropped tidbits about the friend's helpfulness into conversations with other friends, "I do not know what I would do without George's help." When another friend wanted to question the wisdom of the advice because of potential tax consequences, a friend counseled, "Stay out of this! Myra did not ask you for help." Over time, George's counsel proved financially disastrous for Myra. The friend who did not step in, feels that he failed both his deceased friend and Myra by not getting involved or, at least, offering alternatives for her to consider.

Assistance is subject to misinterpretation and comment by others in the friendorbit. The level of assistance can create tension, jealousy, and antagonism between friends, particularly if support becomes something of a competition to see who can do the most for the griever. How much assistance is enough to fulfill the promises? One wife complains,

> Yes, we made some promises to Curt before he died: We'd be there for her. I admit we made some promises to Karen at the funeral home: We'll be here for you. But she has gone overboard. It has been three years since Curt died and she is *still* in mourning! If she has a plumbing problem, does she call a plumber, one of her grown sons, or my husband? Every time it's my husband. It's not like she cannot afford a plumber. Curt left her well off. Lately, I feel like anything but a friend. My husband has neglected things that needed to be done in our home to run over there for some drippy faucet. And then she starts crying and telling him how lonely she is. Why doesn't she call her sons? She is taking advantage of our friendship, but I cannot get Carl to see that!

Some grievers seem so self-sufficient that it is difficult for friends to believe they need help. Moreover, requests for help may become troublesome if the widow/er begins dating or becomes romantically involved, prematurely in the opinion of some friends.

ETHNIC PERCEPTIONS OF HELPFULNESS
BY FRIENDS

Helpfulness and assistance are subject to perception. Barrett (1998) notes that the social norm among blacks is not only to prepare food, but to offer money and resources. Given the tendency for blacks to delay rituals until the entire family can gather, the period between death and the services may be a week or more; thus, there is a longer period in which to offer assistance. Those individuals "who provide personal assistance are held in high regard by survivors" (p. 92).

For many conservative blacks, assistance is an unspoken expectation based on the teachings of the Bible; helpfulness is perceived as a religious obligation as well as an act of friendship. Barrett (1998) concludes, "The more personal the sacrifice, the higher the regard for the offering" (p. 92). Black grievers would seldom protest "Oh, don't go to any trouble." One elderly widow observes, "During your time of sorrow you discover who your true friends are." Barnett (1998) adds that friendships

> are often dramatically redefined according to one's participation and conduct during a time of loss and grief. Those who respond appropriately, according to normative expectations, are gathered closer and regarded highly, and those who fail to respond appropriately are often regarded as losses—additional losses to mourn and grieve (p. 93).

Windows of opportunity for friends to offer assistance are extended among Japanese-Americans because of the tradition of forty-nine days of grief work. This lengthy period of formal mourning not only gives time to "install both the living and the dead into their new status" but also gives the community time to provide social support (Klass & Goss, 1998, p. 15). Rarely during these seven weeks are grievers left alone. NonAsians might be amazed that friends could be expected to provide assistance over such a lengthy period. On the other hand, this extended period provides opportunities for assistance by friends who could not initially offer support.

In an Islamic framework, friends do not respond from a convenience mode but from a need mode. In Islamic tradition, friends and other family members never leave the chief mourner alone. Individuals take turns bringing food and staying overnight (Raad, 1998). Raad notes that when she lived in Afghanistan she resisted these customs. However, after her husband's death, as friends and relatives surrounded her, "I realized how much this tradition meant" (p. 55) to the friendgrievers as well as the recipients.

FRIENDS TOUCH

The early Christians, in a radical departure from their contemporaries' stigmatization of the corpse, showed no fear of contamination, particularly by touching or kissing (Davies, 1986). To discount the superstitions associated with the dead, at the close of the burial rite, following the bishop's example, friends kissed the corpse. The practice was based on the Christian admonition, "Greet one another with a holy kiss" (2 Corinthians 13: 12, NIV).

> The greeting that Christians regularly exchange among themselves was now shared with the deceased, a fitting sign of communion between the living and the dead Christian. Although this kiss was a final gesture toward the body, he [Pseudo-Dionysius] insisted that it was not a "farewell," for life in Christ knows no farewell (Rutherford, 1980, p. 24).

MEMORIES OF TOUCH

Some friends have memories of touching/kissing a corpse or of seeing others do so; the memory becomes something of a permission. Tammeus (1998) recalls attending a funeral as a child and watching his maternal grandmother pat the neatly folded hands of her friend (Tammeus' paternal grandmother) in the casket.

For some patting, touching or kissing a friend's corpse helps confront the reality of the death (Wolfelt, 1994). Rupp (1988), as a friend, highly values touch. "We cannot pray the ache out of one another but we can bless it with the touch of our hands, the gift of our hug and our embrace. When we do this, we give the ache in the other the permission to go on its way" (p. 91). Rupp adds, "Touch can penetrate barriers of despair, anguish, hardness or bitterness. A kiss on the cheek, a quiet embrace, arms linked or hands held are powerful movements in our ritualization of goodbyes" (p. 91). Risberg and McCullough (1989) comment on touch:

> One of the times in our lives when we need touch is when we're grieving. Touch that is given in comfort is one of the most allowed kinds. The value of touch to the grieving person can't be measured and we all know how it can relieve despair, depression, and the feelings of loneliness and isolation that accompany grief (as cited in Shaw, 1994, p. 162).

For many grieving friends, touch is something of an emotional shorthand, especially when one does not know what to say. A "window of permission" seems to exist informally. Lipson, Dibble, and Minarik (1996) remind that ethnic groups have norms governing who should touch and how they should touch. For example, a friend standing too close may offend a griever, while acting out the formal, "stiff upper lip" approach can offend others.

If this society is conflicted about grief, it is increasingly confused by touch. Particularly is this true among males. Some adults are aggressive touchers while others are resisters who prefer to select who touches them and under what circumstances. Still in times of grief, individuals who would not ordinarily hug, do so. Eleanor Roosevelt hugged her friend, now-President Truman and called him by his first name, Harry. Although a breech of protocol, it was acceptable.

FOLLOW THE GRIEVER'S LEAD

The dilemma over touch arises in funeral rituals. Should a friend touch, hug, shake hands, touch the arm, or pat the hand? Inappropriate touch may interfere with grief work. Some friends have found the healthy norm to watch the chief mourner for signaled guidance. Apple (1992) describes his experience receiving healthy touch from a friend,

> When trying to respond to a friend who has suffered a loss, perhaps the first thing to remember is this—when grief is fresh, the less said, the better. There is a grief that is felt so deeply that words cannot touch. I remember placing my head on a shoulder of a friend and saying, "It's over. He is dead and I feel like turning out the lights and going home . . . nothing else matters . . . it's over." All my friend did was to hold me and let me cry on his shoulder. He had no words, he had no scriptures to quote to me, he just held me and let me cry. It meant a lot (p. 7A).

Another describes witnessing the power of touch among a group of young friends:

> It was cold that February day, and a slight breeze caused the tent flaps to move. The young men, most of whom would have felt more at ease shooting baskets in someone's driveway had now carried out their responsibilities. They had carried their pal to his final resting place. Now all that remained of the committal service was for these lanky young men, some in ill-fitting suits, to walk by the casket and place their white boutonnieres on the lid. They fought hard for control, aware of all the eyes focused on them. They were just boys trying to make sense of their first encounter with death of a peer. The first pallbearer slowly placed the flower on the casket then hesitated to move away. Their friend's father stood to thank him. Suddenly, the boy burst into tears and grabbed his best friend's father, wrapping his arms tightly around him. Immediately, those young friends gave up their fight to be brave and reached out to embrace their friend's father. And each other.
> There was no way you could have pried them loose. No one dared look away at such vulnerability. In the awfulness of this boy's death, the beauty of this moment offered the first ray of hope that sad

Saturday. "He loved you guys" the father said over and over. "He really loved you." How long did the hugs last? Probably not long enough. Eventually they broke the hug, straightened their jackets, wiped their eyes, and walked to the limousine. Their last gifts as friends was a simple prolonged hug to a grieving dad. Although friends, they could not hug each other. They needed the father to make it possible for them to hug each other. Most of us who witnessed the rare display of intimacy, walked to our cars convinced we had seen one redeeming moment in what otherwise was one sorry, sad day.

With some grievers, even friends need to seek permission to step into a touch zone. "Would it be all right if I gave you a hug?" Coffin (1997) has learned to recognize the power of touch, whether a hug or a squeezed hand. "That's why immediately after such a tragedy people must come to your rescue, people who only want to hold your hand, not to quote anybody or even say anything . . ." (cited in Theroux, p. 345).

THE FRIEND VALIDATES

Preoccupation with the stages of grief has led to something of an obsession for "doing" grief correctly, particularly via Kübler-Ross' "stages of grief." Moreover, friends who have not had personal losses, have little understanding of how long grief can last (De Loach, 1981). Still friends analyze the grief behaviors and comment on choices grieving friends make. Walter (1999) argues that the shift to privatizing grief, although considered a liberation or deregulation, "leaves mourners without guidelines and in a state of anomie" (p. 131). Repeatedly, friends, in an attempt to comfort, offer some rendition of the five stages of grief, implying, "You should. . . ." As a result, many want "validation of one's chosen style of grieving by one's chosen friends" (p. 131). Different friends in the same friendorbit may espouse different norms, which may lead to rifts at the very time co-grieving friends need support. Thus, some friends may be conflicted when their friend asks, "Do you think I am doing (or did) the right thing?" In fact, a friend may be bewildered and want to say, "I don't know what I would do if I were in your shoes."

Moreover, given the number of decisions that must be made concerning funeral rituals particularly for the unexpected death, grievers may reassess decisions. Thus, they ask friends, "Do you think I spent too much?" or "Should I have spent more?" Honest friends may have to answer, "You did the best you could at the time" or "considering the circumstances." Friends can validate by giving grievers permission to revisit decisions.

One gift to a friendorbit is giving permission to grieve or, at times, to offer alternatives to the map of grief. In many cases, the griever may be asking for someone to listen. A Vermont proverb offers friendgrievers wise counsel, "Talk less and say more." Kolf (1999) reminds friends, "Whether you agree with the methods chosen to express this closure is unimportant. You are not supporting the rituals or the system; you are supporting the grieving people who are left behind" (pp. 52-53). Sometimes friends validate best by saying, "Whatever you do, I will be here for you."

Walter (1999) notes that people may seek validation not just for decisions but for experience, such as sensing the presence of the dead. He notes that some women who have this experience report having "confided in, hesitantly," to a woman friend, "You don't think I am going crazy, do you?" Validation will be influenced by the friend's understanding of continuing bonds.

The friend's ability to fit this grief experience into a long friendship, gives them a vantage point to offer validation. Just as Hoffman (1988) theorizes that a therapist can be something of a "friendly editor" to a client's emerging grief narrative, so a friend can also fill something of that function. Clearly, "the experience of the individual now becomes authoritative in a de-spiritualized, de-ritualized, de-socialized understanding of bereavement" (p. 187). In the absence of the clear "this is the way it should be done" guidelines, the friend has a chance to validate or invalidate choices not just in the immediate ritualizing, but hopefully, over the long integration of a loss into a life story. More than once I have reassured friends, "You are not losing your mind. You are grieving!"

KEY CONCEPTS OF THIS CHAPTER

- Friends promise future assistance.
- Friends touch. However touch is subject to interpretation.
- Friends validate chief mourners and other friends.

IMPLICATIONS FOR CLINICIANS

1. Friends may regret that they were not more helpful at the time of the funeral. The clinician may ask, "What could you do *now* that would be helpful?"

2. Friends tend to store pain and grief somewhere in the body. Some friendgrievers have also found getting a massage to be enormously helpful. An experienced body worker responds to that localizing of pain.

3. I suspect that an absence of validation by friends, or an absence of validity, leads some mourners to seek out therapists as what Yager (1999) calls "safe 'friend'." In fact, clinicians "offer an objectivity and skill that even the best of friends might be unable to provide" (p. 207). If others are not validating grief for a friend, the clinician can offer a "friendly" environment in which to explore the ramifications of the loss.

CHAPTER 13

Remembering Friends

PREVIEW

The fear of being forgotten may be universal among humans, particularly among the childless. Remembering is an important act by a friend. Memory cannot be disenfranchised. Some friendorbits have the equivalent of the official "rememberer." It is important for friends to remember realistically. Some friends will need a clinician's assistance in order to develop a cherishable memory. The clinician may not only give permission to remember, but also suggest creative ways to remember.

> When near your death a friend
> Asked what he could do,
> "Remember me," you said.
> We will remember you (Thomas Gunn, 1992, p. 76).

> As long as we remember, we are all together (Lynn Kelly, 2000, p. 9).

On numerous Civil War monuments in Northern and Southern town squares and cemeteries, in slightly different wording, I find the carved sentiment, "lest we forget." "Honoring and remembrance of the dead is an essential part of closing for the ones left behind" (Menten, 1991, p. 99). The fear of being forgotten may be universal. I have few friends who are afraid of dying but I have some who are afraid of being forgotten. When I spend time with dying friends, I make this promise: I will never forget you, and I will find a creative way to remember you and our friendship.

Remembering has been a particular issue when friends have died from devastating illnesses, especially those with disfigurement such as AIDS or cancer. Some friends avoid going to see an ill friend and insist, "I want to remember her as she *used* to be—not as she was at the end."

How do friends deal with the continual losses? I remember asking one person well-acquainted with death, "How do you cope?" He answered, "I cry a lot, and I do things to remember *each* one." What is true of friends grieving multiple losses, is true of other friendgrievers, too. Friends do psychological damage to themselves and to others in the friendorbit by not remembering; friends enfranchise their own grief when they remember to remember.

INTENTIONAL REMEMBERING ALLOWS
FRIENDS TO HEAL THOROUGHLY

"Healing does not mean I will forget. Actually, it means I will remember. Gently, I will move forward, never forgetting my past" (Wolfelt, 1997, p. 47) or those friends who have populated my past. After President William McKinley was assassinated in 1903, friends in his hometown of Canton, Ohio, clung to words from an editorial penned by a friend: "Memory is the dearest friend now . . ." (Historical plaque, outside *The Repository,* Canton, Ohio). I appreciated this tribute that appeared in *The San Francisco Chronicle.*

> Wilson, Patricia—May 27, 1998, on her birthday. . . .
> She leaves an uncountable number of friends, who together with her family will forever remember her loving heart and the open door to her home (Wilson, 1998, p. D7).

For some "forever remember" is a transitional cliche; for others, an agenda. Silverman (2000, July/August) captures the remembering of her friend, "Mara, I have let you go, but I will miss you always" (p. 8). This culture aggressively discourages "forever" remembering and only grudgingly tolerates transitional remembering. One father decided to have a gathering of the friends of his adolescent son several months after the young man committed suicide. About thirty minutes into it, a participant's father appeared on his doorstep to take his daughter home. He scolded the father, "I wish you would just let this go. These kids need to just get over it and move on with their lives." To many friends, the advice "Best not to dwell on it," however well-meaning, translates "forget!" But if I forget this friend, others will forget me after I have died.

ENFRANCHISING ACTIVE REMEMBERING

Some friends enfranchise active remembering by becoming something of the official "rememberer" in the friendorbit. Lorena Hickok wrote Eleanor Roosevelt after the death of their mutual friend, Tommy Thompson, "You will miss Tommy, as we all will daily for she did so much for those she loved. Nevertheless we will all be happier for her constant memory" (Streitmatter, 1998, p. 281). Carnes (1979) encourages constant remembering: "The dead are not dead if we have loved them truly. In our own lives we give them immortality" (cited in Searle, 2000, p. 38). By being careful stewards of the memories of a friend, you create the possibility that other friends might be "healed by your witness to such a thing" (Benson, 1998, p. 46).

Remembering brings the friend back into our life just as slipping a disk into a computer, returns old writing to a computer screen. Active remembering can be as simple as enjoying a meal and pausing to say, "You know, Mike would have loved this restaurant" especially if a friend ups the memory ante: "Yes, he would . . . do you remember that greasy spoon he loved to drag us to?" "Do I remember? How could I forget?" On some days, I simply offer hospitality to a memory of a friend that has wandered into my consciousness rather than snarl, "Scat!"

In a "here today, gone tomorrow" culture, many die wondering, will my friends—*these* friends in whom I have invested so deeply—remember me? Senak (1998) has prepared wills for many adults who are the sole survivors of what were once particularly tight-knit friendorbits. Such individuals, before dying, lament the loss of a friend to remember the stories of those friendships. So, who in your friendorbit will survive to honor your memory and tell your stories?

One impressive war memorial can be found at Christ Church, Oxford University. Carved in the walls of the entranceway are long rows of names of students summoned for the front lines in France. When war broke out in 1914, many assumed victory would be in hand by Christmas, only months away. That expectation vanished as the British Expedition Force was struck with staggering losses. Entire friendorbits were imploded in the brutality of those early days of World War I. England's finest poets were enlisted to write poetry for the grieving. There was no time to wait for books to be published; newspapers included poetry in the long casualty lists. Laurence Binyon's poems were particularly valued by friendgrievers. Decades later, browsing in a used bookstore, I discovered his writing and recognized a fellow friendgriever with whom I share a mutual vocabulary of loss. Friendgrievers can "piggy-back" on such poems as this:

They shall not grow old, as we that are left grow old.
Age shall not weary them, nor the years condemn.
At the going down of the sun and in the morning
We will remember them (Lawrence Binyon as cited in Partington,
1992, p. 109).

Few veterans of World War I are alive to remember their friends; but, in a sense, the walls at Oxford and other such memorials remember. The active remembering is what amazes me about Memorial Day and Veteran's Day ceremonies. These ceremonies offer many males a sanctioned moment to remember their friends and their courageous exploits on the battlefield and, I suspect, off the battlefield as well. Certainly, Day of the Dead for Hispanics, and Chinese New Year for Chinese, as well as All Saint's and All Soul's Day offer moments to remember. If only that permission could be extended across this society to all friends.

Rando (1992-93) addresses this fear of being forgotten in her list of processes of mourning necessary for healthy accommodation of a loss. One important task in reconciliation is to "recollect and reexperience the deceased and the relationship" (p. 45). Friendgrievers intentionally, aggressively remember—sometimes, in the words of the courtroom oath, "the truth, the whole truth and nothing but the truth." Other friends are so locked into honoring the cultural admonition, "Speak no ill of the dead" that they, in effect, airbrush certain memories.

REMEMBERING THE ABSENCE

I attended a widow-friend's first dinner party. I had been in that home many times when her husband, Jack was alive. Throughout the evening, Jack's absence was everywhere. The next day in a thank you note, I mentioned that I had missed Jack and that it was an "absence called presence." My friend e-mailed me: "Thank you for mentioning Jack. I like the term 'an absence called presence.' I do experience a lot of that these days. I certainly missed his "guidance" when preparing Wednesday night's meal. He was generous with cooking advice after he retired."

Checking a footnote for this book, I discovered that the phrase was not mine. I do not recall having read the phrase in Cicero, but in Sullivan (1998) I discovered the source or, at least, an early wording of the sentiment, "and this is what we mean by friends: even when they are absent, they are with us. . . ." (p. 175). They are with us especially when we remember them. One woman remembers her dead friend by walking in the local walkathon for breast cancer research.

THE COMPONENTS OF REMEMBERING

Rando (1992-93) contends that healthy remembering has two goals: 1) to "review and remember realistically" and 2) to "revive and reexperience the old feelings" (p. 45). With some friends, I sense discomfort when I mention the name of a friend. Some have only grudgingly acknowledged the memory. One friend angrily demanded, "What good does remembering do? Why can't you let the dead be dead? Make some new friends!"

"REMEMBER ME"

It is easier to dance with the memories, then to invest energy trying not to remember. In the Grief Gatherings I facilitate, we extensively use collage-making techniques to stimulate the active remembering of participants so that they can begin to create what Dewey (1988) calls "a cherishable memory" (p. 132). Many friends find making a collage to be a wonderful way to sort through memory bytes to construct a cherishable memory of this friend. Healthy grief relies on revisiting places of importance, viewing photo albums or videos, or telling stories. I remind grievers that a friend is not gone until two things happen (both of which require decisions on the part of the friendgriever): 1) friends stop saying the name and 2) friends stop telling stories about the deceased. Something wonderful can happen when someone says, "Do you remember the time ____ . . . ?"

In the Christian scriptures read during the Eucharist, there is a strong admonition to remember. Jesus, instituting the Eucharist on the eve of his death, prodded friends, "And as often as you do this, remember me" (Paraphrase of 1 Corinthians 11: 24). The Greek tense is imperative: *remember me!* Jesus, facing death, had reason to fear that his friends might, in time, forget him; after all, one friend had already betrayed him. Thus those who practice the Christian religion, have a strong precedent for remembering. In some Hispanic funerals, a roll call of the dead takes place. Individuals call out a name of a deceased person and the friends respond, "presente" (which means present). During the naming, the intensity builds. Then when this latest friend's name is called out, the congregation loudly responds, "Presente!"

Along the corridors of memory, friends are present. We honor the memory of friends by emulating their lives (Johnson, 1999). After Liz Tilberis was diagnosed with cancer, her close friend, Princess Diana was a strong source of encouragement. Tilberis was rocked by Diana's death as well as the death of their mutual friend, Gianni Versace:

Not being a religious person, the only message I can take away from the violent and premature loss of such dear friends, and from facing my own mortality, is: Carpe diem. Seize the day. Diana and Gianni, two brilliant human beings in the prime of life, are gone, and I am thriving. I had imagined the princess attending *my* memorial service, and here I was, attending hers. I don't know how to resolve this conundrum, to make peace with these ridiculous facts, except to embrace the long life that she was denied (Tilberis, p. 282).

Wilcock (1996) through friending the dying concludes:

It may be especially important for people . . . to receive reassurance that they will never be forgotten, that the relationships they are part of here will have contributed to their friends' lives and personalities indelibly; the love they gave, the gift of themselves, is part of life here for ever, and can never be lost (p. 86).

In a "here today, gone tomorrow" world with disposable, toss-away products, many adults have disposable friendships; others never invest the energy to transition a "casual" friendship into a "close" friendship. Rubin places friends into two categories: "friends of the road" ("the people who pass through, whom you are not destined to know forever") who share particular times and places in our lives and "friends of the heart," (the friendships that "take root") (cited in Goodman & O'Brien, 2000, p. 80)—the friends who populate the boundaries between the world of the living and the world of the dead (Walter, 1999).

Two soldiers, initially friends of the road, became friends of the heart. Lewis Puller and Bob Kerrey, both severely wounded in Vietnam ended up in the same hospital. A friendship developed after Puller came to visit Kerrey and pointedly quizzed him about his pain. Puller eventually won the Pulitzer Prize for his Vietnam memoirs but after a prolonged battle with alcoholism and depression, Puller committed suicide. In an elegant eulogy Kerrey, then a U.S. Senator from Nebraska, addressed the need for remembering a friend:

You remind us of something else, dear friend, Lewis. You remind us that we should take a little time to do the important work of saving the lives of those we love. You didn't die of cancer or a heart attack or an automobile accident. You died because you did not feel your life was worth living.

It *was* worth living. I am angry at you for not seeing that, for leaving all of us behind to search without hope of finding the answer. But when the anger subsides, I must face this question: Could I have saved your life? Oh, I wish the answer were an easy no. I wish the word *yes* didn't float so stubbornly into view (cited in Theroux, 1997, p. 302).

REMEMBERING MAKES PAINFUL DEMANDS ON A FRIEND

Sullivan (1998) reveals that he had never cried "for the dozens of acquaintances who had died, the handful of friends I had mourned or resisted mourning" in what he terms "the plague years" (p. 24) early in the AIDS epidemic. Then, one night, watching *Nightline,* he listened intently as Senator Kerrey talked about life after Vietnam and after Puller's death.

> Kerrey grasped, because he had experienced, what it was to face extreme danger, and witness in the most graphic way possible the death of his closest friends and colleagues, only to come home and find those experiences denied or simply not understood. And as he spoke, I felt something break within me (Sullivan, p. 25).

The easy alternative to the pain of remembering is to forget and "move on" (or in this case to switch channels). But not remembering, avoiding the something-breaking-within-us moments, also has consequences. Kerrey, by modeling remembering in front of a large viewing audience, gave Sullivan and, no doubt, others, permission to remember. Clinicians also are permission-givers, especially by providing safe spaces for remembering. Sometimes, the right question opens the door to a memory that needs to be remembered.

WAYS TO REMEMBER

Friends can be good stewards of memory by being creative. Here are ways to remember.

- *Say* your friend's name aloud when telling a story or talking about her.
- *Attend* the rituals honoring your friend.
- *Adopt* one of your friend's charities. Loss of donors through death hurts great causes, institutions, and organizations. A donation— even if small—on the birth date or death date or Memorial Day or a religious holiday is a meaningful way to remember a friend.
- *Write* a note to the family with a specific anecdote about your friend. If you send a card, add a handwritten note with an "I will always remember the time, _____. . ." or "one thing that made _____ such a special friend was. . . ."
- *Plan* a post death ritual, such as a storytelling or reception or potluck dinner weeks or months after the death as a way to gather the

friendorbit and honor the grief. One friend threw a picnic-reunion on a friend's grave for the deceased's lifelong friends who came bearing flowers, old letters, balloons, and stories.

- *Journal* or write about your friend. Here are some starters:

  "I will never forget the time my friend. . . ."

  "One thing that made my friend so special to me was . . . ."

  "The best gift my friend gave me was _____."

  " __ and I never got tired of doing _____ together. . . ."

  "If my friend said it once, he said it a thousand times. . . ."

  "One word or phrase that captures my friend is _____."

- *Visit* the grave or scattering site on ordinary days as well as anniversaries.

- *Remember* the anniversary of the death with a card, letter, phone call to others in the friendorbit and to the family.

- *Compose* a doxology prayer or poem expressing gratitude for this friend.

- *Give* to a fund, help find a cure for the disease which claimed your friend. Write Members of Congress from your state or your friend's state urging adequate funding for research.

- *Include* friends in your will. Do not count on your family being generous or to follow through on verbal instructions. Put it in writing.

- *Honor* Memorial Day. Many consider this to be just the first day of summer rather than a day to remember. Make some time in the day to remember your friend.

- *Continue* a tradition initiated by a friend, such as a holiday barbecue, open house, or seasonal party.

- *Plant* or pay for the planting of a tree or bush in honor of your friend.

- *Visit* a favorite restaurant of your friend. If a full meal is too bittersweet, try a salad or dessert and coffee.

- *Adopt* one good habit of your friend.

- *Explore* your grief with a psychologist or counselor or in a support group.

- *Display* photos of your friend in your home and carry photos of your friend.

- *Prepare* your friend's recipes—even though it may not taste quite the same.

- *Pause* when you hear your friend's favorite song; request it on an oldies radio station.

- *Donate* a book or video (or money) in a field of your friend's interest to a library.

- *Buy* something in the name of your friend being sold by a community organization.

- *Before* you visit your friend's grave or scattering area, ask another friend who would like to go but does not want to go alone.
- *Toast* your friend on special occasions—even if you are alone.
- *Go* to a favorite place and celebrate the memory of your friend and the privilege of such a friendship.
- *Check-in* by phone or letter with some of your friends' friends.
- *Go ahead* and say what you were thinking: "_____, my friend, would have loved this" even if only to yourself.
- *Create* something of beauty in honor of your friend. The AIDS Quilt has become an incredible repository of memory and a model of healthy remembering of friends.
- *Honor* the life lesson(s) you learned from your friend.
- *Remember* friends who lose friends by sending a note, card, or phone call.
- *Recognize* variety in grief style. Some friends will choose to "get over with it" and get on with their own lives and are uninterested in healthly grieving. Remember this is how some in the friendorbit *choose* to grieve.
- *Offer* to assist with tasks related to settling the estate of your friend, particularly if the executor is from out of town. You honor your friend by making the executor's tasks a little easier.
- *Do* a good deed in the name of your friend.
- *Participate* in a l0K race or walk in honor of your friend or sponsor someone.
- *Compile* a scrapbook highlighting your friendship.
- *Remember* what your friend always said.
- *Have* a calligrapher take a favorite quotation of a friend and create a memory-in-ink.
- *Update* your will. If you do not have one, make one. Urge friends to have wills.
- *Write* a letter to the editor of the newspaper telling the city what a great friend you've lost.
- *Whenever* you start to say, "If only ___ could see me now" remember, maybe she can.
- *Light* a candle in a church or holy space in honor of your friend.
- *Place* an ornament on your Christmas tree in honor of your friend.
- *Make* copies of special photos for other friends.
- *Place* a memoriam notice on the anniversary of the death or on your friend's birthday.
- *Remember*: Your grief counts! So do what you need to do to grieve healthily.
- *Give* your friendgrief its voice.

IMPLICATIONS FOR CLINICIANS

The clinician is in unique position to encourage the surviving friend to remember actively. The clinician, as "an engaged witness" (Selwyn, 1998, p. 57) accompanies this friend on the road to reconciliation with the loss. In one sense, the clinician acts as a consultant to the griever.

1. In a culture that aggressively encourages "moving on," the friend may have not been encouraged or permitted to remember. The therapeutic relationship offers a safe place to remember—a rarity for some friends. Ask, "Who encourages you to remember? Who discourages you from remembering? How are you remembering your friend(s)?"

2. This culture has symbolized remembering friends with AIDS with a red ribbon; friends who have died with breast cancer may be remembered by a pink ribbon; the dead at Littleton, Colorado, are remembered with a silver and blue ribbon. The clinician may encourage a friend to create a ribbon as a way of remembering a particular friend or to find another creative way to remember.

3. Some friends remember through brief letters to the editor, although these may be more likely to be published if they are mailed soon after the death. The friend does not have to summarize the entire life, perhaps only a key memory. The letter can begin as "I was one of the many friends of the late . . . or I consider _____ to be my best friend." Ask the client to write such a letter, even if it is never submitted for publication. Ask the client to read the letter to you. Ask them to consider sharing it with others in the friendorbit.

4. It is important to remember realistically, which includes "the good, the bad, and the ugly." Sometimes friends collude to forget the negatives. For example, a friend—when drinking—could have been anything but friendly. Friends need to have a balanced memory. The clinician might initiate such an exploration by asking, "What are you *not* missing about your friend?" By giving light to a friend's shadow, a more cherishable memory may emerge.

CHAPTER 14

Conclusion: Anticipating the Recognition of Friendgrief

> I am a young man. . . . I have however, repeatedly experienced the bewilderment and disorientation of the loss of cherished friends in the most horrible of circumstances. Sometimes I feel like I have more friends in heaven than I do on earth. Grief has been an inescapable part of my life for over twenty years . . . . It became clear to me, not after the first tragedy, but after the second, and the third, the fourth, and the fifth, that there really is nowhere in "today's world" to "move on" to, exactly (Dunlap, 1999, September 15, p. 4).

How does a friend like Dunlap grieve in a culture that so enthusiastically privatizes grief around one clear expectation: moving on? How does any friend go against that cultural mandate in order to embrace grief, especially if others in the friendorbit deny, abandon, or mask their grief? How does an individual—particularly a grief-novice—do thorough griefwork for a friend? How does a friend sort through that which resembles grief for other friends in order to recognize the particulars of this friend's death?

In *Friendgrief* I advanced several key premises.

1. *Friendgrief is a far more common experience than professionals acknowledge.* Despite the widespread developments in thanatology, grief for friends meets Doka's (1989) classic criterion for disenfranchisement: "cannot be openly acknowledged, socially validated, or publicly mourned" (p. xv). Sklar and Hartley's assessment is still as telling as when penned in 1990:

> The hidden population of survivor-friends contains many who are at as high a risk for social, emotional, health, economic, and/or legal problems as are the more visible family members. Survivor-friends may carry a double burden and be at great risk: they may experience the social and emotional transformations at bereavement, while they

are forced to suffer the lack of institutional outlets which act as support for these transformations (p. 105).

2. *Friendgrievers must be enfranchised.* How can a griever be enfranchised to thoroughly engage a loss or string of losses? "With advancing age, all of us witness with increasing despair the deaths of our friends and contemporaries. Obligations to attend funerals become more frequent, and we are faced with personal proof of life expectancy statistics" (Carter, 1998, p. 81). Jimmy Carter used blunt talk that day at the Naval Academy addressing fellow members of the Class of 1946. But by raising the topic, Carter gave fellow alumni permission to miss classmates; almost 25 percent of the Class of 1946 have died (p. 81). Without such permission to grieve, few individuals can face a friend's absence at a class reunion or the hundreds of other ways we miss a friend's presence.

3. *Friendgrievers must acknowledge and verbalize their need for support.* To some, friendgrief is an admission of weakness: "If he went to pieces over a friend dying, what will he do when a family member dies?" In a culture that prizes the disposable and expendable, friends grieve without the benefit of formal recognition and risk having their grief discounted and dismissed with platitudes, sometimes by other friends in the social network. On the other hand, one person's courage to grieve may model the way for others.

4. *Friendgrievers must give grief its voice.* Lynch (2000), a funeral director observes, "More and more we are making up new liturgies to say good-bye" (p. 90); friends today can be innovative in expressing grief. Friends must sift through their grief vocabulary, perhaps auditioning words or phrases or creating new words and expressions as well as new rituals—to voice grief for this particular friend. By finding a voice through a ritual, friends own their grief. That insistence, witnessed by an outsider, may give others permission to grieve creatively for their friends. A *Kansas City Star* obituary announces a "remembrance and celebration of life" service to be held in a local park. What caught my attention were the words, "friends are encouraged to attend" (Adams, 2000, August 15, p. B4). What if obituaries and death notices contained these words, "friends are encouraged *to grieve*."

The decision not to have a public viewing impacts friends (McCormick, 2000, August); some develop friend-friendly alternative grief rituals. Clinicians must be aware of post-funeral activities that can provide venues for the friends to examine, express, and re-express their grief. Often the full reality of the absence does not begin to sink in as traditional rituals take place. The funeral or memorial service is a beginning point for friends not closure.

5. *Friendgrievers must integrate the losses into a restored narrative and a renewed commitment to friendship.* The death of a friend, particularly in certain developmental periods of adolescence or childhood or transitions such as down-sizing or divorce, is life shaping (Blieszner & Adams, 1992) and is a "milestone" (Cable et al., 2000). G. Silverman (2000, July/August) describes her out-of-sequence grief following a close friend's suicide: "At 25, we should not be planning a memorial service for a friend. There is little in our experience to guide us, and little in other sources for us to follow. There are no rituals for mourning friends, no ready-made readings that say what we need to say" (p. 6). Most friends live their way into reconciliation with the death of a friend, through delicate engagement with the grief and with the memories, although, as Silverman points out, some in the friendorbit resist thorough grief for a friend. Memory is an essential resource for reconstructing a friendorbit and integrating the loss. What does integration mean? P. Silverman (2000) explains:

> As friends move on with their lives, we see that, like other mourners, this loss has changed them. They carry with them a new appreciation and sensitivity for life, and their friend remains an important part of who they are. They learn to live with the paradox that their friends are gone, yet still live on (p. 185).

In preparing a eulogy, a friend quizzed me: "What should I say?" I suggested that she ask those present to promise to remember. Upwardly mobile individuals sometimes jettison friends and purge friendship rosters. A friend's spouse may remarry or in moving on allow certain friendships to lapse. Others maintain ties with selected friends. After President Kennedy's death, Mrs. Kennedy regularly invited his friends to dinner so that Caroline and John, Jr. could hear stories about their father (Andersen, 2000; Klein, 1998) narrated through the voices of his life long friends. Not only did the children benefit, but by acknowledging the grief of friends, she provided a safe place for them to integrate this significant loss which not only deprived them of a friend but altered their careers in public service.

The death of a friend must be stirred into the emotional batter of our lives. Ask friends who still grieve the deaths of buddies in Normandy, Korea, or Vietnam. Little surprise that the movie, *Saving Private Ryan* rebooted long silenced friendgrief in many veterans. In response to the film, *The Dallas Morning News* ran a editorial cartoon of two war-weary GIs, resting under a tree on a hill, overlooking a military cemetery. One soldier asks, "Willie. . . Y'think anyone'll remember us fifty years from now?" His compatriot answers, "Lord, Joe, I hope so" (DeOre, 1998,

August 2, p. 10J). The deaths of 291,557 military men and women in World War II (Neuharth, 1998, July 31, p. 13A)—and millions of civilians—produced epidemic friendgrief. Wars are a *tsumini,* a tidal wave, of friendgrief that shapes a culture and turns grievers into gatekeepers trying to control memories. In 1944, after the death of two friends, a pilot wrote his parents, "I'm afraid I was pretty much of a sissy about it cause I sat in my raft and sobbed for a while. It bothers me so very much. . . ." That airman, George Bush, penned the expectation of many who lose friends: "Perhaps as the days go by it will all change and I will be able to look upon it in a different light" (Bush, 1999, p. 51).

Saving Private Ryan and the anniversary commemorations unfroze grief that had for decades been zealously guarded. One spouse recounts her husband's response to the movie: "The only words spoken since the movie ended an hour ago were my husband's 'Welcome to my world'" (Bradley, 1998, July 29, p. 10A). "Welcome to my world" is equally true for senior adults in nursing homes, or for youth in America's inner cities grieving repeated deaths of friends from school violence, or for women whose friends die as a result of domestic violence or substance abuse. Many friendgrievers long to say to family members, other friends, and to clinicians, "Welcome to my world of friendgrief."

Few friends can integrate their loss(es) without assistance. Clinicians provide safe spaces for friendgrievers to audition words, to try out thoughts, and to have the words, the narratives, and the emotions witnessed and valued rather than analyzed or critiqued. Clinicians must offer not just professional competency but also hospitality, which shares the same Latin root as hospital and hospice (Owens, 1996). The clinician listens and by that act of hospitality, enfranchises the griever.

Clinicians help grievers "find an appropriate place" for the friend in their emotional lives—"a place that will enable them to go on living effectively in the world" (Worden, 1991, p. 17). Stories take time to unfold; unfortunately, time is a precarious, to-be-protected-at-all-costs commodity in this culture. So, sometimes, over coffee or a beer or while sharing flight time at 30,000 feet, a friendgriever recounts to a stranger what it is like to grieve for a friend. Not all friends talk but some journal, make scrapbooks, and tell the stories.

Who knows the shelf-life of one account? Disclosure enfranchises others to verbalize their griefs just as silence disenfranchises account-making. Roger Rosenblatt (1999, July 26), compared his grief for his friend John Kennedy, Jr., to that experienced by poet John Milton whose young Cambridge friend, Edward King, also died at sea. Milton's opening words in the poem, *Lycidas* gives evidence of multiple griefs for friends:

Yet once more, O ye laurels, and once more,
Ye myrtles brown, with ivy never sere,
I come to pluck your berries harsh and crude . . .
Bitter constraint and sad occasion dear
Compels me to disturb your season due:
For Lycidas is dead, dead 'ere his prime,
Young Lycidas, and hath not left his peer (Milton in Untermeyer,
1942, 1993, p. 447).

For some, this poem fragment can be the "starter" for constructing a grief script. Rudnick (cited in Jacobson, 1996, February-March) explains the urgency felt by many friends: "It's so hard to hold the losses in your mind. It is so overwhelming that if you ever really thought about it completely, I don't know how you would stop weeping" (p. 33). Imagine the experience for friends of John Kennedy Jr., three weeks after his death, when his best friend and executor Lee Radziwill died. How impoverished we would be if friendgrievers like Milton or Rosenblatt had "kept" their grief in their private thoughts. The clinician can use literary or contemporary narratives of friendgrief such as Pope, Bush, or others included in this book, to facilitate the storying. The next "Lycidias" may be written by a friendgriever in your practice or support group.

6. *Friendgrievers—especially the socially marginalized—must have their grief honored.* No one should be forced to the perimeter of caring in the community of grievers. Admittedly, in this text, I cite the experience of the well-known to illustrate friendgrief. In our media-centric age, norms and attitudes on grief and friendship are influenced by the public dissemination of the experience of celebrities, politicians, and athletes; many take their cues from celebrities. Many individuals eavesdrop on the grief of others and adapt behaviors when the need arises. Would individuals have placed flowers at John Kennedy Jr.'s condo door if they had not seen the outpouring of flowers for Princess Diana?

Nevertheless, from the fringe, some friendgrievers vigorously attempt to deny or limit the impact of a friend's death. AIDS has decimated the current generation of gay men at midlife and has led some men to numb-out because of their inability to deal with their grief roster (Isensee, 1991) just as many senior adults numb out their grief.

Little research has been done on non-AIDS related grief in gay men and lesbians (Martin & Doka, 2000); because of societal constraints, that grief has been largely marginalized. Woolwine (2000) and Boisvert (2000) contend that friendship is valued more within the gay community than among the majority of American heterosexuals. Thus it is difficult for some clinicians—and friends—to receive the grief of persons who are not like them. Yet an accurate assessment of the "ordeal" experienced by survivors of multiple losses "is inaccessible without hearing the intimate, real-life experiences of these survivors" (Nord, 1997, p. 3). Sullivan (1998) is blunt about marginalized friendgrief: "When I would tell my straight friends . . . or my work colleagues, or my family, they tried hard to sympathize. But something didn't compute. It was as if they sensed that the experience was slowly and profoundly alienating me from them" (p. 24). Sullivan adds, "There comes a point at which the experience goes so deep that it becomes almost futile to communicate it" (p. 24). Ironically, five decades ago, large numbers of returning G.I.s came to the same conclusion; some are the parents and grandparents of today's friendgrievers.

Some friendgrievers fall through the cracks in marginalized communities because an individual does not self-identify as a member, interact with others touched by a particular death, or because the grief is not recognized by family or other friends. For example, a woman who sexually partners with women but does not identify herself as a lesbian (Rankow, 1995) may go unsupported when grieving a lesbian friend who dies of breast cancer; the same is true of the closeted gay man with minimal contacts with the gay community. To grieve openly might raise questions.

When a new resident in a senior residence facility loses a newly-made friend, that grief may be challenged, "Why you hardly knew her!" Family dismiss rather than recognize grief resulting from a brief but intense friendship. Indeed, friendgrief may be a disproportional burden on the elderly. "The older you become, . . . the more likely it is that you will have to cope with the death of your friends" (Yager, 1999, p. 147). I failed to "hear" my mother as she repeatedly told me, "A whole lot of people are leaving here" until I leafed through her address book and found name after name crossed out. My mother's friendorbit had all but disappeared by the time she died. In her nursing home, residents' deaths went unacknowledged.

Some friends self-disenfranchise, "She was *only* a friend." One wonders about the impact of the deaths of 156 homeless people on the streets of San Francisco in 1998 ("Deaths of homeless increase on San Francisco streets," 1998, December 21, p. A9). Where does the homeless griever find social support following a street pal's death—probably not at a funeral or memorial service, in a private practice, or in a support group. The death of a drinking buddy or fellow resident in a homeless shelter may actually increase drinking and drug abuse; indeed, the loss of a shared partner in a daily routine organized around securing a bottle or a place to spend the night, may leave the friend at high risk for death (Wright, Jones, & Wright, 1999).

Who comforts staff members in support facilities who develop friendships—or friendly relationships—with participants and clients? Malone (1996) describes her experience with "frequent flyers," people, often without health insurance, who are heavy users of emergency rooms with whom nurses, over time, develop a friendship. When those individuals die, some degree of friendgrief results. Although many professionals are expected to reflect, "He was *only* a client or patient," the grief for a client-friend generally goes unrecognized.

7. *Friendgrief must be recognized by government, business, industry, the military and especially by those who work with the nation's young.* Among the young, the loss(es) of friends are so troubling, particularly those resulting from acts of violence. Even one death makes a significant erasure—especially if the friend was a pillar of support in a crisis or developmental transition. Isensee (1991) identifies the particular upheaval following the death of a "coming out" friend who offered support when family and other friends rejected; the same is true of the "war buddy" or the friend who was fiercely loyal during a messy divorce. The death of a lifelong "turn to" buddy is profoundly significant. One elderly woman when asked what she misses most about friends who have died, replies, "There is no one to call me Rosie anymore" (Wolpe, 1999, p. 5). Wolpe comments, "Her nickname was lost with the last of her friends. Her world had grown colder" (p. 5). Moreover, no one is left in Rosie's circle of friends to remember, or care, *how* she got her nickname.

Often only after—sometimes long after the death and the socially recognized window to express grief ends—does an individual begin to "recognize the role that a particular friendship has played in our life" (Michaelis, 1983, p. 9) or could have played over time. Only in a prolonged absence do we fully appreciate the presence. Discovery may come long after other friends have seemingly finished or abandoned their grief and now insist that we, too, move on.

In the closing days of the 1992 presidential campaign, George Bush, the incumbent, trailing Bill Clinton, energetically campaigned. On October 22, Bush's longtime friend Betty Liedtke died. The President describes the loss in campaign notes, "There goes another close friend, one that we love very, very much" (Bush, 1999, p. 570). When he informed aides that he would attend the funeral, close advisers protested that attendance would be imprudent at this critical stage of the campaign, and "Can't Barbara go?" The President finally ended the discussion, "No, this is our friend and it matters and it counts" (p. 570). The Bushes attended the funeral. George Bush honored his friendship and his friendgrief; Yager (1999) would say that he acknowledged the friend*shift*. Perhaps, in some distant day, an individual, learning of the incident in Bush's life, will rearrange her schedule to attend a friend's funeral.

Admittedly, the social and cultural gatekeepers—government, business, industry, and the military—who have opportunity to recognize and enfranchise through entitlements such as time off with pay, support services, or inheritance—close ranks against the recognition. Sklar (1991-92) argues this disenfranchisement reduces the possibility that friends will "make legal claims on a "family's" economic property" (p. 115) or siphon away support from the family. To too many cultural gatekeepers, friendgrief is an unwelcomed intrusion into the rights of the family. Functional funerals and the smooth settlements of estates are highly prized in this culture; friendships are not.

8. *Friendgrievers can be supported by clinicians in the process of good grieving.* Clinicians enfranchise the grief for friends by hearing out and validating the narrative of a friendship made, maintained, and lost. Clinicians help clients explore creative ways to continue the bonds of friendship. Sherman (1991) finds a narrow but essential difference between merely talking about a friend's death and telling the narrative of a friend's death, the latter far more emotionally engaging and comforting. When friendgrievers relate the essential facts of a friend's death, most people will, at least initially, politely listen. Few applaud a friendgriever's courage. Fortunate is the individual who reports, "My friend died . . ." and hears, "Tell me about your friend" or "How are you handling that loss?"

In Wendell Berry's novel, *Watch With Me,* after Nightlife gets an opportunity to tell friends his story of alienation, the narrator observes, "The others knew what he was talking about. They knew he was telling what it was to be him. And they were moved" (Berry, 1994, p. 207). Some clinicians know what the client is talking about and choose to be moved; others intensify the professional boundary.

9. *A process for communicating the core expectations of a friend during a time of grief must be developed for contemporary, multicultural society, particularly to protect friendgrievers from being drawn away from their grief by an agenda of helpfulness and distraction.* Traditional responses following a friend's death compose a socially sanctioned, core framework for the expression of manners and condolences by friends. However, every generation of friendgrievers must redefine and renew those responses. Friends participate in rituals to the degree defined and permitted by the chief mourner. Families and some professionals "implicitly assume that friends are there to support the bereaved family" (Vande Kemp, 1999, p. 363). Thus, friends can be so attentive to the grief of others that they dishonor their own grief. Maybe we need bumper stickers, "Real friends grieve." Friends must pay attention to their own

grief, even while offering what slain South American Bishop Oscar Romero called "acompanamiento" (Brett, 1988)—accompanying family and other friends on the grief pilgrimage.

10. *Friendgrievers are as entitled to grief as anyone.* A grieving friend has a right to expect support. Friendgrief is not the minor league of grief. Yager (1999) advices friends,

> It is pivotal that others recognize that you are in mourning for your departed friend, and that you are entitled to feeling grief and sadness the same as those who lose a spouse, parent, grandparent, or any other close relative. Friends grieve just like family members and relatives (p. 150).

The assessment of Sklar and Hartley (1990) is accurate: "The difficulties triggered by the death of a close friend may be as severe, and in some cases more severe, as those found in the loss of an immediate family member" (p. 104), a conclusion supported by Roberto and Stanis (1994).

Friendgrief is heightened by the mobility of the American public, the "lite" definitions of friendship, limited expectations of friends, and the prevalence of dysfunctional families. Many individuals enhance friendorbits by investing deliberately and energetically in friendships. Moreover, if the deceased was the magnet friend, the friendorbit may disintegrate, leaving the person jettisoned friendless or lost in grief.

The major barrier to the recognition of friendgrief is economic. This culture's "hyperfamilism" (Fishburn, 1991), or obsession with the family, makes family members "one another's affective property." Family members have "an automatic legal interest in one another's economic assets" (Sklar, 1991-92, p. 113); friends are blocked from inheriting. The notion that "Blood is thicker than water" motivates costly legal searches for some missing relative, third cousin, twice removed, in order to settle an estate, in effect, disowning the family of investment: friends. If friendgrief were to be socially recognized, and legally sanctioned, the historic inheritance patterns would be threatened. Liberalizing corporate policy to accommodate bereavement leave for grieving friends would impact corporate profitability. One clinician friend reminds me, "It all comes down to the money."

Professionals involved with death want a clear delineation between family and friends. At a friend's funeral I watched a highly dysfunctional family escorted to the front, while friends, who had been intimately woven into the fabric of the deceased's daily life during her illness— who, in fact, had become her family—were scattered across the chapel. Not once did the minister address the grieving friends or recognize their heroic care. All the focus was on the grieving family "who have been through so much." After sitting through that pained hour, I reread Sklar's (1991-92) assessment of the consequences of socially ignored friendgrief:

> Society does them "symbolic violence." It imposes the belief that only families grieve and forces them to submerge their sorrow, deny the validity of their emotions, forego significant public display, and watch as family members, many of whom are neither socially nor emotionally close to the deceased, are granted opportunities they are not (p. 110).

So, while the family ate fried chicken in the church fellowship hall, friends scattered, some to fast food meals eaten alone, others back to professional responsibilities. Life goes on.

In the stressed pace of contemporary life, Putnam (2000) argues that the sense of community is unraveling; one piece of evidence he points to is that Americans spend less time with friends than they did in previous generations. Moreover, with the development of death professionals who insist, "Leave everything to us," grieving friends, in some settings, have been turned into passive spectators or observers along the sidelines rather than active participants in the ritual dramas. Friends passively sign the guest book, listen to the music, the eulogy, and the sermon, then disperse—an almost totally spectator sequence. Little wonder that some friends conclude, why bother rearranging a schedule or being inconvenienced to attend?

S. Klein (1998) asserts that friends do not want to get on with their lives; they want to grieve, but are often uncertain of the script, and no one steps forth to offer explicit permission to grieve. Friends

> want to have a safe and comfortable place to talk about the person(s) who died. They do not necessarily want to move on and let go. They also want to spend time speaking with others who knew the deceased. . . . It seems that some people talk about the person who died in order to detach, while others speak of the dead in order to open a space inside them to house the feelings, thoughts, and memories of the person (p. 137).

Clinicians must find ways to help friendgrievers create internal and external spaces to grieve. The core task of clinicians, as well as those in the shared friendorbit, is to hear out a friend's narrative, to work to make meaning of the death, to offer insight as the griever works to realign the friendorbit, and, according to Dissanayake (1995), to find ways to "make special" in celebrating and remembering a friendship.

The clinician must be patient with the friendgrievers' meaning-making. Because friends have been turned away, ignored, or had their narratives and anxieties discounted, friendgrievers may be reluctant to share their grief narrative again and clinicians may only uncover the friendgrief some time into the counseling relationship. The act of hospitality "recognizes and welcomes the unfamiliarity of the stranger" (Owens, 1996, p. 34) and the stranger's experience. Something incredible may happen when a clinician says, "Tell me about your friend. . . ."

In order to work effectively and creatively with friendgrievers, the clinician must confront personal assumptions about friendship and grief which impact practice (Corey & Corey, 1998). Clients grieving for a friend often bring wonderful gifts and insights that will make clinicians more sensitive to and more creative with future friendgrievers, and may prove invaluable when clinicians become friendgrievers.

SCROOGE AS A FRIENDGRIEVER

As I complete this chapter, local dramatists are presenting Dickens' timeless story of Ebenezer Scrooge. I have enjoyed *A Christmas Carol* across the years, yet this time a careful examination of the text stunned me. Dickens' play is not solely about the stinginess of Scrooge. Like a submerged river, disenfranchised friendgrief—Scrooge's grief for his friend, Marley—(as well as his grief for his parents) flows through the production. Near the end of the play, I lean forward to hear a chastised Scrooge promise: "I will honor Christmas in my heart, and will try to keep it all the year. I will live in the past, the present, and the future. The spirit of all three shall strive within me. I will not shut out the lessons that they teach" (pp. 53-54).

In a moment of reflection, I alter Dickens' script:

- I will honor *friendgrief* in my heart . . .
- I will live in the past, the present, and the future . . .
- I will not shut out the lessons that *friendgrief* can teach.
- I will remember.

The only alternative to friendgrief is to avoid friendship and to keep everyone familiar strangers (Pogrebin, 1996). No one is immune from friendgrief, sooner or later it becomes a reality for everyone. But not everyone will be open to the lessons that friendgrief can teach.

As a grief educator and as a friendgriever, I keep re-embracing the hope Sklar (1991-92) verbalizes: "Institutions change, and within American society survivor-friends may in time come to occupy a visible, legitimate role" (p. 118). I so want words spoken two millennia ago, "Blessed are those who mourn, for they shall be comforted" (Matthew 6:4) to be true for *all* grievers.

Change does happen. In the first chapter, I lamented the absence of friendgrief in the literature. In the three years since that gathering, several new resources point to a growing awareness of friendgrief. Cook and Oltjenbruns (1998) significantly address the issue of friend death among adolescents and among adults. Grollman and Malikow's (1999) *Living When a Young Friend Commits Suicide* as well as the chapter, "Invisible Mourners: The Death of a Friend" in Silverman (1999) are valuable resources. Barasch's (1998) delightful children's book on friendgrief, *Old Friends* is a resource for both children and adults. A friend e-mailed me, "Check out *Friendshifts*" (Yager, 1999). Moreover, at the 2000 meeting of the Association for Death Education and Counseling a workshop, "Friendgrief—who cares?" (Smith & Klein, 2000) and a symposium, "Death of a friend—the hidden sorrow" (Cable et al., 2000) were offered. And the theme of the summer 2000 issue of *The Forum* was friendgrief.

By recognizing the grief for friends, clinicians help make Ascher's (1992) experience a reality for all who grieve: "I have been trying to make the best of grief and am just beginning to learn to allow grief to make the best of me!" (p. 98).

Friends need midwives as they reconstruct their lives; in time, because of the support they receive, they can become midwives to other friends. Clinicians are natural midwives who say: Your grief for a friend counts!

References

A brief life: An interview with Jonathan Pryce. (1994, March). *Premiere*, p. 82.

Abernathy, R. D. (1989). *And the walls came tumbling down*. New York: Harper and Row.

Adams, M. R. (2000, August 15). [Obituary]. *The Kansas City Star*, p. B-4.

Aguilar, I., & Wood, V. N. (1976). Therapy through a death ritual. *Social Work, 21*(1), 49-54.

Allen, G. (1989). *Friendship: Developing a sociological perspective*. Boulder, CO: Westview Press.

Alpert, B. (1997). *The love of friends: A celebration of women's friendship*. New York: Berkley Books.

Alty, A. (1995). Adjustment to bereavement and loss in older people. *Nursing Times, 91*(12), 35-36.

Ambrose, S. E. (1991). *Nixon: Volume Three: Ruin and recovery, 1973-1990*. New York: Simon & Schuster.

Ambrose, S. E. (1999). *Comrades: Brothers, fathers, heroes, sons, pals*. New York: Simon & Schuster.

An American satirist in Paris: An interview with David Sedaris. (2000, June). *Borders*, pp. 8-9.

Andersen, C. (1998). *The day Diana died*. New York: William Morrow.

Andersen, C. (2000). *The day John died*. New York: William Morrow.

Anderson, D. C. (1996, March 13). Dear Abby: Funeral processions due respect. *The Kansas City Star*, p. D-2.

Anderson, R. (1994, March 3). In A. E. Dean (Compiler). *Proud to be: Daily meditations for lesbians and gay men*. New York: Bantam.

Andriote, J. M. (1999). *Victory deferred: How AIDS changed gay life in America*. Chicago: University of Chicago Press.

Apple, D. (1992, February 1). Consoling a friend during tragedy. *The Olathe [Kansas] Daily News*, p. 7A.

Applewhite, A., Evans, W. R., III, & Frothingham, A. (Eds.). (1992). *And I quote*. New York: St. Martin's Press.

Aries, P. (1974). *The hour of our death* (P. M. Ranum, Trans.). Baltimore: Johns Hopkins University.

Aristotle. (1987). *The Nicomachean ethics* (J. E. C. Welldon, Trans.). Amherst, NY: Prometheus Books.

Arts, H. (1983). *With your whole soul: The Christian experience of God*. New York: Paulist Press.

Ascher, B. L. (1992). *Landscape without gravity: A memoir of grief*. Harrison, NY: Delphinum Books.

Attrell, L. (1996). Newberg, Oregon. *A personal letter to pallbearers*.

Atwell, R. R. (1987). From Augustine to Gregory the Great: An evaluation of the emergence of the doctrine of Purgatory. *Journal of Ecclesiastical History, 38*(2), 173-186.

Augustine. (1991). *Confessions* (H. Chadwick, Trans.). Oxford: Oxford University Press.

Austin, C. D., & McClelland, R. W. (1998). Writing: The maturing of ideas. *Families in Society: The Journal of Contemporary Human Services, 79*(6), 641-643.

Bacall, L. (1994). *Now*. New York: Knopf.

Badone, E. (1989). *The appointed hour: Death, worldview, and social change in Brittany*. Berkeley, CA: University of California Press.

Balk, D. E. (1991a). Death and adolescent bereavement: Current research and future directions. *Journal of Adolescent Research, 6*(1), 7-27.

Balk, D. E. (1991b). Sibling death, adolescent bereavement: Current research & future directions. *Journal of Adolescent Research, 6*(1), 7-27.

Banker, J. R. (1988). *Death in the community: Memorialization and confraternities in an Italian commune in the late middle ages*. Athens, GA: University of Georgia Press.

Barasch, L. (1998). *Old friends*. New York: Francis Foster Books/Farrar, Straus, & Giroux.

Barrett, J. (1999, March 16). A mother's mission. *Advocate*, pp. 20-38.

Barrett, R. (1994, October). Affirming and reclaiming African-American funeral rites. *The Director, 66*(10), pp. 36-40.

Barrett, R. K. (1998). Sociocultural considerations for working with blacks experiencing loss and grief. In K. J. Doka & J. D. Davidson (Eds.), *Living with grief: Who we are, How we grieve* (pp. 83-96). Philadelphia: Brunner/Mazel.

Barrett, R. K. (1999). *Celebrating the cultural tradition of black funeral rites*. Keynote, Association for Death Education and Counseling, San Antonio.

Barroso, J. (1997). Social support and long-term survivors of AIDS. *Western Journal of Nursing Research, 19*(5), 554-582.

Bartlett, J. (1855/1980). *Familiar quotations: A collection of passages, phrases and proverbs traced to their sources in ancient and modern literature*. E. M. Beck (Ed.). (15th. ed.). Boston: Little, Brown & Company.

Basilios IV, Archbishop of Jerusalem. (1991). Burial rites and practices. In A. S. Atiya (Ed.), *The Coptic encyclopedia* (Vol. 2, pp. 425-426). New York: Macmillan.

Bass, D. C. (2000). *Receiving the day: Christian practices for opening the gift of time*. San Francisco: Jossey-Bass.

Bastis, M. K. (1999). *Adapting traditional Buddhist meditation practices for the dying and bereaved*. Workshop presented at the Association for Death Education and Counseling, San Antonio, TX.

Baugher, R. (1998-99). Heavenly hurts: Surviving AIDS-related deaths and losses by Sandra Jacoby Klein. [A book review]. *Omega, 38*(1), 69-71.

Baxter, L. A. (1985). Accomplishing relationship disengagement. In S. Duck & D. Perlman (Eds.), *Understanding personal relationships* (pp. 243-265). London: Sage.

Bayly, A. F. (1961). Lord, Whose love through humble service. In B. Polman, M. K. Stulken, and J. R. Sydnor (Eds.), *Amazing grace: Hymn texts for devotional use* (p. 249). Louisville, KY: Westminster John Knox Press.

Bebe Rebozo, Nixon friend, dies at age 85. (1998, May 9). *The Kansas City Star*, p. A6.

Bennett, L., & Kelaher, M. (1993). Variables contributing to experiences of grief in HIV/AIDS health care professionals. *Journal of Community Psychology, 21*(3), 210-217.

Benson, R. (1998). *Living prayer*. New York: Tarcher/Putnam.

Berkeley, B. (1998, October 11). Judgement day. *The Washington Post Magazine*, pp. 10-29.

Berry, C. R., & Traeder, T. (1995). *Girlfriends: Invisable bonds, enduring ties*. Berkeley, CA.: Wildcat Canyon Press.

Berry, W. (1994). *Watch with me*. New York: Partheon.

Bessette sisters (1999, July 25). Hometown remembers Bessette sisters. *The Kansas City Star*, p. A17.

Bingham, S. (1989). *Passion and prejudice: A family memoir*. New York: Knopf.

Binyon, L. (1988). For the fallen. In A. Partington (Ed.), *The Oxford Dictionary of Quotations* (p. 109). New York: Oxford University Press.

Black, H. (1898/1999). *The art of being a good friend*. Manchester, NH: Sophia Institute Press.

Blakeman, K. (1988, April 22). Woman tells of evening before friends's slaying. *The Kansas City Times*, p. B-2.

Blieszner, R., & Adams, R. (1992). *Adult friendship*. Newbury Park, CA: Sage.

Boettner, L. (1984). Purgatory. In W. A. Elwell (Ed.), *Evangelical dictionary of theology* (p. 987). Grand Rapids, MI: Baker Book House.

Boisvert, D. L. (2000). *Out on holy ground: Meditations on gay men's spirituality*. Cleveland, OH: Pilgrim.

Boller, P. F., Jr. (1988). *Presidential wives*. New York: Oxford University Press.

Bono eulogies filled with sentiment, Wit. (1998, January 10). *The New Orleans Times-Picayune*, p. A12.

The book of common prayer and administration of the sacraments and other rites and ceremonies of the church. (1979). New York: Seabury Press.

Booth, L. (1995). Spirituality and the gay community. *Journal of Gay & Lesbian Social Services, 2*(1), 57-65.

Borlik, A. K. (1999, Winter/Spring). Plan would ensure small honor guard at funerals. *TAPS*, p. 3.

Boswell, J. (1980). *Christianity, social tolerance, & homosexuality*. Chicago: University of Chicago Press.

Bowers, S. P. (1999). Gender role identity and the caregiving experience of widowed men. *Sex Roles, 41*(9/10), 645-654.

Bowman, L. (1959). *The American funeral: A study in guilt, extravagance, and sublimity*. Washington, D.C.: Public Affairs Press.

Boyd, M. (1990). *Are your running with me, Jesus?: A spiritual companion for the 1990s*. Boston: Beacon.

Bradley, D. (1999, March 28). 'The Mayor of Independence' gets fond farewell from neighbors. *The Kansas City Star*, pp. B-1, B-2.

Bradley, M. (1998, July 29). Tears and thanks. [Letter to the editor.] *USA Today*, p. 10A.

Bragg, R. (1998, September 20). A flash in time is buried in Alabama. *The Dallas Morning News*, Section 4, p, 2.

Braun, M. L., & Berg, D. H. (1994). Meaning reconstruction in the experience of bereavement. *Death Studies, 18*(1), 105-109.

Brener, A. (1993). *Mourning & Mitzvah: A guided journal for walking the mourner's path through grief to healing*. Woodstock, VT: Jewish Lights.

Breslin, M. McS. (1998, March 22). Moods of funerals changing. *The Chicago Tribune*, Section 4, pp. 2-3.

Brett, D. W. (1988). *Murdered in Central America: The stories of eleven American missionaries*. Ann Arbor, Books on Demand.

Brokaw, T. (2000). *The greatest generation speaks: Letters and reflections*. New York: Random House.

Broner, E. M. (1994). *Mornings and mourning: A Kaddish journal*. San Francisco: HarperSan Francisco.

Broun, S. N. (1998). Understanding 'Post-AIDS Survivor Syndrome:' A record of personal experiences. *AIDS Patient Care and STDs, 12*(6), 481-488.

Brown, L. (Ed.). (1993). *The New Shorter Oxford English Dictionary on Historical Principles*. Volume 1: A-M. Oxford, England: Clarendon Press.

Brown, T. L. (1998). *The life and times of Ron Brown: A memoir by his daughter*. New York: William Morrow.

Burch, B. (1993). *On intimate terms: The psychology of difference in lesbian relationships*. Urbana, IL: University of Illinois Press.

Bureau of the Census. (1998). *Statistical abstract of the United States: 1998*. Washington, D.C.: U.S. Government Printing Office.

Bush, G. H. (1999). *All the best: My life in letters and other writings*. New York: Scribner.

Cable, D. G., Doka, K. J., Heflin-Wells, N., Martin, T. L, Nichols, Pine, V. R., Redmond, L. M., Sanders, C., & Schachter, S. R. (2000). *Death of a friend, The hidden sorrow*. Workshop at The Association for Death Education and Counseling, Charlotte, North Carolina.

Caldwell, C., McGee, M., & Pryor, C. (1998). The sympathy card as cultural assessment of American attitudes toward death, bereavement and extending sympathy: A replicated study. *Omega, 37*(2), 121-132.

Caltagirone, C. L. (1988). *Friendship as sacrament*. New York: Alba House.

Cannon, A. (1995, November 11). Arlington Ladies' family is wide. *The Charlotte Observer*, p. 2A.

Carlson, M. (1996, April 22). Washington diary: Grief analysis. *Time*, p. 24.

Carlson, M. (1999, August 2). Farewell, John. *Time*, pp. 30-35.

Carmack, B. J. (1992). Balancing engagement/detachment in AIDS-related multiple loss. *Image: Journal of Nursing Scholarship, 24*(1), 9-14.

Carnes, P. (2000). Memorial service. In E. Searl (Ed.), *In Memoriam* (2nd ed., p. 38). Boston, MA: Skinner House Books.

Caroline, H. A. (1993). Explorations of close friendship: A concept analysis. *Archives of Psychiatric Nursing, 7*(4), 236-243.

Carroll, L. (1960). *Through the looking-glass.* New York: New American Library.

Carson, V. B. (1999). The grief experience: Life's losses and endings. In E. Arnold & K. U. Bogg (Eds.), *Interpersonal relationships: Professional communication skills for nurses* (3rd ed., pp. 169-194). Philadelphia: W. B. Saunders.

Carter, J. (1982). *Keeping faith: Memoirs of a president.* New York: Bantam.

Carter, J. (1998). *The virtue of aging.* New York: Ballentine.

Caspari, W. (1949). Burial. In S. McC. Jackson (Ed.), *The new Schaff-Herzon encyclopedia of religious knowledge* (Vol. 2, pp. 308-309). Grand Rapids, MI: Baker.

Chan, C. S. (1996). Cindy. In J. S. Weinstock & E. D. Rothblum (Eds.), *Lesbian friendships: For ourselves and others* (Ch. 20, pp. 266-271). New York: New York University Press.

Change of address? Less likely. (2000, July 12). *The Kansas City Star,* p. A6.

Chen, D. W. (1998, October 18). Taiwan's old soldiers forsaken in New York. *The New York Times,* pp. 1, 43.

'Children lying everywhere.' Two boys held in attack at Arkansas school. (1998, March 25). *The Kansas City Star,* pp. A-1, A-7.

Chin, F. K. (1995). The funeral in America: Chinese funeral traditions. *The American Funeral Director, 118*(11), pp. 50, 66.

Christ-Janer, A., Hughes, C. W., & Smith, C. S. (1980). *American hymns old and new.* New York: Columbia University Press.

Ciardiello, J. (1993, November/December). The writer's life. *New Age Journal,* pp. 82-85, 88-91.

Cicero. (1971). *On the good life* (M. Grant, Trans.). New York: Penguin.

Clark, D. (1997). *Loving someone gay* (rev. ed.). Berkeley, CA: Celestial Arts.

Clinton, B. (1996, April 10). *Remarks by the President in eulogy at the funeral of Secretary of Commerce Ron Brown.* Washington, D.C.: The White House Office of the Press Secretary.

Clinton, B. (1998). Introduction. In Brown, T. L. (1998). *The life and times of Ron Brown: A memoir by his daughter* (pp. xiii-xv). New York: William Morrow.

Close, H. T. (1969). A funeral service. *Voices, 1,* 82-83.

Cochran, M. M. (1998). Reflections: Tears have no color. *American Journal of Nursing, 98*(6), 53.

Coffin, H. S. (1997). Alex's death. In P. Theroux (Ed.), *The book of eulogies* (pp. 344-347). New York: Scribner.

Cohen, M. Z. (1995). The meaning of cancer and oncology nursing: Link to effective care. *Seminars in Oncology Nursing, 11*(1), 59-67.

Collinson, P. (1992). The late medieval church and its reformation. In J. McManners (Ed.), *The Oxford illustrated history of Christianity* (Ch 7: pp. 233-266). New York: Oxford University Press.

Combe, V. (1999, June 30, p. 9). World pays tribute to Father Basil. (London) *Weekly Telegraph*, p. 9.

Conlon, J. (1998). *Ponderings from the precipice: Soulwork for a new millennium*. Leavenworth, KS: Forest of Peace Publishing.

Cook, A. S., & Oltjenbruns, K. A. (1998). *Dying and grieving: Life span and family perspectives* (2nd ed.). Fort Worth, TX: Harcourt Brace College Publishers.

Corey, M. S., & Corey, G. (1998). Becoming a helper (3rd ed.). Pacific Grove, CA: Brooks/Cole Publishing.

Corr, C. A. (1998-99). Disenfranchising the concept of disenfranchised grief. *Omega, 38*(1), 1-20.

Corr, C. A., Nabe, C. M., & Corr, D. M. (1997). *Death & dying, life & living* (2nd ed.). Pacific Grove, CA: Brooks/Cole.

Crayton, R. (1998, May 12). Friends remember slain man at vigil. *The Kansas City Star*, p. B5.

Cremation. It's all a matter of choice. [Ad]. (1997, March). *The Southern Funeral Director*, p. 3.

Cronin, X. A. (1996). *Grave exodus: Tending to our dead in the 21st century*. New York: Barricade Books.

Cross, F. L., & Livingstone, E. A. (1974). *The Oxford dictionary of the Christian church*. (2nd ed.). New York: Oxford University Press.

Culbertson, P. (1992). *New Adam: The future of male spirituality*. Minneapolis, MN: Fortress.

Daniels, S. (1996, February). Wirthlin study tracks consumer attitude trends. *The Director, 68*(2), pp. 6-8, 30-31.

Dansforth, L. M. (1982). *The rituals of ancient Greece*. Princeton, NJ: Princeton University Press.

Davies, H. (1970/1996). *Worship & theology in England*. Book I, Volume I: *From Cranmer to Hooker, 1534-1603*. Grand Rapids: Eerdmans.

Davies, H. (1962/1996). *Worship & theology in England*. Book II, Volume IV: *From Newman to Martineau, 1850-1900*. Grand Rapids: Eerdmans.

Davies, J. G. (1986). Burial: The early church. In J. G. Davies (Ed.), *The new Westminister dictionary of liturgy and worship* (p. 117). Philadelphia: Westminister.

Davies, R., & Rupp, G. (1965). *A history of the Methodist Church in Great Britain*. (Volume 1). London: Epworth Press.

Dean, E. T., Jr. (1997). *Shook over hell: Post-traumatic stress, Vietnam, and the Civil War*. Cambridge, MA: Harvard University Press.

Deaths of homeless increase on San Francisco streets. (1998, December 21). *The Kansas City Star*, p. A9.

Deck, E. S., & Folta, J. R. (1989). The friend-griever. In K. J. Doka (Ed.), *Disenfranchised grief: Recognizing hidden sorrow* (pp. 77-89). Lexington, MA: Lexington Books.

DelBene, R., with Montgomery, M., & Montgomery, H. (1991). *From the heart*. Nashville, TN: Upper Room Books.

De Loach, M. T. (1981). *Ministry to the elderly recently bereaved widows and widowers in a local congregation*. Unpublished doctoral dissertation/project, San Francisco Theological Seminary.

DeOre, B. (1998, August 2). Saving the memories. *The Dallas Morning News*, p. 10J.

de Paula, T., Lagana, K., & Gonzalez-Raminez, L. (1996). Mexican Americans. In J. G. Lipson, S. L. Dibble, & P. A. Minarik (Eds.), *Culture & nursing: A pocket guide* (Chap. 20, pp. 203-221). San Francisco: UCSF Nursing Press.

DeSpelder, L. A., & Stickland, A. L. (1996). *The last dance: Encountering death and dying* (4th ed.). Mountain View, CA: Mayfield Publishing.

Devore, W. (1990). The experience of death: A Black perspective. In J. K. Parry (Ed.), *Social work practice with the terminally ill: A transcultural perspective* (pp. 100-107). Springfield, IL: Charles C. Thomas.

Dewey, D., III. (1988). When a congregation cares: Organizing ministry to the bereaved. *Death Studies, 12*(2), 123-135.

Di Bernardino, A. (Ed.). (1992). *Encyclopedia of the early church* (Vol. 1) (A. Walford, Trans.). New York: Oxford University Press.

Dickens, C. (1843/1990). *A Christmas carol*. New York: Random House.

Dillard, A. (1999). *For the time being*. New York: Knopf.

Dissanayake, E. (1995). *Homo aestheticus*. Seattle, WA: University of Washington Press.

Doctor is convicted of killing friend in 1976. (1997, October 23). *The Kansas City Star*, p. A-2.

Doka, K. (1989). Disenfranchised grief. In K. Doka (Ed.), *Disenfranchised grief: Recognizing hidden sorrow* (pp. 3-11). Lexington, MA: Lexington Books.

Doka, K. J. (1998). Who we are, How we grieve. In K. J. Doka & J. D. Davidson (Eds.), *Living with grief: Who we are, How we grieve* (pp. 1-5). Philadelphia: Brunner/Mazel.

Doka, K. J., & Morgan, J. D. (Eds.). (1993). *Death & spirituality,* Death, value & meaning series, (Series Editor: J. D. Morgan). Amityville, NY: Baywood.

Doty, M. (1996). *Heaven's coast: A memoir*. New York: HarperCollins.

Driskill, M. J. (1998, November 9). [Obituary]. *The Kansas City Star*, p. B2.

Duncan, Dr. K. P. (1999, June 30). *The Times of London*, p. 24.

Dunlap, R. S. (1999, September 21). Letters: Response to grief. *Pacific Sun*, p. 4.

Dunlop, A. I. (1993). Burial. In D. F. Wright, D. C. Lachman, & D. E. Meek (Eds.), *Dictionary of Scottish church history & theology*. Downers Grove, IL: InterVarsity Press.

Earle, A. M. (1977). Death ritual in colonial New York. In C. O. Jackson (Vol. Ed.), *Contributions in family studies: Number 2. Passing: The vision of death in America*. Westport, CT: Greenwood Press.

Empereur, J. L. (1998). *Spiritual direction and the gay person*. New York Continuum.

Euster, G. L. (1991). Memorial contributions: Remembering the elderly deceased and supporting the bereaved. *Omega, 23*(3), 169-179.

Ex-Dodger executive Campanis dies. (1998, June 22). *The Kansas City Star*, p. C-1.

Family-placed death notices. (1998, April 1). *The Atlanta Constitution*, p. B7.

Fan, H., Conner, R. F., & Villarreal, L. P. (2000). *AIDS science and society* (3rd ed.). Sudbury, MA: Jones & Bartlett.

Farewell to the Mick. (1995, August 16). *The Kansas City Star*, p. A-1.

Farrell, W. (1975). *The liberated man, beyond masculinity*. New York: Random.

Fehr, B. (1996). *Friendship processes*. Thousand Oaks, CA: Sage.

Ferrell, R. (1994). *Harry S. Truman, a life*. Columbia, MO: The University of Missouri Press.

First funeral draws hundreds. (1999, April 24). *The Dallas Morning News*, p. 30A.

Fischer, C. S. (1982). What do we mean by "friend"? An inductive study? *Social Network, 3*(4), 287-306.

Fishburn, J. (1991). *Confronting the idolatry of family: A new vision for the household of God*. Nashville, TN: Abingdon Press.

Fisher, J. J. (1989, January 28). Aged cyclist meets his death on the highway. *The Kansas City Star*, p. C-8.

Fishman, M. (1990). Let me say good-bye. In V. R. Pine, O.S. Margolis, K. Doka, et al. (Eds.), *Unrecognized and unsanctioned grief: The nature and counseling of unacknowledged loss* (pp. 76-78). Springfield, IL: Charles C. Thomas.

Fitzgerald, H. (1994). *The mourning handbook: A complete guide for the bereaved*. New York: Simon & Schuster.

Foege, A., Huhn, M., & Hunter, R. (1995, September 21). Funeral for a friend. *Rolling Stone, 717*, 23-28.

Foley, D. P. (1980). The social psychological functions of the visitation. *Journal of Pastoral Counseling, 15*, 19-27.

Folta, J. R., & Deck, E. S. (1976). Grief, the funeral & the friend. In A.H. Kutscher (Ed.), *Acute grief and the funeral* (pp. 231-240). Springfield, IL: Charles C. Thomas.

Foster, D. (1999, April 24). In memory of John Tomlin. *The Denver Rocky Mountain News*, p. 4A.

Fox, K. L., & Miller, P. Z. (1992). *Seasons for celebration*. New York: Perigee Book.

Freed, L. E. (1998, May 3). [Obituary]. *Kansas City Star*, p. B-3.

Freeman, R. (1999). *Seminar on grief presented at Saint John Church-Baptist*, Chicago, Illinois on August 7, 1999.

Friends describe boys' parents as ordinary people. (1999, April 26). *The Dallas Morning News*, p. 10A.

Funeral: Last victim laid to rest. (1999, April 30). *The Kansas City Star*, p. A12.

The funeral rites of Cardinal George Basil Hume, Archbishop of Westminster. (1999, June 25). London, England.

Gaidies, M. (1999, July). The Columbine tragedy: Part III: The search for understanding and healing in the wake of tragedy. *The Director, 71*(7), p. 54.

Gallup International Institute. (1997). *Spiritual beliefs and the dying process: A report on a national survey conducted for the Nathan Cummings Foundation and Ftezer Institute.*

Gamino, L. A., Sewell, K. W., & Easterling, L. W. (1998). Scott & White grief study: An empirical test of predictors of intensified mourning. *Death Studies, 22,* 333-355.

Gandhi, M. K. (1965). In T. Merton (Ed.), *Gandhi on Non-Violence.* New York: New Directions.

Garrett, J. E. (1987). Multiple losses in older adults. *Journal of Gerontological Nursing, 13*(8), 8-12.

Gathering, Comprehensive. (1994). *"May the angels."* Chicago: GIA, p. 858.

Gaunt, W. (1971). *Turner.* London: Phaidon.

Geddes, G. E. (1981). *Welcome joy: Death in Puritan New England.* Ann Arbor, MI: University of Michigan Research Press.

George, A. R. (1986). Burial: Methodist. In J. G. Davies (Ed.), *The new Westminster dictionary of liturgy and worship* (p. 127). Philadelphia: Westminster.

Gerhardt, P. (1676/ 1994). Commit thou all thy griefs. In B. Polman, M. K. Stulken, & J. R. Syndron (Eds.), *Amazing grace: Hymn tests for devotional use* (pp. 44-45). Louisville, KY: Westminster/John Knox Press.

Gibbons, M. B. (1993). Listening to the lived experience of loss. *Pediatric Nursing, 19*(6), 597-599.

Gibbs, E. C. (1974). *A ministry to persons experiencing grief.* Unpublished D.Min. dissertation, San Francisco Theological Seminary.

Gilanshah, F. (1993). Islamic customs regarding death. In D. P. Irish, K. F. Lundquist, & V. J. Nelsen (Eds.), *Ethnic variations in dying, death, and grief* (Ch 10, pp. 137-144). Washington, D.C.: Taylor & Francis.

Glasse, C. (1989). *The concise encyclopedia of Islam.* San Francisco: Harper & Row.

Glasser, C. (1991). *Coming out to God: Prayers for lesbians and gay men, their families and friends.* Louisville, KY: Westminster/John Knox Press.

Goldberg, E., Comstock, G. W., & Harlow, S. D. (1988). Emotional problems and widowhood. *Journal of Gerontology, 43*(4), S206-S208.

Goldberg, H. (1979). *The new male: From self-destruction to self-care.* New York: William Morrow.

Goodman, E. (1998, July 6). Linda was no 'friend' of Monica's. *The Kansas City Star,* p. B-5.

Goodman, E. (1998, August 2). Mourning gets the bum's rush. *The Kansas City Star,* p. B7.

Goodman, E., & O'Brien, P. (2000). *I know just what you mean: The role of friendship in women's lives.* New York: Simon & Schuster.

Gootman, M. E. (1994). *When a friend dies: A book for teens about grieving & healing.* Minneapolis, MN: Free Spirit.

Gordon, J. (1997). Till death do us part: When death affects the workplace, are you prepared to help your staff cope? *Sales & Marketing Management, 149*(11), 78-83.

Gordon, S. (1997). *Life support: Three nurses on the front lines*. Boston: Little, Brown and Company.

Grabowski, J., & Frantz, T. T. (1993). Latinos and Anglos: Cultural experiences of grief intensity. *Omega 26*(4), 273-285.

Greising, D. (1998). *I'd like the world to buy a Coke: The life and leadership of Robert Goizeuta*. New York: John Wiley.

Grollman, E. (1974). The Jewish way in death and dying. In E. Grollman (Ed.), *Concerning death: A practical guide for the living*. Boston: Beacon Press.

Grollman, E. A. (1993). Death in Jewish thought. In K. J. Doka with J. D. Morgan (Eds.), *Death and spirituality* (Ch. 3, pp. 21-32). Amityville, NY: Baywood.

Grollman, E. A. (1998). What you always wanted to know about your Jewish clients' perspectives concerning death and dying—but were afraid to ask. In K. J. Doka & J.D. Davidson (Eds.), *Living with grief; Who we are, how we grieve* (Ch. 2, pp. 27-37). Philadelphia: Brunner/Mazel.

Grollman, E.A., & Malikow, M. (1999). *Living when a young friend commits suicide: Or even starts talking about it*. Boston: Beacon Press.

Grout, L. A., & Romanoff, B. D. (2000). The myth of the replacement child: Parents' stories and practices after perinatal death. *Death Studies, 24*, 93-113.

Grumbach, D. (1991). *Coming into the end zone: A memoir*. New York: W.W. Norton.

Guest, L. (2000). *The Payne Stewart story*. Kansas City: Woodford Press/Stark Books/Andrews McMeel.

Gunn, T. (1992). *The man with the nights sweats*. New York: Farrar, Straus, & Giroux.

Gurley, G. (1992, November 26). A not so gentle reminder. *The Kansas City Star*, p. C-1.

Gusewelle, G. W. (1995, March 6). George Burg bossed staff with fairness, humor, generosity. *The Kansas City Star*, p. B-1.

Habenstein, R. W., & Lamers, W. M. (1962). *The history of American funeral directing* (rev. ed). Milwaukee, WI: Buflin.

Hallock, K. (1994). Reflections: Trying escargot. *American Journal of Nursing, 94*(3), 88.

Hanson, K. R. (1996). Minister as midwife. *The Journal of Pastoral Care, 50*(3), 249-256.

Harley, L. R., Jr. (1998, June). Embalming. *The Director, 70*(6), p. 5.

Harris, J. W. (Ed.). (1999). *Remembrances and celebrations: A book of eulogies, elegies, letters, and epitaphs*. New York: Pantheon Books.

Hatchett, M. J. (1995). *Commentary on the American Prayer Book*. New York: HarperCollins.

Havner, V. (1999). "If you can't pray." In D. Zarda & M. Woodward (Eds.), *Forever remembered* (p. 54). Seattle, WA: Compendium.

Hayslip, B., Jr., Ragow-O'Brien, D., & Guarnaccia, C. A. (1998-99). The relationship of cause of death to attitudes toward funerals and bereavement adjustment. *Omega, 38*(4), 297-312.

Heckenlively, C. (1999, April 2). [Letter to the editor]. *Kansas City Star*, p. B-5.

Heller, R., & Hindle, T. (1998). *DK Essential Manager's Manual.* New York: D[orling] K[indersley].

Herman, J. L. (1992). *Trauma and recovery.* New York: Basic Books.

Hines, P. M. (1991). Death and African-American culture. In F. Walsh and M. McGoldrick (Eds.), *Living beyond loss: Death in the family* (pp. 186-191). New York: Norton.

Hocker, W. V. (1990). Characteristics of unsanctioned and unrecognized grief, and appropriate helping strategies. In V. R. Pine et al. (Eds.), *Unrecognized and unsanctioned grief: The nature and counseling of unacknowledged loss* (Ch. 13, pp. 104-121). Springfield, IL: Charles C. Thomas.

Hoffman, K. (1998, September 25). Single-word question haunts killer, mother and his victim's widow. *The Kansas City Star*, pp. A-1, A-16.

Hoffman, L. (1988). Like a friendly editor: An interview with Lynn Hoffman. *Networker*, Sept/Oct.

Hoffman, P. L. (1995). *AIDS and the sleeping church.* Grand Rapids: W. B. Eerdmans.

Hollingsworth, B. (1998, July 2). From Dena to many: Gifts for better lives. *The Kansas City Star*, p. C-1.

Hostetler, J. A. (1963/1993). *Amish society* (4th ed.). Baltimore: Johns Hopkins University Press.

House, J. S. (1981). *Work stress & social support.* Reading, MA: Addison-Wesley.

How, W. W. (1864/1994). For all the saints. In B. Polman, M. K. Stulken, and J. R. Sydnor (Eds.). *Amazing grace: Hymn texts for devotional use* (p. 293). Louisville, KY: Westminster John Knox Press.

Howard, S. (1976). The Vietnam warrior: His experience, and implications for psychotherapy. *American Journal of Psychotherapy, 30*(1), 121-135.

Huscher, C. A. (1998, May 4). [Obituary]. *Kansas City Star*, p. B-3.

Hymer, S. (1988). *Confessions and psychotherapy.* New York: Gardner.

Imhoff, E. A. (1993). *Always at home: A southern Illinois childhood.* Carbondale, IL: Southern Illinois University Press.

International Commission on English in the Liturgy. (1990). *Order of Christian funerals* (rev. study ed.). Chicago: Liturgy Training Publications.

Irion, P. E. (1990-91). Changing patterns of ritual response in death. *Omega, 22*(3), 159-172.

Irion, P. (1996, February). Not even technology can replace care. *The Director, 68*(2), 62.

Isaacs, F. (2000). *My deepest sympathies: Meaningful sentiments for condolence notes and conversations, Plus a guide to eulogies.* New York: Clarkson/Potter.

Isensee, R. (1991). *Growing up gay in a dysfunctional family: A guide for gay men reclaiming their lives.* Englewood-Cliffs, NJ: Prentice-Hall.

Island, B. (1998). *Jane's naval history of World War II.* New York: HarperCollins.

Jackson, C. O. (Ed.). (1977). *Passing: The vision of death in America.* Westport: CT: Greenwood Press.

Jacobson, B. (1996, February-March). The seminal Paul Rudnick: Part 2. *A & U,* issue 20, pp. 32-36.

James, C. (1999, July 24). Networks in a generation apply a coating of significance to celebrity. *The New York Times*, p. A13.

Jarolmen, J. (1998). A comparison of the grief reaction of children and adults: Focusing on pet loss and bereavement. *Omega, 37*(2), 133-150.

Jensen, R. H. (1993). The private life and public death of David Schwartz. *The National Law Journal, 45*(21), 30-31.

Jim McDougal prepares for prison. (1997, May 20). *The Kansas City Star*, p. A-5.

Johannsen, R. W. (1997). *Stephen A. Douglas*. Urbana, IL: University of Illinois Press.

Johnson, E. A. (1999). *Friends of God and prophets: A feminist theological reading of the communion of saints*. New York: Continuum.

Johnson, J. W., & Johnson, J. R. (1925/1969). Swing low, Sweet chariot. *The Book of American Negro spirituals*. New York: Da Capo Press.

Jones, M. B. (1998). *"If she weren't my best friend, I'd kill her!": Almost 600 ways women drive their girlfriends crazy*. Kansas City, MO: Andrews McMeel.

Kahn, R. L., & Antonucci, T. C. (1980). Convoys over the life course: Attachment, roles, and social support. In P. B. Baltes & O. G. Brim, Jr. (Vol. eds.), *Life span development and behavior* (Vol. 3, pp. 253-283). New York: Academic Press.

Kapleau, P. (1998). *The Zen of living and dying: A practical and spiritual guide*. Boston: Shambhala.

Kastenbaum, R. (1969). Death and bereavement in later life. In A. H. Kutscher (Ed.), *Death and bereavement* (pp. 28-52). Springfield, IL: Charles C. Thomas.

Katz, P., & Bartone, P. (1998). Mourning, ritual and recovery after an airline tragedy. *Omega, 36*(3), 193-200.

Kavanaugh, R. E. (1972). *Facing death*. Los Angeles: Nash.

Kelley, H. K. (1997, March). This is now: Alternatives contribute to cremation's slow, steady growth. *The Southern Funeral Director, 153*(3), 8-9.

Kelley, P. (1997). *Companion to grief: Finding consolation when someone you love has died*. New York: Simon & Schuster.

Kelly, L. (2000). *Don't ask for the dead man's golf clubs: Advice for friends when someone dies*. Littleton, CO: Kelly Communications.

Kemp, D. R. (1995). Employers and AIDS: Dealing with the psychological and emotional issues in the workplace. *American Review of Public Administration, 25*(3), pp. 263-279.

Kenworthy, T. (1998, October 10). Gay student near death after Wyo. attack. *The Washington Post*, pp. A1, A9, A15.

King, A. (1998, March 9). Eulogy: Henny Youngman. *New York*, p. 52.

Klass, D., & Silverman, P. R. (1996). Introduction: What's the problem? In D. Klass, P. R. Silverman, & S. L. Nickman. (1996). (Eds.), *Continuing bonds: New understandings of grief* (Ch. 1, pp. 3-27). Washington, D.C.: Francis & Taylor.

Klass, D., Silverman, P. R., & Nickman, S. L. (1996). (Eds.). *Continuing bonds: New understandings of grief* (Ch. 1, pp. 3-27). Washington, D.C.: Francis & Taylor.

Klass, D., & Goss, R. E. (1998). Asian ways of grief. In K. J. Doka & J. D. Davidson (Eds.), *Living with grief: Who we are, how we grieve* (Ch. 1, pp. 13-26). Philadelphia: Brunner/Mazel.

Klein, A. (1998). *The courage to laugh: Humor, hope, and healing in the face of death and dying*. New York: Jeremy P. Tarcher/Putnam.

Klein, E. (1998). *Just Jackie: Her private years*. New York: Ballentine.

Klein, S. J. (1998). *Heavenly hurts: Surviving AIDS-related deaths and losses*. Amityville, NY: Baywood.

Klein, S. J., & Fletcher, W., III. (1986). Gay grief: An examination of its uniqueness brought to light by the AIDS crisis. *Journal of Psychosocial Oncology, 4*(3), 15-25.

Kleinfield, N. R. (1999, July 24). Doors closed, Kennedys offer their farewells. *The New York Times*, pp. A1, A12.

Kligman, D. (1998, August 15). No obits of AIDS victims: That's news. *The Kansas City Star*, p. A-9.

Knight, D. (1991). *Purgatory—Another chance to say yes*. St. Meinrad, IN: Abbey.

Kolbenschlag, M. (1979). *Kiss Sleeping Beauty good-bye: Breaking the spell of feminine myths and models*. New York: Doubleday.

Kolf, J. C. (1999). *How can I help?: How to support someone who is grieving*. Tucson, AZ: Fisher Books.

Kramer, J. (1970). *Lombardi: Winning is the only thing*. New York: World.

Lageman, A. G. (1986). The emotional dynamics of funeral services. *Pastoral Psychology, 35*(1), 16-22.

Lambe, J. (1998, October 22). Ex-intimate convicted of murder. *The Kansas City Star*, pp. C-1, C-2.

Lamendola, F., & Wells, M. (1991). Patient's advocate: Letting grief out of the closet. *Registered Nurse, 54*(5), 23-25.

Lamm, M. (1969). *The Jewish way in death and mourning*. New York: Jonathan David Publishers.

Lanoue, N. (1991). Fighting spirit. In M. Stocker (Ed.), *Cancer as a women's issue: Scratching the issue* (pp. 59-68). Chicago: Third Side Press.

le Goff, J. (1981). *La naissance du purgatoire*. Paris: Gallimard.

Lehigh, S. (1998, April 2). Sen. Kennedy recalls Powers at funeral for JFK's devoted friend. *The Boston Globe*, p. 3.

L'Engle, M., & Shaw, L. (1997). *Friends for the journey*. Ann Arbor: Servant Publications.

Levine, A. (1994). *To comfort the bereaved: A guide for mourners and those who visit them*. Northvale, NJ: Jason Aronson Inc.

Levinger, G. (1980). Toward the analysis of close relationships. *Journal of Experimental Social Psychology, 16*, 510-544.

Levinger, G. (1983). Development and change. In H. H. Kelley, E. Berscheid, A. Christsen, J. H. Harvey, T. L. Huston, G. Levinger, E. McClintock, L. A. Peplau, & R. D. R. Peterson (Eds.), *Close relationships* (pp. 315-359). New York: W. H. Freeman.

Levinson, D. J. (with Darrow, C. N., Klein, E. B., Levinson, M. H., & McKee, B.) (1978). *The seasons of a man's life*. New York: Ballentine.

Lewis, C. S. (1944/1962). *The problem of pain*. New York: Macmillan Paperbacks.

Lewis, C. S. (1960). *Four loves*. New York: Harcourt, Brace and Company.

Lewis, C. S. (1946, 1966). Preface. In D. Sayers, J. R. R. Tolkien, C. S. Lewis, A. O. Barfield, G. Mathew, & W. H. Lewis, *Essays presented to Charles Williams* (pp. vi-xiv). Grand Rapids, MI: William B. Eerdmans.

Lieb, D. A. (1998, August 12). Boys sentenced to juvenile center in school shootings. *The Kansas City Star*, p. A3.

Lifton, R.J. (1993). From Hiroshima to the Nazi doctors: The evolution of psychoformative approaches to understanding traumatic stress syndromes. In J. P. Wilson & B. Raphael (Eds.), *International handbook of traumatic stress syndrome* (pp. 295-308). New York: Plenum Press.

Limbo, R. K., & Wheeler, S. R. (1986). *When a baby dies: A handbook for healing & helping*. LaCrosse, WI: Resolve Through Sharing.

Lincoln, H., III. (1990). Grief and the funeral director: We, too, hurt sometimes. In V. R. Pine, O. S. Margolis, K. Doka, A. H. Kutscher, D. J. Schaefer, M. Siegel, & D. J. Cherico (Eds.), *Unrecognized and unsanctioned grief: The nature and counseling of unacknowledged loss* (pp. 158-160). Springfield, IL: Charles C. Thomas.

Lipson, J. G., Dibble, S. L., & Minarik, P. A. (Eds.) (1996). *Culture & nursing: A pocket guide*. San Francisco: UCSF Nursing Press.

Littlewood, J. (1992). *Aspects of grief: Bereavement in adult life*. London: Tavistock/Routledge.

Lofland, L. H. (1982). In W. J. Ickes & E. S. Knowles (Eds.), *Personality, roles, and social behavior* (pp. 219-241). New York: Verlag.

Long, T. G. (1997, October). The American funeral today—Trends and issues. *The Director, 69*(10), 10-16.

Lovegren, M. (1996). Widows and widowers: Life satisfaction and social support networks. *The Journal of Pastoral Care, 50*(3), 289-296.

Lynch, T. (1997). *The undertaking: Life studies from the dismal trade*. New York: Norton.

Lynch, T. (2000). *Bodies in motion and at rest: On metaphor and mortality*. New York: Norton.

Madigan, T. (1997, January). The love I'll never forget. *Reader's Digest, 150*(897), pp. 65-67.

Magida, A. J. (Ed.) (1996). *How to be a perfect stranger: A guide to etiquette in other people's religious ceremonies*. Volume 1. Woodstock, VT: Jewish Lights Publications.

Maier, A., & Calkins, L. B. (1995, August 21). How to bury a millionaire. *People*, pp. 40-43.

Makrevis, C. S. (1994). Difficult patient: Learning from Ann. *Nursing94, 24*(8), 42, 44.

Malloch, D. (1925/1950). A comrade rides ahead. In B. E. Stevenson (Ed.), *The Home Book of Modern Verse* (pp. 1000-1001). New York: Henry Holt.

Malone, R. E. (1996). Research: Almost 'life family': Emergency nurses & 'frequent flyers.' *The Journal of Emergency Nursing, 23*(3), 176-183.

Mansell, J. S. (1998). *The funeral: A pastor's guide*. Nashville, TN: Abingdon.

Marius, R. (1999). *Martin Luther: The Christian between God and death*. Cambridge, MA: Belknap Press of Harvard University.

Markides, K. S. (1981). Death-related attitudes and behavior among Mexican Americans: A review. *Suicide and Life-Threatening Behavior, 11*(2), 75-85.

Marks, A., & Piggee, T. (1998-99). Obituary analysis and describing a life lived: The impact of race, gender, age, and economic status. *Omega, 38*(1), 37-57.

Martin, T. L., & Doka, K. J. (1998). Revisiting masculine grief. In K. J. Doka & J. D. Davidson (Eds.), *Living with grief: Who we are, How we grieve* (pp. 133-142). Philadelphia: Brunner/Mazel.

Martin, T. L., & Doka, K. J. (2000). *Men don't cry . . . women do: Transcending stereotypes of grief*. Philadelphia: Brunner/Mazel.

Marty, M. E. (1999, August 25-September 1). Memo: The inner history. *The Christian Century*, p. 831.

Maslin, S. J. (Ed.). (1979). *Gates of Mitzvah: A guide to the Jewish life cycle*. New York: Central Conference of American Rabbis.

Mason, B. A. (1999). *Clear Springs: A memoir*. New York: Random House.

Mathewes-Green, F. (1999). *At the corner of East and now*. New York: Jeremy T. Tarcher, 1999.

Maxwell, N. (1996). Responses to loss and bereavement in HIV. *Professional Nurse, 12*(1), 21-24.

Mayne, M. (1998). *Pray, love, remember*. London: Darton, Longman, & Todd.

McBrien, R. P. (1995). *The HarperCollins encyclopedia of Catholicism*. San Francisco: HarperSan Francisco.

McClintock, J., & Stagg, J. (1891). Dead, prayers for the dead. In *Cyclopedia of biblical, theological and ecclesiastical literature* (Vol. 2, p. 710). New York: Harper & Brothers.

McConnell, S. D. (1998). Christians in grief. In K. J. Doka & J. C. Davidson (Eds.), *Living with grief: Who we are, how we grieve* (Ch. 3, pp. 39-46). Philadelphia: Brunner/Mazel.

McCormick, M. (1998, October). She was always there. *The American Funeral Director, 121*(3), 94.

McCormick, M. (1999, October). The Norman Funeral Home. *The American Funeral Director, 122*(10), 142-149.

McCormick, M. (2000, August). The broken necklace. *The American Funeral Director, 123*(8), 78.

McLean, A. M. (1996). Death. In H. J. Hillerbrand (Ed.), *The Oxford encyclopedia of the Reformation* (Vol. 1, pp. 468-469). New York: Oxford University Press.

McCullough, D. (1992). *Truman*. New York: Simon & Schuster.

McGoldrick, M. (1991). Irish families. In F. Walsh & M. McGoldrick (Eds.), *Living beyond loss: Death in the family* (pp. 179-182). New York: W.W. Norton.

McImse, A., Bartels, L., & Foster, D. (1999, April 25). Closest friends were deceived. *The Rocky Mountain News*, p. 25AA.

McNaught, B. (1997). *Now that I am out, what do I do?* New York: St. Martin's Press.

Meeks, W. A. (1983). *The first urban Christians: The social world of the apostle Paul*. New Haven, CT: Yale University Press.

Menten, T. (1991). *Gentle closings: How to say goodbye to someone you love*. Philadelphia: Running Press.

Merton, T. (Ed.) (1965). *Gandhi on non-violence: Selected texts from Mohandas K. Gandi's non-violence in peace and war*. New York: New Directions.

Metcalf, P., & Huntington, R. (1991). *Celebrations of death: The anthropology of mortuary ritual* (2nd ed.). New York: Cambridge University Press.

Metress, E. (1990). The American wake of Ireland: Symbolic death ritual. *Omega, 21*(2), 147-163.

Michaelis, D. (1983). *The best of friends: Profiles of extraordinary friendships*. New York: Murrow.

Miller, M. (1974). *Plain speaking*. New York: Berkeley.

Miller, S. (1983). *Men and friendships*. Los Angeles: Jeremy P. Tarcher.

Milton, J. (1942/1993). Lycidas. In *A treasury of great poems*. Compiled by L. Untermeyer. New York: Galahad Books.

Moe, T. (1997). *Pastoral care in pregnancy loss: A ministry long needed*. New York: Haworth Pastoral Press/Haworth Press.

Monroe, M., & Baker, R. C. (1997). The relationship of homophobia to intimacy in heterosexual men. *Journal of Homosexuality, 33*(2), 23-37.

Moore, P. (1997). *Presences: A bishop's life in the city*. New York: Farrar, Straus, & Giroux.

Morgan, E. (1994). Bereavement. In J. Morgan (Ed.), *Dealing creatively with death: A manual of death education & simple burial*. New York: Zinn Communications.

Murphy, K. (2000, June 6). Town remembered bloody price of D-Day. *The Kansas City Star*, pp. A-1, A-8.

Murphy, N. M. (1999). *The wisdom of dying: Practices for living*. Boston, MA: Element.

Myss, C. (1996). *Anatomy of the spirit: The seven stages of power and healing*. New York: Three Rivers Press.

Nardi, P. M. (1999). *Gay men's friendships: Invincible communities*. Chicago: The University of Chicago Press.

Nardi, P. M., & Sherrod, D. (1994). Friendship in the lives of gay men and lesbians. *Journal of Social and Personal Relationships, 11*, 185-199.

Nava, M. (1996). *The death of friends*. New York: Putnam.

Neimeyer, R. A. (1998). *Lessons of loss: A guide to coping*. New York: McGraw-Hill/Primis Custom Publishing.

Neimeyer, R. A. (1999). *Meaning reconstruction and the experience of loss*. Workshop presented at the Association for Death Education and Counseling, San Antonio, TX.

Neuharth, A. (1998, July 31). 'Ryan' movie misses the cause of WWII. *USA Today*, p. 13A.

Neuharth, A. (1998, November 27). Thanksgiving: Life, and the right to die? *USA Today*, p. 11A.

Neville, J. M., Jr., & Greif, G. L. (1994). When a therapist and client are HIV positive. *AIDS Patient Care, 8*(5), 260-264.

Niebergall, A., & Lathrop, G. (1986). Burial: Lutheran. In J. G. Davies (Ed.), *The new Westminster dictionary of liturgy and worship* (pp. 124-127). Philadelphia: Westminster.

Niederland, W. G. (1971). Introductory notes on the concept, definition, and range of psychic trauma. In H. Krystal, & W. F. Niederland (Eds.), *Psychic traumatization: After effects in individuals & communities* (pp. 1-10). Boston: Little, Brown.

Nieves, E. (2000, June 25). In San Francisco, more live alone, and die alone, too. *The New York Times*, Section 1, page 12.

Noonan, J. (1996). *The church visible: The ceremonial life and protocol of the Roman Catholic Church*. New York: Viking.

Nord, D. (1997). *Multiple AIDS-related loss: A handbook for understanding & surviving a perpetual fall*. Washington, D.C.: Taylor & Francis.

Nord, D. (1998). Traumatization in survivors of multiple AIDS-related loss. *Omega, 37*(3), 215-240.

Nord, T. (1998, June 13). Hundreds offer farewells to family killed in crash. *The Louisville Courier-Journal*, p. A1.

Oerlemans-Bunn, M. (1988). On being gay, single, and bereaved. *American Journal of Nursing, 88*(4), 472-476.

Oltjenbruns, K. (1995, April). *Building friendships during childhood: Significance of the death of a peer*. Paper presented at the meeting of the Association for Death Education and Counseling, Miami.

One 'damned good funeral' for Goldwater. (1998, June 4). *USA Today*, p. 3A.

Order of Saint Benedict. (1989). *Order of Christian funerals: Vigil service/evening prayer*. (1989). (Leaders' edition). Collegeville, MN: The Liturgical Press.

Order of the Golden Rule. (1987). *Before and after the funeral service*. Bridgestone, MO: Order of the Golden Rule.

Organ music should have a 'consoling radiance.' Interview with Virgil Fox. (1969). *American Funeral Director, 12*, p. 30.

Orth, M. (1999). *Vulgar favors: Andrew Cunanan, Gianni Versace, and the largest failed manhunt in U.S. history*. New York: Delacourte.

Osborne, C. (2000, July/August). Death of an adult friend: Catalyst for changing my perspective. *Forum, 26*(4), 5.

Owens, D. M. (1996). *Hospitality to strangers: Toward an integrative model of empathy in the physician-patient relationship*. Unpublished doctoral dissertation, Vanderbilt University.

Oxford English dictionary. (1978). Volume IV: F-G. Oxford: Clarendon Press.

Pang: Relatives look for more answers with lawsuits. (1998, February 20). *Seattle Post-Intelligencer*, p. A3.

Parachin, V. (1998, March). Helping grievers survive a loss to homicide. *The Director, 70*(3), pp. 83-84.

Pardo, S. (1998, October 17). 'It's getting too hard to cope,' friends say after students' death. *The Detroit News*, p. 3.

Passages. (1992, December 20). *The Seattle Times*, p. A16.

Payton, W. (1999, November 21). Payton scores one for his dad. *The Los Angeles Times*, p. D8.

Pelikan, J. (1978). *The growth of medieval theology (600-1300)*. Volume 3 of *The Christian tradition: A history of the development of doctrine*. Chicago: The University of Chicago Press.

Penn, S. (1998, May 8). Customers, friends mourn store owner. *The Kansas City Star*, pp. C-1, C-3.

Pilsecker, C. (1994). Essay: Starting where the client is. *Families in Society: The Journal of Contemporary Human Services, 75*(7), 447-452.

Pitts, L., Jr. (1998, October 26). Love the sinner, but hate the sin? It all looks like hate from here. *The Kansas City Star*, p. B5.

Pitts, L., Jr. (1998, November 27). There's a little celebrity stalker in all of us. *The Kansas City Star*, p. C7.

Platt, S. (Ed.) (1989). *Respectfully quoted: A dictionary of quotations requested from the Congressional Research Service (1989)*. Washington, D.C.: Library of Congress.

Pogrebin, L. C. (1987). *Among friends: Who we like, why we like them, and what we do with them*. New York: McGraw-Hill.

Pogrebin, L. C. (1996). *Getting over getting older: An intimate journey*. Boston: Little, Brown.

Pokorski, D. (1995). *Death rehearsal: A practical guide for preparing for the inevitable*. Springfield, IL: Octavio Press.

Pollock, C., & Pollock, D. (1996). *The book of uncommon prayer*. Dallas, TX: Word.

Pooley, E. (1999, July 26). The art of being JFK, Jr. *Time*, pp. 34-41.

Post, E. L. (1992). *Emily Post's etiquette* (15th ed). New York: HarperCollins.

Puckle, B. S. (1926). *Funeral customs: Their origin and development*. London: T. Werner Laurie, Ltd.

Putnam, R. D. (2000). *Bowling alone: The collapse and revival of American community*. New York: Simon & Schuster.

Raad, S. A. (1998). Grief: A Muslim perspective. In K. J. Doka & J. D. Davidson (Eds.), *Living with grief: Who we are, how we care* (Ch. 4, pp. 47-56). Philadelphia: Brunner/Mazel.

Rabbinical Assembly. (1998). *Siddur Sim Shalom for Shabbat and festivals*. [No place of publication identified.] The United Synagogue of Conservative Judaism.

Radford, E., & Radford, M.A. (1969). *Encyclopedia of superstitions*. Edited and revised by Christina Hole. Chester Springs, MD: Dufour Editions.

Raether, H. (1997, November). Deaths and cremations—1995, 1996 and beyond. *The Director, 69*(11), pp. 77-78.

Raether, H. (1999, September). Death, the funeral home & the funeral practitioner. *The Director, 71*(9), 26, 28.

Rakowsky, J. (1997, August 24). Mourners pay tribute to slain troopers: Funeral draws officers, others to N.H. school by the thousands. *The Boston Globe*, Section B, p. 1.

Rando, T. A. (1984). *Grief, dying, and death: Clinical interventions for caregivers*. Champaign, IL: Research Press.

Rando, T. A. (1988). *How to go on living after someone you love dies*. New York: Bantam Books.

Rando, T. A. (1992-93). The increasing prevalence of complicated mourning: The onslaught is just beginning. *Omega, 26*(1), 43-59.

Rankow, E. J. (1995). Breast and cervical cancer among lesbians. *Women's Health Issues, 5*(3), 123-129.

Rawlins, W. K. (1992). *Friendship matters*. Hawthorne, NY: Aldine de Gruyter.

Righter, W. G. (1998). *A pilgrim's way*. NY: Knopf.

Risberg, G., & McCullough, V. E. (1989). *Touch: A personal workbook*. Oak Park, IL: Open Arms Press.

Rivers, J. (1997). *Bouncing back: I've survived everything . . . and I mean everything and you can, too*. New York: HarperCollins.

Roberto, K. A., & Stanis, P. I. (1994). Reactions of older women to the death of their close friends. *Omega, 29*(1), 17-27.

Robeson, R. B. (1999). "I'll never forget you, young soldier." In *Amy writing awards: 1999 prize winning entries* (pp. 30-32). Lansing, MI: Amy Foundation.

Rocco, S. R. (1998, March). Legal rights to a deceased's burial: Who decides? *The Director, 70*(3), 68-74.

Rodabough, T. (1981-82). Funeral roles: Ritualized expectations. *Omega, 12*(3), 227-240.

Rofes, E. (1996). *Reviving the tribe: Regenerating gay men's sexuality and culture in the ongoing epidemic*. Binghamton, NY: Harrington Park Press.

Rogers, W. (1993). *When I think of Bobby: A personal memoir of the Kennedy years*. New York: HarperCollins.

Rorem, N. (1999). "Leonard Bernstein." In J. W. Harris (Ed.), *Remembrances and celebrations: A book of eulogies, elegies, letters, and epitaphs* (pp. 133-135). New York: Pantheon.

Rosen, H. (1996). Meaning-making narratives: Foundations for constructivist and social constructionist psychotherapies. In H. Rosen & K. Kuehlwein (Eds.), *Constructing realities* (pp. 3-54). San Francisco: Jossey-Bass.

Rosenblatt, R. (1999, July 26). Look homeward angel, Once again. *Time*, p. 88.

Roshan, M. (1997, December 15). Surviving at the top. *New York*, pp. 39-41.

Rosten, L. (1972). *Leo Rosten's treasury of Jewish quotations*. New York: Bantam.

Rothman, R. A. (1998). *Working: Sociological perspectives* (2nd ed.). Upper Saddle River, NJ: Prentice Hall.

Roush, M. (1999, July 31). Moving images. *TV Guide*, pp. 40-43.

Rubin, L. (1983). *Intimate strangers: Men & women together*. New York: Harper & Row.

Rupp, J. (1988). *Praying our goodbyes*. Notre Dame, IN: Ava Maria Press

Rush, A. C. (1969). Burial, II (early Christian). In *New Catholic encyclopedia* (Vol. 2, pp. 894-986). San Francisco: McGraw-Hill.

Rutherford, R. (1980). *The death of a Christian: The rite of funerals*. New York: Pueblo Publishing.

Sanders, C. (1995). The grief of children and parents. In K. J. Doka (Ed.), *Children mourning, mourning children* (pp. 69-84). Washington, D.C.: Hospice Foundation of America/Taylor & Francis.

Sanders, C. (1998). Gender differences in bereavement expression across the life span. In K. J. Doka & J. D. Davidson (Eds.), *Living with grief: Who we are, how we grieve* (pp. 121-132). Philadelphia: Brunner/Mazel.

Sandys, S. (Ed.). (1993). *Embracing the mystery: Prayerful responses to AIDS.* Collegeville, MN: The Liturgical Press.

Saunders, C. (1997, October). Death and the developmentally abled. *The Director, 69*(10), 49-50, 52.

Saunier, 1966, The Bibble Pages, 1996 Christian Lokick, InterNet.

Sawyer mystery solved. (1999, August 9). *The Kansas City Star*, p. A2.

Saxer, V. (1992). Dead, cult of the. In A. Di Bernardino (Ed.), *Encyclopedia of the early church* (Vol. 1, pp. 221-222) (A. Walford, Trans.). New York: Oxford University Press. (Original work published 1992.)

Schaller, L. E. (1999). *Discontinuity and hope: Radical change and the path to the future.* Nashville: Abingdon.

Schelps, R., & Klein, S. J. (1998). Negative consequences: Issues for HIV-negative gay/bisexual men. *Journal of Gay & Lesbian Social Services, 8*(2), 51-68.

Schiedermayer, D. L. (1996). A physician's experience. In J. F. Kilner, A. B. Miller, & E. D. Pellegrino (Eds.), *Dignity and dying: A Christian perspective* (pp. 3-20). Grand Rapids, MI: William B. Eerdmans.

Schoenberg, B. M. (1980). When a friend is in mourning. In B. M. Schoenberg (Ed.), *Bereavement counseling: A multidisciplinary handbook* (Ch. 13, pp. 239-249). Westport, CT: Greenwood.

Schulman, H. (1998, May 18). The habitual aborter. *Time,* pp. 76-79.

Schwartzberg, N., Berliner, K., & Jacob, D. (1995). *Single in a married world: A life cycle framework for working with the unmarried adult.* New York: Norton.

Scott, T. E. (1994). King Joey. *Nursing94, 24*(2), 54-55.

Scriven, J. (1855, 1994). What a friend we have in Jesus. In B. Polman, M. K. Stulken, & J. R. Syndron (Eds.), *Amazing grace: Hymn tests for devotional use* (p. 233). Louisville, KY: Westminster John Knox Press.

Searl, E. (2000). *In memoriam: A guide to modern funeral and memorial services* (2nd ed.). Boston: Skinner House Books.

Seaver, G. (1957). *David Livingstone: His life and letters.* New York: Harper & Brothers.

Senak, M. (1998). *A fragile circle: A memoir by Mark Senak.* Los Angeles: Alyson.

Seefried, E. L. (1999). In J. Kane and C. G. Warner (Eds.). *Touched by a nurse: Special moments that transform lives* (pp. 156-157). Philadelphia: Lippincott.

Selwyn, P. A. (1998). *Surviving the fall: The personal journey of an AIDS doctor.* New Haven, CT: Yale University Press.

Shatan, C. F. (1973). The grief of soldiers: Vietnam combat veterans' self-help movement. *American Journal of Orthopsychiatry, 43*(4), 640-653.

Shaw, E. (1994). *What to do when a loved one dies.* Irvine, CA: Dickens.

Sherman, E. (1991). *Reminiscence and the self in old age*. New York: Springer.

Silverman, G. S. (2000, July/August). Avelut: A year of mourning. *Forum, 26*(4), 6-8.

Silverman, P. R. (1999). *Never too young to know: Death in children's lives*. New York: Oxford University Press.

Sklar, F. (1991-92). Grief as a family affair: Property rights, grief rights, and the exclusion of close friends as survivors. *Omega 24*(2), 109-121.

Sklar, F., & Hartley, S. F. (1990). Close friends as survivors: Bereavement patterns in a 'hidden' population. *Omega 21*(2), 103-112.

Sloyan, V. (Ed.). (1990). *Death: A sourcebook about Christian death*. Chicago: Liturgical Training Publications.

Smith, D. W. (1990). *Men without friends: A guide to developing lasting & meaningful friends*. Nashville, TN: Thomas Nelson.

Smith, H. I. (1993). *The impact of a storytelling seminar for friend-grievers*. Unpublished D. Min. dissertation-project, Asbury Theological Seminary.

Smith, H. I. (1996). *Grieving the death of a friend*. Minneapolis, MN: Augsburg.

Smith, H. I. (1998). *"We make you kindly welcome:" Helping gay and lesbian grievers feel welcome in traditional grief groups*. Workshop presented at the Association for Death Education and Counseling, Chicago, IL.

Smith, H. I. (2000, July-August). Friendgrief: The consequence of friending. *Forum, 26*(4), 1, 3-4.

Smith, H. I., & Klein, S. J. (2000). *Friendgrief: Who cares?* The Association for Death Education and Counseling, Charlotte, NC.

Smith, W., & Cheetham, S. (Eds.). (1875). Burial of the dead. In *A dictionary of Christian antiquities* (Vol. 1, pp. 251-254). Boston: Little Brown.

Snelling, J. (1991). *The Buddhist handbook: A complete guide to Buddhist schools, teaching, practice, and history*. Rochester, VT: Inner Traditions.

Snow, J. (1987). *Mortal fear: Meditations on death & AIDS*. Cambridge, MA: Cowley Press.

Society of Saint John the Evangelist. (1997). *The rule of the Society of St. John the Evangelist, North American Congregation*. Cambridge, MA: Cowley Press.

Solberg, C. (1984). *Hubert Humphrey: A biography*. New York: Norton.

Sprang, M. V., McNeil, J. S., & Wright, R., Jr. (1993). Grief among surviving family members of homicide victims: A casual approach. *Omega, 26*(2), 145-160.

Stairwell death. (1998, October 7). *The Kansas City Star*, p. C-3.

Stanley, J. L. (1996). The lesbian's experience of friendship. In J. S. Weinstock & E. D. Rothblum (Eds.), *Lesbian friendships: For ourselves and others* (Ch. 3, pp. 39-59). New York: New York University Press.

Stannard, D. R. (1975). *Death and dying in central Appalachia*. Philadelphia, PA: University of Pennsylvania Press.

Stannard, D. R. (1977). *The Puritan way of death: A study of religion, culture, and social change*. New York: Oxford University Press.

Staudacher, C. (1991). *Men and grief: A guide for men surviving the death of a loved one*. Berkeley, CA: New Harbinger.

Steele, S. (1973). Death's aftermath: Group experience in early grief & bereavement. *Communitas*. Arundel, MD: Arundel Community College.

Steinsaltz, A. (1999). *Simple words: Thinking about what really matters in life.* E. Schachter & D. Shabtai (Eds.). New York: Simon & Schuster.

Stephanopoulis, G. (1999). *All too human: A political education.* Boston: Little, Brown & Company.

Stone, S. (1999). *Where's Harry? Steve Stone remembers his years with Harry Carey.* New York: Taylor.

Strong, D. M. (1994, December 13). Remembrance of things past. *The Advocate*, p. 35.

Stowe, A., Ross, M. W., Wodak, A., Thomas, G. V., & Larson, S. A. (1993). Significant relationships and social supports of injecting drug users and their implications for HIV/AIDS services. *AIDS Care, 5,* 1409-1413.

Streitmatter, R. (Ed.). (1998). *Empty without you: The intimate letters of Eleanor Roosevelt and Lorena Hickok.* New York: Free Press.

Stuart, E. (Ed.). (1992). *Daring to speak love's name: A gay and lesbian prayer book.* London: Hamish Hamilton.

Sudnow, D. (1967). *Passing on: The social organization of dying.* Englewood Cliffs, NJ: Prentice Hall.

Suilleabhain, S. O. (1967). *Irish wake amusements.* Dublin: Mercier.

Sullivan, A. (1990, September 17). Gay life, gay death. *The New Republic*, pp. 19-25.

Sullivan, A. (1998). *Love undetectable: Notes on friendship, sex, and survival.* New York: Knopf.

Syme, D. B. (1988). *The Jewish home: A guide for Jewish living.* New York: Union of American Hebrew Congregations.

Tammeus, B. (1998, June 21). Storm sheds new light on a familiar place. *The Kansas City Star*, p. K-3.

Taylor, B. B. (1998). *When God is silent.* Boston, MA: Cowley Press.

Tennyson, A. L. (1895). *In memoriam.* New York: E. P. Dutton.

Tennyson, A. L. (1971). The passing of Arthur. In R. W. Hill, Jr. (Ed.), *Tennyson's poetry: Authoritative texts, juvenilia and early responses, criticism* (pp. 420-430). New York: Norton.

The Hartmans—A life of turmoil. Wife's temper led to fights, friends say. (1998, May 29). *The San Francisco Chronicle*, p. A2.

Texas continues to mourn bonfire collapse victims. (1999, November 23). *The Kansas City Star*, p. A-2.

Theroux, P. (1990, October 21). The life and death of a Mayor. *The Washington Post*, p. C5.

Theroux, P. (Ed.). (1997). *The book of eulogies: A collection of memorial tributes, poetry, essays, and letters of condolence.* New York: Scribner.

Thoits, P. A. (1982, June). Conceptual, methodological, and theoretical problems in studying social support as a buffer against life stress. *Journal of Health & Social Behavior, 23,* 145-159.

Thomas, L. (1987). Funeral rites. In M. Eliade (Ed.), (K. Anderson, Trans.). *The encyclopedia of religion* (Vol. 5, pp. 450-459). New York: Macmillan.

Tilberis, L. (1998). *No time to die*. Boston: Little, Brown & Company.

Trillin, C. (1993). *Remembering Denny*. New York: Farrar, Straus, & Giroux.

Trollinger, W. V., Jr. (1998, November 11). My friend's execution. *Christian Century, 113*(31), 1058-1061.

The United Methodist Church. (1989). *The United Methodist hymnal: Book of the United Methodist worship*. Nashville, TN: United Methodist Publishing House.

Unruh, D. (1983). Death and personal history: Strategies of identity preservation. *Social Problems, 30*(3), 340-351.

Untermeyer, L. (Comp.). (1942/1993). *A treasury of great poems*. New York: Galahad Books.

Upton, J. (1990). Burial, Christian. In P. E. Fink (Ed.), *The new dictionary of sacramental worship* (pp. 140-149). Collegeville, MN: The Liturgical Press.

Valdiserri, R. O. (1994). *Gardening in clay: Reflections on AIDS*. Ithaca, NY: Cornell University Press.

van den Boom, F. (1991, December 5). Point of view: AIDS in the family: A personal reflection. *AIDS Patient Care, 5*(6), 273.

Van Buren, A. (1996, August 25). Why not carry out uncle's wish for pallbearers? *The Dallas Morning News*, p. 4F.

Van Doren, C. (1938). *Benjamin Franklin*. New York: Viking Press.

Vande Kemp, H. (1999). Grieving the death of a sibling or the death of a friend. *Journal of Psychology and Christianity, 18*(4), 354-366.

Vanezis, M., & McGee, A. (1999). Mediating factors in the grieving process of the suddenly bereaved. *British Journal of Nursing, 8*(14), 932-937.

Vanzant, I. (1998). *One day my soul just opened up*. New York: Fireside.

Venturella, J. (1998, December). A Christmas tribute. *RN*, pp. 37-38.

Walfoort, N. (1998, November 27). Newcomers fuel increase in housing, services. *The Louisville Courier Journal*, pp. A-1, A-5.

Wallbank, S. (1996). *Facing grief: Bereavement and the young adult*. Cambridge, England: Lutterworth.

Walker, W. (1966). In G. C. Wilcox (Ed.), *The southern harmony*. Los Angeles: Pro MusicAmericana.

Walter, T. (1999). *On bereavement: The culture of grief*. Philadelphia: Open University Press.

Watts, I. (1859). *Psalms & hymns adapted to social, private, & public worship in the Cumberland Presbyterian Church*. Nashville, TN: Cumberland Presbyterian Board of Publication.

Ware, T. (1963/1993). *The orthodox church*. New York: Penguin.

Webster's ninth new collegiate dictionary. (1983). Springfield, MA: Merriam-Webster.

Weinbach, R. W. (1989). Sudden death and the secret survivors: Helping those who grieve alone. *Social Work, 34,* 57-60.

Weinstock, J. S., & Rothblum, E. D. (1996). What we can be together: Contemplating lesbians' friendships. In J. S. Weinstock & E. D. Rothblum (Eds.), *Lesbian friendships: For ourselves and others* (Ch. 1, pp. 3-30). New York: New York University Press.

Weiss, Hali. (1997, September 10). Loosening the rules of mourning. *The Los Angeles Times*, p. A11.

White, E. (2000). *The married man*. New York: Knopf.

White, L. M. (1990). Burial. In E. Ferguson (Ed.), *Encyclopedia of early Christianity* (pp. 161-163). New York: Garland.

Whitley, D. (1999, October 30). Thousands mourn Stewart. *The Kansas City Star*, p. D1.

Wieseltier, L. (1998). *Kaddish*. New York: Knopf.

Wilcock, P. (1996). *Spiritual care of dying and bereaved people*. Harrisburg, PA: Morehouse.

Williamson, M. (1994). *Illuminata: Thoughts, prayers, rites of passage*. New York: Random House.

Willmott, P. (1987). *Friendship networks and social support*. London: Policy Studies Institute Research.

Wilson, P. (1998, May 29). [Obituary]. *The San Francisco Chronicle*, p. D7.

Wiltshire, S. F. (1994). *Seasons of grief and grace: A sister's story of AIDS*. Nashville, TN: Vanderbilt University Press.

Wiseman, J. P. (1986). Friendship: Bonds and binds in a voluntary relationship. *Journal of Social & Personal Relationships, 3*, 191-211.

Wolfe, B. (1993). AIDS and bereavement: Special issues in spiritual counseling. In K. J. Doka & J. D. Morgan (Eds.), *Death & spirituality* (Ch. 20: pp. 257-280). Death, Value & Meaning Series (Series Editor: J. D. Morgan). Amityville, NY: Baywood.

Wolfelt, A D. (1988). *Death and grief: A guide for clergy*. Muncie, IN: Accelerated Development.

Wolfelt, A. D. (1994). *Creating meaningful funeral ceremonies: A guide for caregivers*. Fort Collins, CO: Companion Press.

Wolfelt, A. D. (1997). *The journey through grief*. Fort Collins, CO: Compassion Press.

Wolfelt, A. D. (1998, June). Creating meaningful funeral ceremonies: Part 1: Their purpose. *The Director, 70*(6), 18-22.

Wolfelt, A. D. (1998, November/December). Companioning versus treating: Beyond the medical model of bereavement caregiving: Part 3). *The Forum, 24*(6), 3, 15.

Wolfelt, A. D. (1999, February 11). *Understanding grief: Helping yourself heal*. Presentation, Olathe, Kansas.

Wolmuth, E. (1983). *The overnight guide to public speaking: The Ed Wolmuth method*. Philadelphia: Running Press.

Wolpe, D. (1999). *Making loss matter: Creating meaning in difficult times*. New York: Riverhead Books.

Wood, T. (1999, August 1). New ways to say goodbye. *The Kansas City Star*, pp. G1, G2.

Woodward, K. L. (1997, September 22). The ritual solution. *Newsweek*, p. 62.

Woodward, K. L. (1999, June 14). The making of a martyr. *Newsweek*, p. 64.

Woolwine, D. (2000). Community in gay male experience and moral discourse. *Journal of Homosexuality, 38*(4), 5-37.

Worden, J. W. (1991). *Grief counseling and grief therapy: A handbook for the mental health practitioner.* (2nd ed.). New York: Springer.

Wright, J. H. (1967). Prayers for the dead. In *The new Catholic encyclopedia* (Vol. 4, pp. 672-673). New York: McGraw-Hill.

Wright, P. H. (1982). Men's friendships, women's friendships and the alleged inferiority of the latter. *Sex Roles, 8*(1), 1-20.

Wright, R. D., Jones, A., & Wright, S. E. (1999). Dying homeless but not alone: Social support roles of staff members in homeless shelters. *Illness, Crisis & Loss, 7*(3), 233-251.

Wyse, L. (1995). *Women make the best friends.* New York: Simon & Schuster.

Yager, J. (1999). *Friendshifts: The power of friendship and how it shapes our lives.* (2nd ed.). Stamford, CT: Hannacroix Creek Books.

Yeats, W. B. (1951/1974). The municipal gallery revisited. In *The collected poems of W. B. Yeats: Definitive edition, with the author's final revisions* (pp. 316-318). New York: Macmillan.

Zadra, D., with Woodard, M. (Eds.). (1999). *Forever remembered.* Seattle, WA: Compendium.

Zeggelink, E. (1993). *Strangers into friends: The evolution of friendship, network, using an individual oriented modeling approach.* New York: Kinderhook.

Zizzo, D. (1998, October 13). Pilot in fatal crash asked to return to airport after takeoff. *The Daily Oklahoman [Oklahoma City],* p. 7.

Zurakowski, T. L. (2000). The social environment of nursing homes and the health of older residents. *Holistic Nurse Practitioner, 14*(4), 12-23.

Index